Getting Your
Business
Wired

Getting Your Business Wired

Using Computer Networking and the Internet to Grow Your Business

WILLIAM KILMER

American Management Association

New York • Atlanta • Boston • Chicago • Kansas City • San Francisco • Washington, D.C.
Brussels • Mexico City • Tokyo • Toronto

This publication is designed to provide accurate and authoritative
information in regard to the subject matter covered. It is sold with
the understanding that the publisher is not engaged in rendering
legal, accounting, or other professional service. If legal advice or
other expert assistance is required, the services of a competent
professional person should be sought.

Library of Congress Cataloging-in-Publication Data
Kilmer, William E.,
    Getting your business wired: using computer networking and
the internet to grow your business/William Kilmer.
        p.   cm.
    Includes bibliographical references and index.
    ISBN 0-8144-7007-6
    1. Small business—Computer networks.   2. Internet marketing.
    3. Electronic commerce.   4. Intranets (Computer networks)   5.
    Local area networks (Computer networks)   I. Title.
        HD30.385.K54   1999
        658'.0546—dc21   99-12179
                                                                   CIP

Printing number

10   9   8   7   6   5   4   3   2   1

Contents

List of Figures and Tables

FIGURES

TABLES

Foreword

IF YOU OWN YOUR OWN BUSINESS, CONSIDER YOURSELF LUCKY, VERY LUCKY. You are an entrepreneur at the very best time in history to be one. Not only are there millions of folks like you; there are many millions more who are eager to try your wares and services. Could it get any better than that?

Yes, it could. People are taking new ideas and growing them into great companies every day. And most owe it to technology. In fact, a recent Roper survey conducted for Ernst & Young revealed that technology is thought to be the overriding factor in the blossoming of entrepreneurial enterprises. Technology has not only made it easier and cheaper to grow your business but has also created entirely new industries and ways of doing business.

Technology once designed only for bigger businesses is now being used in even the smallest companies. Networking isn't just for the big boys anymore. Starting a neighborhood business takes on a new meaning when the neighborhood is the world. And almost anyone can launch an Internet website. Still, most entrepreneurs don't even know what they don't know, so figuring it out can be intimidating. But to thrive in today's marketplace you have no choice. It's time to learn about technology and use it to help your business. If you're in business and you're not wired, you are in trouble. Big trouble. You are at a competitive disadvantage, and worse, you are deliberately making your business slower and less efficient than it could be.

Well, no more excuses! In *Getting Your Business Wired,* William Kilmer tells you not only exactly why you should get connected but, more important, how you can do it. Here, in language even I can understand (and, believe me, I'm no techie), is your guide to taking your business to the next level, to being techno-savvy without being techno-geeky.

I hate to fall back on a cliche, but in business, time is money. If you make the time to read this book, that investment will pay off in more ways than one.

Rieva Lesonsky
Vice President
Editorial Director
Entrepreneur Magazine

Preface

CHANCES ARE THAT IF YOU WORK IN A SMALL BUSINESS, YOU HAVE A NUMBER of roles that you perform every day. In the morning you may work as the human resources department, reviewing resumes. During the lunch hour you may be part of the sales department, meeting with a potential client. In the afternoon, you may be the marketing department, developing a brochure for your new product or service. You are never short on responsibilities, only on time.

That challenge of juggling roles and responsibilities is part of the fun and excitement of working in a growing business. But it is also part of the difficulty and frustration. You struggle with the lack of resources and compete in a tough business environment—not enough people, not enough money, and certainly not enough hours in the day.

Because of these challenges, you probably look for help wherever you can. And if your company is like most others, you are already using personal computers to improve your business. You probably use computers to create a professional image with desktop publishing software, keep your company's books with accounting software, and even manage your list of customers in a contact manager. Computers have changed and improved the way you do business.

But now there is a new technological wave moving around you: computer networking and the Internet. You have seen it, no doubt, whether advertisements that include Internet addresses for more information or your competitor's website. You hear friends talk about how a network has saved their company money or an Internet website has brought them extra business. It sounds interesting and helpful, but you don't have the time or the knowledge to investigate how a network can help your business. Maybe you don't fully appreciate the big picture of what a network is or how it can help you. Or perhaps you are skeptical, thinking that any investment in networking or the Internet is too complicated, too difficult, and too expensive. Maybe it is something you have heard so much about that you feel you should know more.

Whatever the reason that you don't have a network or have not fully used the Internet to your advantage, you have picked up the right book.

About This Book

NETWORKING IS PROBABLY NOT YOUR FAVORITE SUBJECT, AND IT STILL WON'T be after you finish this book. But a working knowledge of today's network technology can be essential to the competitiveness of your small business.

As part of my work developing products for small businesses, I have spoken with many small-business owners and mangers. Over and over, I hear the same thing: "I really want to [fill in the solution], but I don't know where to start." In other words, they want to improve their business with a network but don't have the information on where to begin, whom to talk to, or even what a network will really do for them.

This book is the place to start. If you own, manage, or work in a smaller business, this book was written for you. It's for businesspeople who want to improve their business by taking advantage of computer networks and the Internet. Like other books, it will give you some information on the technology as a foundation. But it goes beyond that. It provides you with ideas and solutions to improve your business and the tools to succeed. In short, it will help you begin to leverage the technology of networking and the Internet to help your business be more competitive.

As a side note, I use the term "your company" often throughout this book. I don't necessarily assume you are the owner or manager. However, no matter what your position, you have a stake in the business's success. What you do has an impact on the company's success. In that respect, the company belongs to everyone that works there.

ASSUMPTIONS

Since this book is written for the nontechnical user, I don't assume much about your knowledge or interest in technology. In fact, your interest in technology is only triggered by how you can use it to help your company. However, I do assume two things. The first is that you already have more than one personal computer in your office and that you know how to use them with some degree of proficiency. This book is based on the idea that you are already using computers and want to do more.

The second assumption is that you want to understand networking and the Internet only from the perspective of their business application and advantages. If you want to read an in-depth section on Internet protocols, put this book down and slowly back away—you're a closet engineer. The information here is not for you. If you got shivers just reading the word protocol, keep on reading. This book was written for you with minimal technical descriptions. And when technical topics are covered, they are done so in terms anyone can understand.

HOW TO USE THIS BOOK

This book is set up as a resource and a guide for the lay user and businessperson. You can use it two different ways: If you are interested in getting the big picture, you may start at the beginning and read through the entire book. You will get a step-by-step overview of networking and Internet technologies, applications you can use in your business, planning ideas for setting up a network, and other valuable information. Or, if you are interested in finding out more information on a particular topic, such as how to use e-mail in your business, you may use the table of contents or the index to look up a specific topic. The book is divided into logical topics and solutions so that you may look up a particular area of interest as needed. You will find that you may come back to the book over and over again as your needs change and your company evolves.

HOW THIS BOOK IS ORGANIZED

This book is structured around easy-to-read topics that will guide you through the technology, solutions, and implementation steps that will give your business a competitive edge. The book is organized as follows:

■ **"Section One: Today's Small Business"** lays the foundation for networking and the Internet in small businesses. It describes the new small-business environment and why it is time for small businesses to begin adopting technology that has made large corporations more efficient and profitable. It also covers some basics on the benefits that your business can expect from networking.

■ **"Section Two: Small-Business Guide to Local Area Networks"** covers the essentials of connecting the computers in your office together to form a Local Area Network (LAN). It includes the technology essentials that will explain everything you need to know about LANs. It also includes information on planning your LAN, where to go for help, where to buy equipment, and what to look for in a networking consultant.

■ **"Section Three: Small-Business Guide to Wide Area Networks"** explains the basics of a Wide Area Network (WAN) that connects multiple offices or sites together. It introduces examples of how a WAN may help if you are running multiple sites; it also describes key WAN technologies and equipment and offers guidance on finding a solution for your needs.

■ **"Section Four: Small-Business Guide to the Internet"** covers the hottest buzzword in networking: the Internet. You will learn about Internet technology and how to use it for communication, research, setting up a website, and even selling over the Internet. You will also learn how to choose a good service provider for your Internet connection.

■ **"Section Five: Planning and Justifying Your Network"** shows you how to make sound decisions about wiring your business, whether you work in a small business or are the owner of one. This final section covers the essentials for prioritizing and planning your network. You will also learn how to justify the investment in a network, show a return on your investment, and budget for future years.

■ Finally, the Appendixes at the end of the book provide you with additional information and tools that you need to move forward. Included are forms for network planning, a list of several vendors that you may want to consider, and a glossary of networking terms.

After reading this introduction, I hope that you can move into this book with some confidence. Then, when you finish it, my hope is that you'll have garnered a good understanding of how you can improve your business with networking, including the Internet. With this book in hand, you can make informed decisions about your business's networking needs and how to cost-justify them, even with a small budget. In short, you will be able to make sound business decisions and get your business wired.

Acknowledgments

I WOULD LIKE TO ACKNOWLEDGE THE MANY INDIVIDUALS WHO HAVE CONtributed to this book. First of all, I want to thank my coworkers and friends at Intel Corp. who contributed to and reviewed the material: Steve Ashby, Steve Bateman, Daren Fackrell, Tom Hogan, Stacey Parish, Brad Romney, Sean Varley, and Steve Workman. I am grateful for these and other dedicated individuals and have benefited greatly from their knowledge and contribution.

I'd also like to thank Jeanne Talbot and Jessica Daughetee of Intel; Scott Aaron of MCI, for his help with the material on wide area networks; Richard Weeks of Burgoyne Computers, for his insights into the world of computer resellers; Chun Bahl and the Visio Corporation, for the use of their software in creating many of the book's network diagrams; Steve Spiro from HotOffice Technologies; David Brandt and Benjamin Solomon of Dell Computer; and Shannon Harmon Shupe of Novell Inc.

My thanks also go out to the many small-business employees who have opened up their companies' doors to me and helped me understand their business environments and needs. They have brought me to an appreciation of how important small businesses are to our economic system and how difficult it is to be an entrepreneur.

Above all, I would like to thank my dear wife and son, who are my inspiration. Without their sacrifice, encouragement, and support, this work would never have been possible.

Today's Small Business

CHAPTER 1

The Wired Small Business

THERE IS NO DOUBT THAT SMALL BUSINESSES JUST AREN'T WHAT THEY USED to be. Gone are the days when a small business was thought of as a local hardware store or the corner mom-and-pop store selling bread and milk. Businesses are leaner, meaner, and faster than ever, and they are competing on an increasingly larger geographic scale with businesses of all sizes.

To thrive, or sometimes just survive, small businesses have turned to many sources for help, including technology. For small businesses, the competition has never been fiercer. But the technical tools available have never been more extensive.

The Small-Business Environment

IF YOU ARE WORKING IN A SMALL BUSINESS, YOU ARE CERTAINLY NOT ALONE. There are about 7.5 million small businesses (defined as companies with fewer than 100 employees) in the United States, and that number is growing.[1] Corporate downsizing, a good economic environment, and the ever-present dream of being your own boss have all contributed to those numbers. In addition, it has never been easier to start a small business. With favorable laws for small businesses, low interest rates, and more opportunities to find your niche, the possibilities are endless.

However, starting a business is a lot different from staying in business. Certainly you have heard all of the morbid statistics of the number of businesses that go out of business every year. While the numbers are often exaggerated, there are many internal and external challenges that small businesses face today.

The internal challenges of owning and managing a business are enough to put anyone on edge. Managing cash flow, profitably pricing products or services, making your company's presence known, hiring and managing employees, customer issues, and a host of other problems come up daily. At best it makes for long days. At worst, the combined problems can make you unprofitable or put you out of business.

And as if the internal pressures of running a business aren't enough, most small businesses face almost insurmountable levels of competition from every angle.

For starters, you have to compete with other small businesses. Small businesses often attract the best and brightest in the business world. Like you, these highly skilled workers are looking for the diversity and challenge of having a large stake in a small business. Oftentimes they have lived for years in the corporate world gaining experience and knowledge before venturing off on their own. Many of these former corporate warriors bring with them an appreciation for technology and what it can do for them.

In addition, small businesses regularly compete with medium-size and large businesses. Your company may be in a niche market, defending itself by holding on to or carving out a specialized business that the larger guys can't afford to go after. Or, you may find yourself in an out-and-out battle with a company that has more people, resources, and money than you do.

In addition, the playing field has gotten geographically bigger. Businesses today are reaching out further and further across the world, increasing competition for global customers. As a result, your new competitor could come from across town or across the world.

With these internal and external challenges facing small businesses, there is no doubt that you need to increase your competitive posture to survive. Overcoming your internal challenges can include measures such as increasing the efficiency of your internal processes, communicating better with co-workers, suppliers, and customers and cutting costs to maintain profitability. From an external perspective, you need to keep up with customer demands and provide a better product or service than the competition.

Networking and Small Businesses

YOU MAY BE ASKING YOURSELF HOW A COMPUTER NETWORK CAN BE THE answer to your problems. After all, you have done well so far without one. How is connecting your computers together or to the Internet going to make or break your company? It can because a network can help your business become more profitable, more efficient, and more competitive.

For years, small businesses have adopted technology to survive. Just look around at the telephone and the calculator on your desk and the postage machine in your shipping area. All of these devices were once too big, too expensive, or too complicated for general use by all businesses, and all eventually made their way to your business when they became simpler and less expensive.

The personal computer is a great example of a technology tool adopted by small businesses that has improved many areas of operation. A recent study of small businesses by the consulting and research firm Charles River Strategies, Inc., found that overall, small businesses that used multiple personal computers generated $110,000 in sales per employee per year, while those with no computers only made $83,000 per employee.[2] That difference is an indication of the power of computers in business.

Look at the other technologies you have learned to rely on as well, such as fax machines, voice mail, cellular phones, and pagers. You could probably live without some of these devices, but it would be extremely difficult for you to be as productive as companies that use them. Imagine if you had to tell your customers that you couldn't fax a proposal to them because you don't have a fax machine, or the look on their face if they received a document produced on an old manual typewriter. They would expect you to be running your business out of a cave, and your competitors would be running all over you.

Many businesses have the attitude that they can't afford networking technology. But it won't be long before networking and the Internet will be just as critical to the competitiveness of your business as that fax machine sitting in your office. Networking is becoming a strategic investment, one that reaps quick returns on investment and lifts companies to a new level of competitiveness. Table 1-1 shows how this can be the case.

The second part of the Charles River Strategies study shows that those businesses with computer networks saw even more sales per employee than those with just standalone computers. In fact, while those companies with multiple computers generated $110,000 in sales per employee per year, those with networks generated $134,000 in sales per employee.[3]

Table 1-1. *Small-Business Sales per Employee*

	Average Sales Per Employee by Technology in Company ($000s)			
Industry	*No PCs*	*One PC*	*Multiple PCs*	*Networked PCs*
All industries	83	96	110	134
Service	39	58	72	92
Construction	120	140	152	173
Wholesale	139	159	172	192
Manufacturing	72	92	105	125
Retail	40	59	73	93
Finance	58	79	91	100

After adjusting for other factors. These factors include percentage of white-collar employees, years in business, number of employees, percentage of college graduates, and major industry.

Source: Charles River Strategies

Networks help businesses become more productive because they leverage the resources and capabilities of computers and other devices, letting users share resources, files, applications, hardware, information, and ideas. Networking provides three distinct advantages (which will be discussed further in Section Two). Those advantages are (1) resource cost savings; (2) increased communication/collaboration and sharing of information; and (3) increased productivity.

Because networks, including the Internet, have become such an important tool, they are a staple in the corporate world. But while large companies have reaped the benefits of networking, it is still a mystery to most small businesses, something that seems so foreign to them that they don't even know where to start.

So, you're asking yourself, if networking is so great, why aren't all small businesses networked? The main reason is that until recently, networking hasn't been all that easy to understand. In the past it has seemed as if you needed a Ph.D. and an interpreter just to get through all of the acronyms and cryptic technolanguage, and a crystal ball to know what you were doing. But networking has become simpler. Microsoft's Windows 95 was the computer operating system that made it simple to start a basic network. Also, many networking companies have developed products that are designed and priced specifically for small businesses and that are easier than ever to understand, install, and maintain than earlier programs. This combination of new hardware and software is making it easier for small businesses to set up a network and see a return for their investment.

With these improvements, the only gap that remains is small business owners' lack of understanding of what is available to them. That is the purpose of this book: to show you that the technology is available at your disposal. Networking is not difficult to understand, learn, or implement. The benefits of networking are measurable and tangible. All you need is an understanding of your options, an ability to assess your needs, and knowledge of where to start. With that, let's get started.

Notes

1. Ray Boggs and Warren Childs, International Data Corporation, "Small Business Networking: Building Momentum," IDC/LINK# 15655 (March 1998).
2. "Technology Effectiveness Model," Charles River Strategies, Inc. Wellesley, Massachusetts, 1995.
3. Ibid.

CHAPTER 2

Networking Overview

THIS CHAPTER BEGINS YOUR NETWORK EDUCATION. IN IT YOU WILL LEARN more about the benefits of networking and the three basic types of networks covered in this book. But first, we take a little detour for a lesson in English.

TLAs

JUST A WORD OF WARNING HERE: THIS IS THE FIRST CHAPTER WHERE YOU ARE introduced to TLAs. That is technical speak for three-letter acronyms. If you have ever read or heard anything about networking, then you know that the networking language is just filled with them. You may have already asked yourself, what's with the acronyms? Why can't anyone speak plain English?

Well, many people sympathize with you. But it doesn't make the acronyms go away. You will find that this book uses acronyms as sparingly as possible, and when they are used they are accompanied by an explanation. Remind yourself that acronyms serve a good purpose; they make it easier to communicate, as long as both persons know what the acronym means. Imagine, for example, that you worked for the federal government and had to say Federal Bureau of Investigation all the time instead of the acronym FBI. It is much simpler to say the FBI as long as everyone knows what it stands for.

As you read this book, try to learn the acronyms as best you can and focus on the concept behind the acronym rather than on the exact wording. Many people in the networking world understand what an acronym means, even when they don't necessarily know what each letter stands for. If you know the meaning, you too can be on the inside looking out.

What Is a Network?

A SIMPLE DEFINITION OF A NETWORK IS TWO OR MORE COMPUTERS connected together for the purpose of sharing. This definition is broad enough to include a connection between two personal computers that sit in the same office, or a system as vast, complex, and disorganized as the Internet. A network provides a connection between your computer and other computers and resources. Once you're connected, there are four basic things you can do with a network:

1. *Share hardware resources.* Hardware sharing includes any devices that can connect to the network. In the past, that mostly meant sharing printers. But today, peripheral devices can include just about anything, such as printers, modems, hard drives, CD-ROM drives, removable media storage, scanners, and even cameras.

2. *Share files.* Sharing files is another great networking application. Think of all those times you have gone to someone and asked for a specific file from his or her computer. You have to walk over to the person's desk, hand your coworker a floppy, and wait for that person to copy the file and give it to you. Then you take it back to your desk and copy it to your computer. This type of file sharing is a big waste of time. And with the increasing size of some files today, they are often too large to fit on one floppy disk, making the process even harder. A network provides a link between computers that lets users share files quickly and easily.

3. *Share applications.* Networks also let you share applications across the network. You can buy a network license to put an application on a high-speed server and run the application from any or all desktop computers across the network. This is often more cost-effective than buying separate applications for everyone in the office.

   It is illegal, however, to share a single-user copy of a software application across the network. This should only be done with an application for which you have a network license. Read software license agreements before sharing any software on a network.

4. *Share information.* How many times have you walked into your office and found your computer has been used as a $2,000 bulletin board, covered with those little sticky notes from your cowork-

ers? Or perhaps you have a pile of memos that someone has typed out and placed on your desk. Instead of using the outside of your computer, why not use your computer to send and receive messages electronically across a network?

Information sharing across the network can be done using electronic mail (e-mail) or groupware such as Lotus Notes, or by posting information for others to read from their own computer. This latter solution is often known as an "intranet." These solutions are explained further in Chapter Six.

Benefits of Networking

NETWORKING CAN BENEFIT ALMOST ANY BUSINESS. THE BIGGEST BENEFITS to businesses are:

1. *Cost savings.* One of the most obvious and tangible benefits to networking is the cost savings achieved by sharing resources. These resources can include both hardware (e.g., printers) and network applications. Oftentimes these savings are by themselves large enough to pay for the cost of the original network investment.

   Take a simple example of five users with computers. All five users want to use a high-quality laser printer for their work. But good laser printers cost more than $1,000 each. It would certainly be infeasible to buy a separate laser printer for each user's computer. Yet it is unproductive to connect a printer to a single computer. Other users would have to go to that computer with the attached printer, kick the owner off, insert a disk containing their file, and print it. Imagine doing that several times per day. The person on that computer would never get anything done. But for a fraction of the price of a second laser printer, all five computers can share the single printer simultaneously without interrupting anyone's work.

   Software cost savings can be equally dramatic. Say you have a particular application that everyone in your office uses. Instead of purchasing a single-user copy of the software for each person, you can buy a multiple-user version for the network (usually at a lower cost per user) and run it on the network.

2. *Informed, collaborative employees.* Networks give users a medium to improve communication and collaboration. Do you need to get information to everyone in the company on a new policy or a big sales proposal? Do you want to let employees know the time for a meeting? Send it to the entire company through e-mail and you will make sure it gets to everyone in less time than walking around to each individual.

You will also find that a network will improve collaboration. For example, say that you have a question or problem that you want to hear everyone's opinion on, but you don't feel the need to hold a long meeting. Poll everyone by electronic mail and wait for the responses to come back. Or you may have a proposal that you are sending out to a client and you want a few key people to review it first. Send it out to them over the network and they can review it and get it back to you, with changes to the actual document. With a network you can keep people more informed and they, in turn, can work better together.

How many times has someone in your company said, "I never got that information," or "I didn't know where to find that"? With a network, you can remedy that situation through various ways of sharing and publishing information so that it is available to anyone or everyone. You can give others access to documents, spreadsheets, sales literature, presentations, policies, photographs, anything. If you can put it in electronic format, you can share it over the network.

Networks, specifically the Internet, also give you the ability to access information from outside resources. Workers can access information on a wealth of topics, such as market research, competitive information, tax and copyright laws, and hundreds of thousands of other topics on the World Wide Web. This information allows workers to make better informed, more accurate decisions.

3. *Increased productivity.* If you have ever had to share a file with someone, you know that it isn't a big deal. You take the file, copy it onto a disk (as long as it fits on the diskette), and walk it over to the other person's desk. They take the disk and put it into their computer and use it. This is affectionately known in the networking world as "sneakernet"—you let your feet act as the network. It works pretty well for sharing a single file. But imagine what

happens when the people you've lent your disk to are done modifying your file: They go through the same process to get it back to you. Then you realize you forgot to add something to the file, so you go through the process again, and on, and on, and on. Now take that time that you spend waiting for the file to copy, walking it over, having that person copy the file, and multiply it by the number of people going through the same process in your company. Then add in the number of people doing the same thing to print to someone else's printer. Now add in all the time that people are walking around putting sticky-note memos on each other's computers. Are you starting to see the pattern? There is a lot of time involved in walking around with information that could be sent electronically in a fraction of the time, saving time for more productive activities. You can also save some wear and tear on the office carpet.

Once you understand the impact of these benefits, you can review your own needs and determine how to justify your company's investment in a network. (Note: For readers from the accounting side, keep all of these benefits in mind for a later discussion.)

Types of Networks

OKAY, SO YOU HAVE THE IDEA OF JUST HOW HELPFUL A NETWORK CAN BE. So what networking options are available? When people hear the word *network* they may think about different things. Some picture a huge corporate network stretching across many floors of a building. Others think about a series of networks on a university campus, connected together into one large communications infrastructure or the Internet, with its vast resources and ability to search out important information or even the most ludicrous, unproductive material. Still others think about a couple of computers connected together so that they can play their favorite game with a player on another computer. (Hey, we all have our needs.)

Although the lines between networks are becoming blurred, there are essentially three types of networks: local area networks, wide area networks, and the Internet.

LOCAL AREA NETWORKS

A local area network is just what the name implies. It is a network that is local, meaning that it is within a close proximity. A local area network, or LAN (rhymes with pan), connects computers and other resources together. It usually operates in a fairly small environment—for example, within a single room or a single building. On a few occasions, a LAN may go between buildings that are very close to each other.

A LAN uses special cabling that goes only a short distance, usually within a few hundred meters at the most. However, LANs are usually quite fast, enabling you to easily share files and other resources.

WIDE AREA NETWORKS

A wide area network (WAN) is much broader in scope than a LAN. It is designed to connect multiple LANs, each in a different geographic location. For example, if you have an office with a LAN in New York and another office with a LAN in San Francisco, you can use a WAN to connect the two networks together. WANs use special connections through the telephone company and are also usually much slower than LANs.

THE INTERNET

Though technically a WAN, the Internet is something quite different from what is normally understood by the terms LAN and WAN. It is a conglomerate of interconnected computers and networks throughout the world. The Internet includes computers, servers (high-speed computers), mainframes, and other devices. Unlike a LAN or a WAN, it is not something you can implement; it is something that you connect to. You are one of a vast number of connected devices to an extremely large worldwide network.

The Internet is comprised of many different organizations that use it for many different purposes. Schools, government agencies, small and large businesses, nonprofit organizations, and even individuals connect to the Internet. There are as many reasons to use the Internet as there are people on it.

A Word About Network Speeds

Before going further, we need to touch on an important topic: network speed. You will find speed discussed throughout this book, so it is important to understand it.

Network speeds are rated in bits per second (bps). A bit is the most basic unit of information for a computer to process, designated as a 0 or a 1. When we talk about bps, it translates to how many of those bits can theoretically be sent or received per second across the network.

Prefixes such as *kilo* (thousand), *mega* (million), and *giga* (billion) along with a number designate how fast a network runs. Thus, if a network can run at 10 megabits per second (10 Mbps), it can send and receive 10 million bits per second through the network cable. That doesn't mean much to you. I know, because it doesn't really mean much to me. But it does help us understand relative speed. That relativity will help you evaluate how much faster, for example, your 10 Mbps network is than your 56 Kbps (kilobits per second, or thousand bits per second) modem connection to the Internet.

Where Do I Go From Here?

IF I HAVEN'T SCARED YOU AWAY YET WITH THIS BRIEF OVERVIEW OF NETWORK types, then you are ready to move on. You may already have an idea of what is best for your needs and even how it may benefit you. For example, if your company doesn't have more than one location, you probably don't need a wide area network. Or, if you need to communicate with customers, you may want to read up on the Internet to find out how to make best use of this resource. The rest of this book is assembled so that you can move from subject to subject and find specific areas that may help you. Don't worry about jumping ahead and ruining the ending because the conclusion—that networks are important for your small business—is the same no matter how you get there.

My suggestion is that you use the next three sections of the book to develop a more in-depth view of the types of networks that you think may benefit your company. Each section is independent of the others, with information on the technology, explanations, and examples to give you an idea of how networks are implemented. Taken together, the chapters in this book will help you to get started so that you can know what decisions you need to make.

This book was designed to start you on the right path to implementing the solutions your business needs. So follow through the information provided, look at what will work for your business, and begin improving your business through networking and the Internet.

Small Business Guide to Local Area Networks

CHAPTER 3

Local Area Network Essentials

YOU MAY HAVE SEVERAL COMPUTERS IN YOUR COMPANY THAT YOU USE thoroughly for processing and storing different information, such as spreadsheets, documents, and presentations. But if the computers in your office stand alone, they have only reached part of their potential. Without being networked, computers are limited to what you can plug into them. However, when connected to other computers through a network, each individual computer is able to leverage the resources of other computers and share their resources to gain a new level of synergy. This chapter and the five chapters that follow will show you how to increase the power of your computers through Local Area Networking.

Characteristics of Local Area Networks

A LOCAL AREA NETWORK, OR LAN, IS A CONNECTION OF COMPUTERS AND other devices within a short distance, usually on the same premises. Local area networks use cabling to connect computers and other devices so users can share information and resources. Here are some of the characteristics of a local area network:

■ *LANs are contained within a close proximity*. A LAN usually operates within a building, office, or a floor of a building.
■ *LANs are high-speed networks*. LANs are relatively fast compared to other types of networks.

19

■ *LANs use special cabling made just for networking.* Although some networks are wireless, most use special networking cabling to connect everything together.

This definition does not mean that a local area network cannot have connections to the Internet or even a wide area network. In today's interconnected world, there is a fine line between where one type of network starts and another begins.

There are many different things you can do with a local area network. For example, you can:

■ **Share files.** Networks allow you to share files and documents with other computer users.

■ **Share information.** Beyond just sharing files, a network allows you to share information. There are few businesses where employees *don't* complain that they are lacking information; a network can facilitate information flow and increase collaboration and cooperation. Many applications such as electronic mail (e-mail) can increase the communications in your company, make employees more productive, and cut down on the number of meetings. Who wouldn't like to get out of some meetings?

■ **Share applications.** Many software companies let you buy a network license for a software package that lets you put the software on a network server so that a specified number of people can use it.

■ **Share hardware.** With a network you can give everyone in the company access to a single printer and save the expense of buying extra printers for every computer. The same can be done for CD-ROMs, modems, scanners, and just about every other type of computer equipment.

These are only some of the things that you can do with a local area network. You will learn about these and other applications for LANs in this and subsequent chapters.

Some people reading this book may dread what comes up next: a discussion of the technology. In reality, learning about the technology behind networking is painless. Some of you may actually enjoy it. So sit back, open your mind, and prepare to learn.

Network Topologies

WHEN WE TALK ABOUT NETWORKING, ONE OF THE FIRST THINGS TO ADDRESS is the network topology. Topology is a description of how computers are physically connected together. A topology looks like a map of your network from above. There are three main types of network topologies: bus, star, and ring.

BUS TOPOLOGY

A NETWORK THAT USES A BUS TOPOLOGY IS CONNECTED TOGETHER IN A LINEAR manner, with all of the computers on the network connected through a single line of cable, one after the other, as shown in Figure 3-1. The advantage of the bus topology is that it is simple and fairly inexpensive to implement. Bus topology uses coaxial cable that looks similar to the cable that connects to the back of your television set.

Figure 3-1. *Bus Topology*

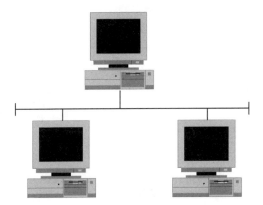

The bus topology also has several disadvantages. The first is that if you remove a computer from the network, you have to disconnect the cabling that connects the entire network. This means that if you break the network connection, no one can access the network until the connection is restored. Also, adding new computers to the network requires you to redirect that single line of cable to that user's location to connect that machine to the network. If that new computer is across the building, it is not easy to stretch the cable to the other end of the company. Finally, the cable that

21

is used for bus topology doesn't upgrade well to newer technologies. In fact, no new network technologies support it. Because of these difficulties, bus topology is a way of the past and is only recommended for very small networks—such as a network with only two or three computers.

STAR TOPOLOGY

A STAR TOPOLOGY CONNECTS EACH COMPUTER TO A CENTRAL DEVICE CALLED a hub. As shown in Figure 3-2, a star network resembles the spokes of a wagon wheel. It uses flexible cabling much like thick telephone wire that is easy to install and move. Star networks are very easy to change and expand. This simplicity explains why the star is the most popular network topology today. Star networks are the also a popular choice because they are easier to upgrade.

Figure 3-2. *Star Topology*

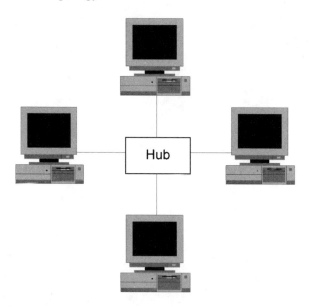

RING TOPOLOGY

A RING TOPOLOGY ACTS—YOU GUESSED IT—LIKE A RING. FIGURE 3-3 SHOWS that all the computers are connected in a ring. In reality, a ring is physically set up like a star network with a central hub. However, the way the computers speak to each other is as if all of the computers were connected together in a circle. Each computer is allowed to speak only when it is spoken to—that is, when it receives a token, or opportunity to communicate. Token ring, the most popular type of ring networks, was developed and pushed by IBM Corp. during the 1980s and early 1990s, but its popularity has waned in recent years.

Figure 3-3. *Ring Topology*

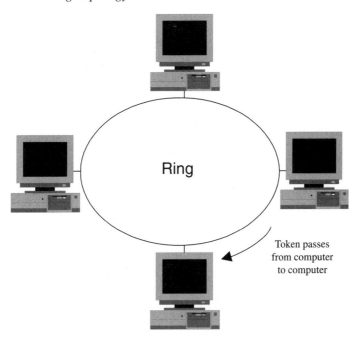

Ring

Token passes
from computer
to computer

PSEUDO NETWORKS

IN ADDITION TO THE STANDARD NETWORK TOPOLOGIES DESCRIBED SO FAR, there is a final category of pseudo networks. These networks often use a connection through the serial port at the back of your computer to daisy chain the computers together for rudimentary file sharing, printer sharing, and even Internet access. Pseudo networks are sometimes known as zero-slot networks because they don't use an adapter that takes up an expansion slot inside your computer. An example of a zero-slot network is shown in Figure 3-4.

Figure 3-4. *Zero-Slot Network*

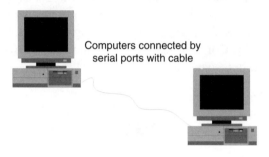

Computers connected by
serial ports with cable

Zero-slot networks are not recommended under any scenario. You may save a few minutes or a few dollars with this type of network, but you will regret your decision down the road when you want to expand your network or run faster applications. With other networks getting cheaper, easier to use, and faster, there is no need to look at zero-slot networks.

Networking Standards

A NETWORK STANDARD DEFINES ALL THE ESSENTIAL INFORMATION ABOUT A network, such as what type of cabling you can use, the way the computers connect together, the minimum and maximum cable length, the maximum number of computers on the network, and how devices talk to each other and access the network. A network standard is not something that you go out to the store and buy, like an application for your computer. Instead, it is a common set of rules that is supported by the networking devices (i.e., the cables, adapters, and other equipment) that you buy.

There are many factors to consider when choosing a network standard that could potentially make it a complex decision. Corporate information systems managers spend lots of time and money deciding which standard is right for their needs and then reevaluate it often. Fortunately, this can become a more clear-cut decision for most businesses because of the overwhelming popularity of one network standard: Ethernet.

Ethernet is clearly the most popular networking standard in the world today. There are essentially three flavors of Ethernet networks available: Ethernet, Fast Ethernet, and Gigabit Ethernet. There is also a variation of Ethernet that is called switched Ethernet. Table 3-1 lists the different types of Ethernet and their advantages and disadvantages.

Table 3-1. *Ethernet Types*

Network Type	Speed	Description	Available Switched
Ethernet	10 Mbps	Most popular network protocol. Used for basic networks with low needs.	Yes
Fast Ethernet	100 Mbps (10x Ethernet)	Excellent for networks with more users or more data traffic. Often used for connections to network servers. Inexpensive enough to use for basic networks.	Yes
Gigabit Ethernet	1 Gbps (100x Ethernet)	Primarily used for "backbone" applications and connections to servers.	Yes

ETHERNET

ETHERNET, KNOWN AS BASIC ETHERNET OR SLOW ETHERNET, WAS INVENTED back in the 1970s by Digital Equipment Corp., Intel Corp., and Xerox Corp. Ethernet transmits information at a rate of 10 megabits (million bits) per second, or 10 Mbps. One of its key attributes is the way devices, such as computers, "talk" on the network. This is called its access method. The Ethernet access method is similar to how someone might have used a "party" telephone line several years ago. With a party-line phone system, everyone in a given area shared the same telephone connection. To place a phone call, you picked up your phone and listened to see if anyone else was on. If the line was available, you could make your phone call. However, if someone was on the phone when you wanted to call, you hung up and tried to make the call later.

This very simple explanation is known by a very complex term in networking—Carrier Sense Multiple Access with Collision Detection, or CSMA/CD. You don't need to remember that, but do remember that it treats the network like a big party line, with only one computer speaking at a time. Before your computer wants to send any information on the network it listens to see if anyone else is already using the network "line." If not, your computer sends its information. If someone else is using the network, your computer waits until later and tries again. If more than one computer tries to send information at the same time, a "collision" occurs and both computers wait a random amount of time before trying to resend their information.

FAST ETHERNET

FAST ETHERNET IS BASED ON, AND SIMILAR TO, THE ETHERNET STANDARD developed two decades ago. The difference is that Fast Ethernet is, well, faster. It is actually ten times faster than regular Ethernet (ten times faster means 100 megabits per second, or 100 Mbps). Fast Ethernet is used for networks that frequently transmit information such as graphics or other large files. Fast Ethernet used to be expensive, but prices have dropped dramatically over the last few years so that it is now just a little more expensive than standard Ethernet.

Eventually Ethernet networks will be overtaken by Fast Ethernet as the market standard, although it will take a while before most existing networks are converted to Fast Ethernet. If you can afford Fast Ethernet, it is worth the premium.

GIGABIT ETHERNET

GIGABIT ETHERNET IS BASED ON THE ETHERNET STANDARD ALSO. ETHERNET runs at 10 megabits per second, Fast Ethernet runs at 100 megabits per second, and Gigabit Ethernet runs at 1,000 megabits (one gigabit) per second. It is only now beginning to be used by large corporations in areas for special applications. However, it is too fast and too expensive for connecting desktop computers together, at least for now.

SWITCHED ETHERNET

REMEMBER THE PARTY-LINE EXAMPLE USED PREVIOUSLY TO EXPLAIN Ethernet technology? Well, think of why we no longer use a party telephone line. It is a pain to wait until the line is free to get on and call someone. The same can be said for networks. That is why switched Ethernet was invented.

Switched Ethernet is the direct-dial system of Ethernet networking. It can be used with regular Ethernet, Fast Ethernet, or Gigabit Ethernet. Switched Ethernet knows where devices, including computers, are on the network through their network addresses, and it handles network traffic by delivering information only to its intended recipients. This is done with a device called a switch, which divides up a network into segments. When you send information to someone on the network, it is sent just to the network segment that person is using and nowhere else. This way, demanding users can be segmented from less-demanding users on the network so that others will not be slowed down by intensive network traffic. It is often used in situations where many people regularly use the network.

Why Ethernet?

Ethernet is clearly the choice of most networks in the world. Fast Ethernet is a great alternative if you can afford the slight price premium, want more speed, and want to be ready for the future. Here are six reasons why Ethernet or Fast Ethernet should be your main choice in networking. Ethernet is:

1. *The most popular.* Even if you like being a rebel, your network is not the place to exercise your freedom. Ethernet is the most popular networking type in the world, so learn to fit in. Tens of million of computers are connected to Ethernet networks, far more than any other type of network. That means it has been tested by time and it is easy to find someone who knows something about it if anything goes wrong.
2. *The most flexible.* Ethernet also provides the most flexibility in options. For example, Ethernet can be set up in either the bus or the star topology. Ethernet is also flexible in its ability to connect to other network standards. Other networking types aren't as flexible in connecting to each other.

3. *The most supported.* More vendors make Ethernet networking products than any other type of network. That means that you will find more Ethernet products and devices, such as printers, that connect directly to Ethernet.

4. *Cost-effective.* Because there are so many vendors that make and sell Ethernet products, it is a highly competitive market. That translates to lower prices and better products for you.

5. *Upgradeable.* Ethernet has several variations that provide faster speed, including Fast Ethernet, Gigabit Ethernet, and switched Ethernet. They are all variations of the same basic technology, so it is much easier to upgrade as your needs change.

6. *Easy to install.* Because Ethernet has become so popular, many vendors have focused on making it easier to use. Many other networking types are built for very high-end or specialized applications and tend to be less user-friendly than Ethernet.

With all of these things going for it, Ethernet is the right choice for most networks. For those with the ability and budget to pay a slight premium, Fast Ethernet is also a great option.

THE "OTHER" STANDARDS

OKAY, TO BE FAIR THERE ARE ALTERNATIVES TO ETHERNET, AND TO GIVE them their due I will explain a few of them. However, I need to warn you up-front that this entire book uses Ethernet networks in every example. These other network types all have one or more difficulties that put them out of the mainstream. Most are either older technology, too advanced for ordinary needs, or too expensive. With that in mind, the alternatives are:

■ **Token ring.** Like Ethernet, token ring has been around for many years. It uses the ring topology, as you could probably guess (see, this stuff is intuitive). The only time a device can "talk" is when it receives the token that circulates around the network, stopping at each device. This access method is called token passing. It is efficient and makes token ring perfect for all of you Type-A personalities.

One of token ring's advantages is that it is faster than Ethernet. In fact, it is 60 percent faster (16 Mbps) than standard Ethernet. However, token ring is not as popular as Ethernet, so it is more difficult to find products or people who know about it, and when you do, they are both likely to be more expensive. Unless you enjoy collecting Beta format VCRs, I would recommend that you stay away from token ring.

■ **ATM.** Asynchronous Transfer Mode (ATM) is an emerging technology that, in practical terms, is still several years from mainstream LAN implementation, if ever. ATM runs at speeds between 25 Mbps and 155 Mbps, with potential speeds of up to 622 Mbps or more.

■ **FDDI.** Fiber Distributed Data Interface (FDDI) has been available for a number of years as a high-speed networking technology. Established as a standard to run on fiber-optic cable, it is fast (100 Mbps) and can go a maximum distance of 60 miles. It is an older technology, not very popular, and expensive.

■ **100 VG AnyLAN.** 100 VG AnyLAN came and went as fast as any network standard could. Like Fast Ethernet, 100 VG AnyLAN runs at 100 Mbps, but uses a token passing access method just as token ring does. There are few companies that even make AnyLAN products, so you won't want to support it either.

This is just the short list. There are plenty of other network standards available, but Ethernet should be adequate for your needs. Throughout the rest of this chapter and book, when we discuss local area networking, we will be referring to an Ethernet network or a variation such as Fast Ethernet.

Network Components

EXCLUDING COMPUTERS, NETWORKS GENERALLY CONSIST OF FOUR DIFFERENT components. They include hardware (hubs, cabling, adapters, and other devices that connect everything together), software (which provides the ability to connect to and access information and resources), protocols (which are essentially the network language), and servers (which are large computers that run processes and applications for the entire network). We will discuss each of these in more depth.

HARDWARE COMPONENTS

EVERY NETWORK NEEDS SEVERAL BASIC HARDWARE COMPONENTS, WHICH are those devices that physically connect all of the computers together to allow them to communicate. Hardware components include the cabling, the network adapters that go into each computer, and a hub or other central device that connects it all together.

Network Cabling

Unless you want to look at a wireless network (which isn't practical for most networks), your network will require cabling to connect everything together. There are essentially three types of cabling used today: twisted pair, coaxial, and fiber.

■ **Twisted pair.** Twisted pair is the most popular type of networking cable available. Twisted-pair cabling comes in two types: STP (Shielded Twisted Pair) and the more popular UTP (Unshielded Twisted Pair). Sometimes it is also referred to as 10BaseT (pronounced "ten-base-tee") cabling. It consists of copper strands of wiring that are twisted together and coated. As you can see from Figure 3-5, twisted-pair wiring looks similar to phone wire, but it is thicker and uses a larger connector called an RJ-45.

Figure 3-5. *Twisted-Pair Cable*

The advantages of twisted-pair cabling is that it is flexible and relatively low cost. It also runs a fairly long distance, up to 328 feet (100 meters). Twisted-pair cabling is used in a star network topology.

■ **Coaxial.** Coaxial is copper cabling that is covered with a thick black coating. Coaxial cable, shown in Figure 3-6, is often called Thin Ethernet cable or 10Base2 (pronounced as "ten-base-two") and looks similar to wiring for cable television. It is however, a higher-grade wire that allows two-way communications and a different connector called a BNC connector that twists on.

Coaxial cable has the advantage of going longer distances than regular twisted pair, approximately 607 feet (185 meters). However, it is not used very often for new networks, mainly because it is not easy to change or upgrade. Because it is used in a bus topology only, you must break the network connection every time you want to make a change. Coaxial cable should only be used as a cost-effective way to connect a maximum of two or three computers. There is an even older standard, called Thick Ethernet, which is a thicker, yellow cable that goes farther distances but is used even less than Thin Ethernet today.

Figure 3-6. *Coaxial Cable*

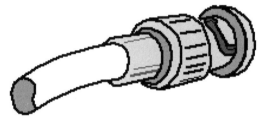

■ **Fiber optic.** Fiber-optic cable is at the top of the network cable pyramid. It is the stuff network managers dream of. Fiber can carry data at very fast speeds and for long distances. It works by transmitting information by light, instead of electricity, through glass strands, so there is less interference from outside electrical sources such as lights, power lines, and electric motors. Can you think of anything more exciting than that? Well, network managers can't. In spite of its exciting capabilities, fiber-optic cable is better left to the dreams of those crazy network guys, especially those that install "campus" networks that connect multiple buildings and LANs. It is too expensive for most smaller LANs.

What About Wireless Networks?

Okay, so by now you may be wondering about the option of a wireless network. Wireless networking is a great idea, in theory. You don't have to string cabling, and air is cheap, although wireless equipment isn't. Wireless networks usually work through one of two mediums: radio waves or infrared (light). There is now even a standard for wireless networks, although many wireless networking vendors continue to develop their own proprietary technology.

Wireless networking is an advantage for those using portable computers around the office. Imagine being able to carry your notebook computer throughout the office and stay connected to printers, electronic mail, the Internet, etc. You could actually get some work done during meetings.

But for most businesses, wireless networks are still not ready for prime time. Wireless is great in overcoming wiring problems. For example, if your office building has asbestos in the walls, you may want to go wireless rather than exposing a health risk or running wires out in the open. Likewise, some applications such as inventory management software benefit from mobile computers with access to the network. If you don't have a specific reason to use a wireless network, stick with a wired network until wireless becomes more standardized, faster, and less expensive.

Network Adapters

Network adapters are also known as network interface cards, or NICs (see Fig. 3-7). They are your computer's connection to the network, relaying information between your computer and the network. Anything

Figure 3-7. *Adapter*

Intel ®PRO/100 adapter. Reproduced by permission of Intel Corporation. Copyright 1999 Intel Corporation.

that you do on the network is sent and received through your network adapter.

Network adapters fit in the expansion slots at the back of your computer. Slots are connections inside your computer where you attach cards that upgrade your computer's functionality. Older pre-Pentium computers use slower ISA slots. Newer machines that run Pentium or Pentium II processors generally use faster PCI slots. There are also other types of slots such as Micro Channel (also known as MCA) from IBM, but they are used only in older machines. If you run Apple Macintosh computers, there are so many different versions of cards that I would take up this book explaining them all.

If you have a portable computer, your expansion slots are probably on the side of the computer. They take small, credit-card-type adapters, called PC cards or PCMCIA cards that supply the computer's network connection.

Hubs/Repeaters

A hub is the central device of most networks using the star topology (see Fig. 3-8). It is the clearinghouse of information; anything that is sent out on the network goes through the hub, which then passes the information on across the network. A hub has connections or ports, either in the front or back, which are used to plug in the network cables.

A repeater is similar to a hub in terms of its function, with one major difference. Rather than just taking the information or signals sent from a computer and passing them through, a repeater rebroadcasts the signal so

Figure 3-8. *Hub*

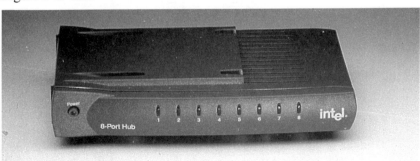

Intel ®Express 220T hub. Reproduced by permission of Intel Corporation. Copyright 1999 Intel Corporation.

that it is strong enough to go longer distances. Repeaters are not very common anymore. Hubs, however, are a necessity for a star topology network.

Cables, network adapters, and hubs are the basic network components. However, as companies grow, their networks grow also. When they do, they often need ways to manage the amount of traffic that builds up on the network once more people start doing more things. So, there are devices for more advanced needs. You may not need them now, but you may use them later on to improve the performance of your network.

Bridges

A bridge separates computers and other devices into distinct groups of computers called network segments. As shown in Figure 3-9, the purpose of a segment is to isolate users into groups. Segments keep local traffic within that segment, so they help reduce network traffic and improve performance within a segment. Only the information that is destined for other segments is transferred out of the segment.

Figure 3-9. *Segmenting With a Bridge*

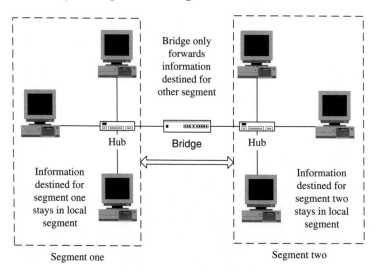

Bridges segment by selectively allowing traffic through based on its destination. While a hub just sends out everything that it receives to everyone, a bridge receives the information and determines the destination segment of the information. The bridge then sends the information only to the intended segment and nowhere else. Bridges usually only have two ports, one for each network segment. Bridges can also be used to connect two different types of networks.

Switches

A switch works like a hub with an individual bridge for each port and is used in switched Ethernet networks. Everything that is plugged into a port of the switch—whether it is a single computer or a hub with several computers—is on a separate segment, which is an isolated group within a network.

Switches are used for networks that have many people using the network often. It sets up segments on each port to decrease traffic and improve network performance.

Routers

Routers are the kings of the networking world. A router is the highest form of intelligent network devices. They are more advanced than bridges and switches. Like bridges, they read addresses and forward "packets" of information based on its destination. However, routers are also smart enough to find the most efficient path to get information to its destination. This isn't very important (or very interesting) for companies with smaller networks. But because of this special function and the router's ability to translate between different network protocols (i.e., languages), a router is often used for connecting wide area networks or for connecting local area networks to the Internet. Routers are one of the best ways to connect a LAN to the Internet, and they are used by companies of all sizes for this purpose.

SERVERS

A SERVER IS A LARGE, POWERFUL, SPECIALIZED COMPUTER THAT CONNECTS to your network. It is generally the most powerful computer on the network, and with good reason—it is used by everyone. Servers run a network operating system, such as Microsoft Windows NT or Novell NetWare, and control the sharing of information and access to resources on the network.

Servers are optional components on a network and are used in client/server networks. They perform many operations for the clients (i.e., desktop computers), such as run applications, store databases and other information, connect printers to the network, store files, run e-mail, send faxes through the network, or connect you to the Internet. In fact, because a server is basically a bigger, faster version of your desktop computer, it can do just about anything that your desktop computer can, and more.

Servers are complex and offer much more power than regular personal computers. However, there are new servers out that are customized just for small businesses. These products are great; they come prepackaged with many of the features a small business needs at a reasonable price. But even though they run small-business software, these small-business servers aren't necessarily easier to set up and maintain than any other network server.

SOFTWARE

ON THE SOFTWARE SIDE, AN OPERATING SYSTEM (OS) PERFORMS THE BASIC services and instructions needed to access and use resources. There are two different types of operating systems, computer operating systems and network operating systems.

Computer Operating Systems

Although it may not be apparent to you when you see the web of cables and devices that make up a network, you are the center of the network; a network begins and ends with your computer. It is designed for you to access information and resources that you don't have on your local computer. That makes your computer operating system an essential part of any network.

A computer operating system controls access to your computer's internal resources, such as the hard drive, memory, and CD-ROM drives. It is also the platform that all your applications run on. Most of the newer operating systems, including Windows 95, Windows 98, Windows NT, and the Mac OS, can also serve as a network operating system. Once you connect to the network, your computer operating system supplies the network operating system as well.

Network Operating Systems

The network operating system (NOS) is similar in operation to your computer's operating system. But instead of controlling access to internal computer resources such as a hard drive, it controls access to resources located on the network. If you want to print to a printer on the network, the NOS sends those instructions over the network to the printer, giving you access to that resource. It also is the platform that network applications run on.

Your network operating system may be a separate software package that runs on a central network server, such as Novell's NetWare or Microsoft's Windows NT Server. When the network operating system runs on a server, the network is called a client/server network. Alternatively, the network operating system may be part of your computer operating system, as it is with Windows 95, Windows 98, and the Mac OS. This type of environment, without a server, is called a peer-to-peer network. These two basic types of networks, peer-to-peer and client/server, are explained next.

Peer-to-Peer Networks

A peer-to-peer network is the simplest type of network. A peer-to-peer network does not use a server. Instead, all of the computers on the network run the network operating system—hence all computers are peers to each other. It's pretty egalitarian.

Peer-to-peer networks have some advantages, especially for smaller networks. First of all, they are simple to set up and relatively inexpensive. In fact, if you are running Windows 95, Windows 98, Windows NT Workstation, or even the Mac OS, you already have the software that you need for basic networking operations. With any of these operating systems you can share files, printers, and even send electronic mail to other computers on the network. More advanced peer-to-peer networking software, such as Artisoft's LANtastic, allow you to share modems and other resources and have improved security.

Peer-to-peer networks are relatively inexpensive to build. Because the software is already built in to your computer, you can connect your computers with a few network adapters, some cabling, and a hub. There is no expensive server to buy.

But peer-to-peer networking also has some disadvantages. First of all, every computer on the network is a client to the others. This increases the load on individual computers and often leads to slower computer performance. In addition, all information is stored on individual computers, so it is difficult to keep information, particularly computer files, organized. This is also a problem when the report you need is on someone else's computer and that computer is turned off (or worse, the report is on a notebook computer and your coworker has taken it out of the office).

Also, peer-to-peer networks have less stringent security than client/ server networks.

Fortunately, a peer-to-peer network is easy to convert to a client/server network without losing your investment in the networking hardware, so it is great for starting out.

WHEN TO CONSIDER A PEER-TO-PEER NETWORK

1. *You have a need for basic networking.* If all you are doing is sharing files and printers, a basic peer-to-peer network is often good enough.
2. *You have a small number of computers (no more than 10 to 15 computers).* Smaller numbers of computers are easier to handle with a peer-to-peer network. However, once you have more than 15 machines, your computer performance may suffer.
3. *You have no need for sharing applications.* Sharing applications is one of the biggest reasons for a server. If you are not planning on running any applications on the network, you may not need one.
4. *You have the same computer operating system running on all your computers.* If all computers are running the same operating system and that OS has built-in peer-to-peer networking, then you already have all the software you need to set up a network.

If you think that a peer-to-peer network is adequate for your needs, you have several software options to choose from. They include:

■ **Windows 95/98.** Several years ago, Windows 95 really helped peer-to-peer networking take off. Because peer-to-peer networking is built into the operating system, it makes it easy for anyone to set up a network. The Windows 95 and Windows 98 computer operating systems contain everything you need to do basic file sharing and printer sharing, including password-based security to protect your files and printers from unauthorized access.

■ **Windows NT Workstation.** Microsoft Windows NT Workstation is designed to be the desktop operating system for large corporations. Like Windows 95 and Windows 98, it has basic networking functions such as file sharing and printer sharing built right in and can be used in a peer-to-peer network.

■ **LANtastic.** Until Windows 95 came along, Artisoft Inc.'s LANtastic product was the preeminent peer-to-peer software package on the market.

LANtastic is a separate application that loads onto your computer in addition to the computer operating system. Today, LANtastic is still an impressive product, although it is not necessary for basic networking.

■ **Mac OS.** The Macintosh operating system, or Mac OS, pioneered built-in networking. Originally, the Mac OS included LocalTalk for connecting Macintoshes together on a network. Although LocalTalk was slow, it was readily available, so many Mac users were connecting their computers long before DOS and Windows users could even spell LAN. Apple has continued that tradition today by including an Ethernet connection on virtually every Macintosh sold, making it very easy to build a quick peer-to-peer network.

Client/Server Networks

Client/server networking is a more advanced form of networking. It includes desktop and notebook computers (i.e., the clients) and a central computer called a server. The server is set up to—you guessed it—"serve" the clients (sounds pretty businesslike, doesn't it?).

The advantage to a client/server network is that everyone can share the resources of a big, powerful computer on the network, so you can do more, faster. In addition, a client/server network lets you store files and applications in a central location and even lets you select different privileges for users on what they can access, when they can access it, and what they can do with it.

The disadvantages of client/server networks are their cost and complexity. Servers are generally faster, more powerful, and more expensive than desktop computers. Add on other costs, such as the network operating system and software licenses, a backup power supply, file backup system, and a cool location (servers can really heat up), and you can see that it becomes a large investment. In addition, client/server networks are much more complex than peer-to-peer networks. That means that you have to pay someone to come in to set up the network and possibly even manage it.

WHEN TO CONSIDER A CLIENT/SERVER NETWORK

1. *You have more than 10 to 15 users on the network.* With more than 10 or 15 computers in a peer-to-peer environment, the computers begin to drain too many resources from each other. A server is necessary to relieve the burdens caused by peer-to-peer networks.

2. *You have shared applications among several users.* Applications that are shared across the network need to be shared on a server that can provide good performance.
3. *You need to run server-based applications.* Many business accounting, manufacturing, inventory, database, and electronic mail applications only run on a server.
4. *You require a central location to store files for universal access.* Sharing files on individual computers works well for smaller groups, but when you need more space or a guarantee that the system will always be available, a server is the best way to go.
5. *You require a high level of security on your network.* Client/server networks can provide more advanced security than a simple peer-to-peer network.
6. *You run computers with different operating systems.* If you are running Windows 95, Windows 3.x, and the Mac OS on the same network, a server can act as an intermediary to connect multiple computer operating systems on one network.

When looking at network operating systems for a client/server network, there are really only two options for most small businesses: Microsoft's Windows NT Server and Novell's NetWare. Both are complicated systems to run, but they both also have small-business versions of their operating systems that include added features and somewhat simpler installation processes.

■ **Windows NT Server.** Windows NT Server is Microsoft's general-purpose network operating system. It is used by small businesses and large businesses alike. Windows NT Server definitely has its advantages, including a great graphical interface similar to Windows 95/98, Internet integration, advanced security, and efficient integration with other Microsoft products such as Exchange messaging software. Windows NT is a great choice for many networks.

There is also a version of Windows NT Server for small networks called BackOffice Small Business Server (SBS). This is the Swiss Army knife of network operating systems, designed specifically for small businesses. SBS gives you virtually everything that you need to get started, including a connection to the Internet (through one or more modems in the server), network faxing, remote access, Internet connection software, Exchange messaging server (for e-mail), printer sharing, and even database capabilities. Software wizards allow you to set up new users, e-mail accounts, and even add hardware with a few mouse clicks.

Small Business Server is a great option if you are looking for a client/server network operating system, but don't kid yourself—SBS is complex enough that it probably needs to be set up by a professional. It comes in license packages for 5 and 25 users. If you have more than 25 users you'll need to use Windows NT Server. Small Business Server can also be upgraded to Windows NT Server if you outgrow the 25-user limit.

■ **Novell NetWare.** Although its networking muscle has weakened a little in the last few years, Novell Inc. is still the undisputed leader in network operating systems. There are more networks running Novell's NetWare than any other NOS in the world. Like Microsoft, Novell has also released a network operating system for small businesses called NetWare for Small Business.

NetWare for Small Business is a scaled-down version of NetWare. It has many features a small business would look for, such as Groupwise (for e-mail, calendaring, and messaging), Internet access, and file and printer sharing. It has also been optimized for easy installation. Like Microsoft's BackOffice Small Business Server, NetWare for Small Business has a 25-user limit, but you can buy it in single-license increments so you don't have to buy more capability than you need. NetWare for Small Business also has an upgrade to regular NetWare when you go beyond 25 users.

Both the small-business versions of NetWare and Windows NT Server are great general operating systems if you are under the 25-user limit. If you are over the limit, then look to the full-blown versions.

While Windows NT and Novell NetWare are the two most likely options that you will have to choose from, there other server operating systems available. UNIX is a very popular operating system used for both high-end computers (workstations) and servers. There are many UNIX versions available from many different vendors.

A new, very popular version of UNIX called Linux is also available. Developed by Finnish programmer Linus Torvalds, this computer and server operating system is popular because it is very stable—meaning that it is less likely to crash. Linux is also available free if you download it from the Internet (which makes it very popular). One of the other advantages of Linux is that it has open source code, which means that anyone has access to operating system's code and can modify it to their needs. This makes it very attractive to those that know how to change

Table 3-2. *Popular Networking Protocols*

Protocol	What It Means	Where It Is Used
IPX	Internetwork Packet Exchange	Used mostly with Novell NetWare computer networks.
TCP/IP	Transmission Control Protocol/Internet Protocol	Used to connect to the Internet and for connecting computers on the LAN. For all types of computers.
NetBEUI	NetBIOS Extended User Interface	Used to connect Windows for Workgroups, Windows 95, Windows 98, and Windows NT computers.

the operating system. Many users who modify Linux make their changes available to other users on the Internet. This creates a very flexible, dynamic, and inexpensive option for experienced programmers. However, it also makes it far too sophisticated and complex for non-technical users.

Finally, if you are running all Macintosh computers at your business, you have the option of running AppleShare IP from Apple Computer Inc. AppleShare IP provides all the built-in services needed for file sharing, printer sharing, hosting web sites, and even e-mail.

PROTOCOLS: THE SECRET LANGUAGE OF GEEKS

BESIDES A NETWORKING STANDARD SUCH AS ETHERNET, EACH NETWORK must run a protocol to control communications. A protocol is nothing more than a common set of rules or the language all network devices use to talk to each other. To go back to our phone analogy, telephones use a set of rules to govern how they connect, what a busy signal means, when to ring each other, and what happens when someone picks up a phone; these rules are similar to our network standard of Ethernet. But people also have another protocol that runs over the phone—what language we speak. The most important thing to know is that like people, computers must all speak the same language in order to communicate. If not, they need a translator, such as a router or a server. Computers, fortunately, can speak different languages at the same time.

There are three popular protocols that are spoken on networks. You don't need to know much about them, except that your computer uses them to communicate with other computers and devices on the network. These protocols are set up when you set up your computer to connect to the network. A list of popular protocols is shown in Table 3-2. Don't try to memorize them, just remember that this table is here if you ever want to know what they mean.

We covered a lot for your first exposure to networking, but if you made it this far and your head isn't completely spinning, you've done well. After reading this chapter, you probably have a pretty good idea about what a local area network is and does. If you think that local area networking can benefit your company, refer to Chapters 4 through 8 to better understand the types of applications that typically run on a LAN and how to plan for your own local area network. The next chapter takes a closer look at what a basic network can do for your business.

CHAPTER 4

Sharing With a Basic Network

IF YOUR BUSINESS IS LIKE MOST OTHERS, COMPUTERS HAVE ALREADY drastically changed the way you do business. They have become the focal point of most offices for getting work done. To prove it, just look at how your computer is set up on your desk. If you're like most people, it is at the center of your work area. It is a powerful tool, but if it is not connected to the other computers in your office, you are only using part of its potential.

Basic Networks

A BASIC PEER-TO-PEER LOCAL AREA NETWORK CAN BE ONE OF THE MOST cost-effective ways to leverage the power of your computers by allowing users to share peripherals and files—without a huge expense, excessive setup time, or even someone to manage it. Even a group of only two or three computers can benefit from a network to share files and peripherals such as printers.

File sharing and peripheral sharing are the most popular functions for peer-to-peer networks. File sharing is simply the ability to access others' files and let others access your files through the network. You probably already do file sharing in your office today, even without a network. But with a network it is much simpler, saving you the bother of copying files onto disks, handing them to your coworkers, and letting them copy the file from the disk onto their computer.

With a network, instead of playing the sneakernet game (where your sneakers do the transfer, physically carrying you and your disk over to the next computer), you set up a folder on your computer of what you want to share, assign a password to it, and just drop the files in it. Then you can give out the password and let users copy the files from your computer over the network or copy theirs to your computer.

Figure 4-1 shows how file sharing is used in a typical company. In this example, an advertising agency has six employees who often collaborate on projects for their accounts. But the employees frequently waste time exchanging information by trading floppy disks. And because their shared files are usually too large to fit on a floppy disk, the company has had to invest in several removable media drives, which can store many times the information of a floppy, to transfer information. Sneakernet for this company is expensive, both in time and hardware costs.

Figure 4-1. *Basic Network for File Sharing*

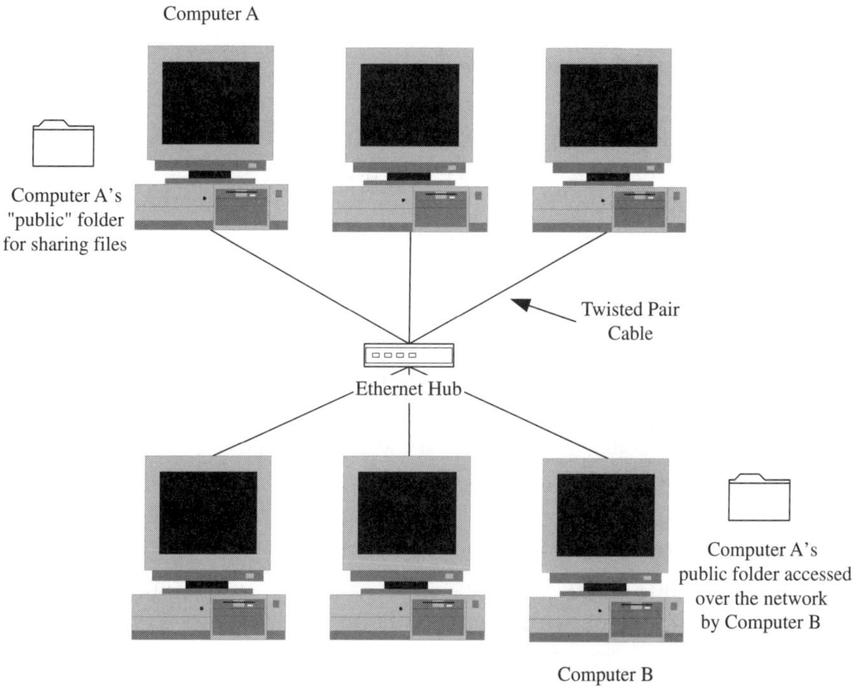

Computer A

Computer A's "public" folder for sharing files

Twisted Pair Cable

Ethernet Hub

Computer A's public folder accessed over the network by Computer B

Computer B

To save costs and time, the company sets up a basic network to improve file sharing. The network consists of a hub, network adapters for each computer, and cabling, along with the company's existing Windows 98 operating system. With the network each employee sets up "public" folders on his or her computer for sharing information. The folders are protected with passwords, so only those with the correct password can log on to someone else's computer for the information. Now, rather than shuffling disks and spending money on more removable media drives, employees access important files on each other's computers with just a few clicks of their mouse.

Sharing hardware, or peripherals, is the second reason for setting up a basic network. This can bring a huge cost savings by allowing many users to share the cost of one peripheral device, such as a printer, rather than having to buy separate printers for each individual computer. Often the money saved by sharing peripherals pays for the cost of the entire basic network.

As Figure 4-2 shows, sometime after installing a basic network, the advertising agency purchased a new laser printer for documents and a color laser printer for making presentations.

With this network, the company can attach the new printers to any computer on the network and share it with everyone on the network. All other users on the network access the printers through the network and are be able to print to them as if the printers were connected directly to their own computer. This gives the company the ability to share expensive printers with everyone on the network and allocate that cost over all employees.

Benefits

EVEN THE MOST BASIC PEER-TO-PEER NETWORK CAN BENEFIT MOST COMPANIES. Among the benefits of a network are:

■ **Improved productivity.** A basic network will help you to avoid the sneakernet syndrome of shuttling disks back and forth from computer to computer. With the network, using a file on someone else's computer is a one-person operation, not two. Say, for example, that you have a business proposal that you have been working on for the last few weeks. You want some input on the proposal from a coworker. To share the file without a network you must insert a floppy disk into your computer, copy the file to

Figure 4-2. *Basic Network for Printer Sharing*

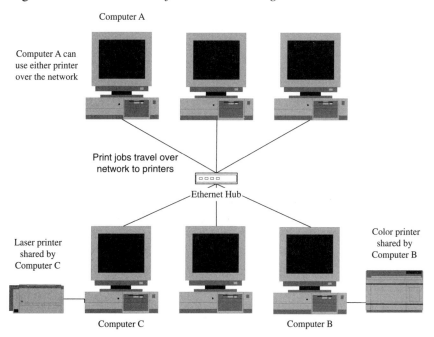

the floppy disk, remove the floppy, and physically carry the disk to your coworker's computer. She must then do the reverse process, putting the file on her computer, viewing it, and making changes.

You may be thinking that this scenario doesn't sound too bad. But let's say that your coworker makes some changes. She brings the disk back to you. You make changes based on her revisions and carry the disk back to her. She makes changes and brings the disk back to you, and so on. Before you know it, there is a path worn in the carpet between your offices.

Now imagine that you can set up a folder on your computer that your coworker can access through her computer. By giving her access to the folder, she can connect to it from her own computer, open the file, and make changes, without either of you ever leaving your desk. It's that simple!

■ **Lower hardware costs.** Sharing printers and other devices on the network saves on hardware costs because you don't have to buy separate devices for each computer. At times, the savings alone is enough to cover the cost of the entire network.

47

The number-one peripheral shared on networks today is printers. Being able to avoid the expense of buying a printer for each computer in your office is itself a significant savings. But the same can be said for many other peripherals as well. You can share almost anything that you would normally use on through your own computer, including hard drives, CD-ROMs, removable storage devices, scanners, and even modems. Even basic file sharing can help save hardware costs. Just imagine that you are working on a presentation for a business proposal. You put together a nice presentation, adding a few graphics and charts to give it that professional edge. Now you want to show off your work or give it to the salesperson down the hall to use on his next trip. So you put in your floppy and start copying, but the file is too big to fit on the floppy diskette. What is your alternative? Buy not one but *two* removable storage devices for the two computers to transfer the large files. Removable storage devices, such as Iomega's Zip drives, hold a lot of data. But it is difficult to justify having to buy them just for transferring files between two computers. Your other alternative, of course, is to install a network and transfer those files over the network.

■ **Improved quality of hardware.** By reducing the number of different devices that you have to put on individual computers, you can also increase the quality of your equipment. For example, if you have five computers in your office, you could be tempted to buy five printers, one for each computer. But with a network, you can take the cost of five individual low-end printers and apply that total amount toward purchasing a bigger, better, faster printer.

■ **Increased communications/collaboration.** By using a network to make it easier to share files and information, you can improve your company's level of communication and collaboration. Communication and collaboration can be extended even further with applications such as electronic mail.

Is It for You?

BASIC NETWORKS CAN BENEFIT ALMOST ANY TYPE OF OFFICE THAT HAS MULTIPLE computers. Since people generally work together in an office environment, there is an opportunity to share information and projects quickly and easily.

WHEN TO CONSIDER A BASIC NETWORK

1. Your office has one or more printers that can be used by multiple employees, or your company has hesitated to buy a good printer because you are not sure how to set it up so that everyone has access to it.

2. Some of your computers have CD drives, removable storage such as Zip drives, or other peripherals that can be shared on the network. If you have invested in various peripheral devices already, you can share them.

3. Your employees regularly work together on projects. If so, your employees can benefit from sharing information such as spreadsheets, documents, databases, or presentations more easily over the network.

4. Your employees regularly transfer files back and forth on floppy disks from computer to computer.

Cautions

WHILE A BASIC NETWORK CAN BRING MANY BENEFITS, THERE ARE SOME concerns that should be addressed. Here are some issues you'll want to consider to ensure that you don't fall into any traps.

SECURITY

Placing computers on the network opens up a new potential security risk. Networks are about sharing, but you don't want to publish every file on your hard drive to everyone in the company. You may have valuable information that you want to share, but a spreadsheet of employees' salaries is not one of them.

The security issue can be resolved by using special folders set up for public use on the network, setting up different rights of access so that people can only read files and not change them, and assigning passwords to protect files from unauthorized users.

PRINTER MANIA

If you plan to have one or more printers on the network, watch out for signs of a printing marathon. Newfound freedoms often bring about new abuses. One of the worst is when people start sending everything they have to the fast, new laser printer down the hall. Before you know it, people are printing out every document on their computers and sending your printing costs through the roof. This especially happens with networked color printers.

One quick way to remedy this situation is to assign password access to printers on the network and only give it out to a select group that needs access to that printer.

CROSSING FILES

As file sharing becomes more popular in the office, problems may occur as a document has multiple revisions on multiple computers. Who owns the document? Where is it? What if I accidentally delete it from someone's computer? Which is the latest version? As you can see, it gets a little complex when multiple persons store a document in multiple sites and make regular changes to it.

To avoid confusion as to the location of files, it is best to establish files in set folders. For example, if you and several coworkers are all working on a marketing plan, keep all files in one folder named Marketing Plan on one person's computer. Make sure that all files are kept in that folder.

The simplest way of identifying the latest version of a file is to use file revision numbers as part of the file name. This involves using a numbering system to identify what version of the file is most current. Therefore, the draft of your marketing plan may be Marketing Plan v0.1. Each time a major revision is made (such as the first distributed copy), the revision number jumps up to the next whole number, such as 2.0, 3.0, etc. Each time a minor revision is made to the file (such as adding a paragraph or some data), the number changes by .1. The second draft of the marketing plan would be Marketing Plan v0.2, and a revision to Marketing Plan v1.0 would be Marketing Plan v1.1. Using file revision numbers is simple and can avoid overwriting someone else's work.

BURDENING INDIVIDUAL COMPUTERS

In many cases, it is easy to share a device that is already connected to your computer—for example, a printer or CD-ROM drive. However, there are times when sharing a device that is connected to your computer can become a burden to the performance of your computer. When that happens, you may want to consider a way to connect the device to the network without having it on your computer. This can become a problem with printers and modems, which can especially burden desktop computers. Using a standalone print server, which connects the printer directly to the network, can solve the problem by making a special connection for the printer to the network. Other, similar devices are available to share modems, CD drives, or other peripherals without having to attach them directly to someone's computer. These devices can also be shared through a server.

Getting Started

BASIC NETWORKS ARE NOT THAT DIFFICULT TO SET UP. IF YOU FEEL COMFORT-able opening your computer to add memory and installing applications, you can do it on your own. There are also plenty of people out there that will do it for you and save you the hassle. Even if you decide to do it yourself, you probably will want to have someone else install the networking cable for you. Unless all your computers are close together, it is not easy to string the cable without it looking like a spaghetti factory. A professional can install cabling so that it looks decent and runs through the walls and ceilings and isn't left out on the open floor.

BASIC GUIDELINES FOR INSTALLING A NETWORK
1. *Decide what you want to share and who should share it.* Do you just want basic file sharing, or do you want to share peripherals? What peripherals are available? Does everyone need to be on the network, or just a few people who work together? Knowing what you have and what you want to do up-front is key. The LAN planning steps outlined in Chapter 8 can help you put your needs in writing.
2. *Determine the most appropriate network topology and protocol for your needs.* Your best choice for flexibility and ease of use is a star network that uses a hub to connect everything together. Your choice for a networking protocol should be Ethernet or Fast Ethernet.
3. *Choose a network operating system (NOS) to give each computer access to network resources.* Your first decision here is whether to run a peer-to-peer or a client/server network. For

start-up networks, a peer-to-peer network using Windows 95, Windows 98, Windows NT, or the Macintosh operating system is the easiest way to get started. Everything you need for file and printer sharing is built in. If you already have one of these operating systems on all of your computers, it is best to stick with it. If you are planning on a client/server network, your NOS options for a server are Novell's NetWare or Microsoft's Windows NT. You can consider the small-business versions of either of these operating systems.

Usually your choice of networking protocols will be determined by your network operating system. For example, if you are using Novell's NetWare, your protocol will likely be IPX. If you are running Windows 95, you will use NetBEUI or TCP/IP. (You can refer back to Table 3-2 for explanations of these popular networking protocols.) Networks can run several network protocols simultaneously.

4. *Write down your equipment laundry list.* Your list should include all the necessary equipment you will need.

NETWORK COMPONENTS YOU WILL PROBABLY NEED

■ **Network adapters.** Network adapters are needed for each computer to connect to the network. The network adapter will plug into a slot inside your computer. Your computer's manual should tell you what type of card you need.

The best choice today, whether you run Ethernet or Fast Ethernet, is to buy adapters that run both, called 10/100 cards. They automatically switch between the two types of Ethernet so they can run Ethernet today and Fast Ethernet in the future, and they cost only slightly more than regular Ethernet cards. Since most networks will eventually move to Fast Ethernet, it is worth the investment to not have to change cards in the future.

■ **Cabling.** Go with twisted-pair cabling that is used with a hub in a star network. Even if you decide to install the network on your own, cabling may still be the one area that you want to turn over to a professional. Use only Category 5 cabling, the highest grade available, because it will work with future technologies as well. The last thing you want to do is pull cabling out of your walls when you want to upgrade.

■ **Hub.** If you use a star topology you will need a hub to connect everything together. When buying a hub, buy for tomorrow's needs, not just today's. If you only need to connect five people, buy an eight-port hub. That way, if you ever add more people or more devices to the network, you will have a few extra ports for growth. The difference in price is usually minimal.

■ **Print server.** When sharing a device such as a printer on the network, you can share it though your computer if it is running Windows 95 or Windows 98. However, there are three disadvantages to this setup. First, when your coworkers use the printer connected to your computer, they steal some of your computer's resources, dragging down its performance. Second, your computer must be on anytime someone wants to use the printer. If not, no one can access the printer. Third, the printer must sit close by the computer, rather than a central location.

A simple, inexpensive solution is to use a print server to connect the printer to the network. A print server is a small, single-function computer with its own processor and memory. It connects to the printer on one side (through a serial or parallel port) and the network on the other side. The print server then accepts print jobs from workers' computers and processes them for printing. Print servers also allow you to put the printer in a central location where everyone can easily access it. A print server only costs a few hundred dollars, so it is a good investment if it saves you some headaches.

Other devices—modems, external CD-ROM drives, and scanners—can be shared on the network with a server as well. If you plan to run a basic peer-to-peer network, shared devices are a simple, easy-to-use solution.

■ **Starter kits.** If you are the do-it-yourself type and have a small number of computers to connect, you may want to consider buying a network starter kit. Network starter kits are all-in-one packages that include network adapters, cabling, hub, and installation instructions. If you have an operating system that only does peer-to-peer networking, these kits are a great way to get started. They are less expensive than buying separate components, but the one-size-fits-all concept comes at a price. You get fixed lengths of cable from 25- to 50-feet long, which may not be the correct length for your needs. You also tend to get a smaller hub, with five or eight connections.

Setting up a basic network does not have to be expensive; the essential components generally run around $100 per computer. For that relatively small amount, a simple network is one of the best investments you can make to improve your workers' productivity and coordination/collaboration while keeping peripheral costs lower. To get started planning your local area network, refer to Chapter 8. The next chapter explains how expanding your network with a server can benefit your company even more.

CHAPTER 5

Using a Network Server

WITH A BASIC NETWORK INSTALLED FOR CONNECTING YOUR COMPUTERS, YOU are able to share files and peripherals between coworkers. When you outgrow the size, performance, or application limitations of your peer-to-peer network, a client/server network with a server is the next step.

Servers

A NETWORK SERVER IS A LARGE, FAST, SPECIALIZED COMPUTER THAT IS SET UP on the network for all users to share. The server is not used by anyone as a desktop computer; it is used by all computers on the network as a shared resource. Figure 5-1 shows an example of a server.

Several different types of servers are available. They are generally categorized into two different types: workgroup and departmental. As you can see, these names are indicative of their use in large companies. Departmental servers are designed for large corporate environments and can handle hundreds of users. Workgroup servers are designed for smaller groups within a company and usually handle under 100 people. There are also new servers out designed specifically for small businesses; these are usually workgroup-class servers bundled with software for small businesses.

No matter what type of server you use, remember that a server is different from a desktop computer; it is much more powerful and more expandable so it can perform many functions simultaneously. Servers generally have faster processors, faster I/O (input and output to devices), more storage, and more memory than desktop computers. Just about anything that you want to share on a network can be put on a server. For example, with a server you can:

Figure 5-1. *Server*

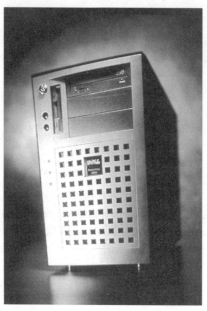

Dell Poweredge 2300 server. Reproduced by permission of Dell Computer Corporation. Copyright 1999 Dell Computer Corporation.

■ **Share applications.** A server can share applications on the network. One of the most popular applications shared on a server is database software, but a server can run many types of software. This is beneficial for three reasons. First, the server is often the fastest computer on the network, so it can often run an application faster than it can be run it on your slower desktop computer.

Second, most companies that sell software offer discounts for companies that buy a license for a certain number of users (called "seats") to run the application at the same time. Discount network licenses can be purchased for accounting software, databases, and more. These licenses save you money and work well for applications that are run sporadically.

Take, for example, Figure 5-2, which shows how application sharing on a server can help a typical business. The company's five employees regularly use software such as a word processor, spreadsheet, and presentation software. Because they are used often, those applications reside on each employee's computer. However, the employees also use a database sporadically. The database software is expensive, costing more than $500 per copy. All employees use it, but no single person uses the software enough to justify the cost of individual applications on each computer. In addition, the users need to share the same database of information, so the data needs to reside in one place. So instead of purchasing a single application for each employee, the company purchases a network license for the software that allows it to run on the server. Everyone can

Figure 5-2. *Application Sharing on a Server*

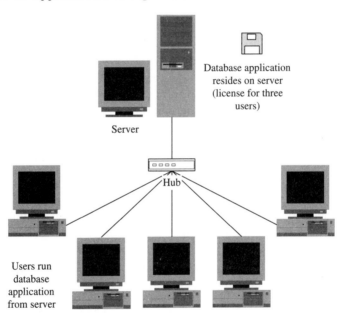

now access the application, but under the agreement no more than three employees use the software simultaneously. The server is powerful enough to handle the application, and everyone can share the software at a reduced cost.

The third benefit to sharing applications on a server is that when it is time to upgrade the software, you only have to load the upgrade onto the server itself, not the individual computers, which can be a major time-saver.

■ **Share files.** Even if you are sharing files on a peer-to-peer network, you may use a server to set up and control file sharing. A server lets you share files in a central location and without having to keep every computer on all the time. It even allows you to back up your most important files from the clients to the server to protect data from crashes.

We all need our own personal space, and network users are no different. One of the benefits of file sharing with a server is that you can set up directories for each person on the network. It becomes their own personal area to put important files. Users can even "map" a drive on the server to their computer so that when they log onto the network they see the directory as one of their computer's drives. This is helpful because computer hard drives fill up faster than you can imagine, so you can use the server to free up space on individual computers. Also, it is good to back up important files to the server in case anything happens to the computer. This is particularly the case with notebook computers that are more susceptible to being stolen or damaged.

File sharing on servers can help to keep things organized as well. Companies can organize folders on the server by clients, projects, file types, months, or a number of other ways. Some employees can have access to some folders and not others. Some users may also have rights to copy or change files while others can only read them. This level of organization keeps file sharing optimized.

■ **Share peripherals.** Servers can also be used to share peripherals. In fact, one of the first uses of servers was for sharing printers. Novell Inc. became a networking giant largely because of two main features in its NetWare network operating system: file and printer sharing.

Today's network operating systems also allow you to share modems (for access to the Internet and faxing), CD-ROM drives, removable media drives, and more. Servers can also share modems used to give users the ability to dial into the network from a remote location with a notebook or desktop computer and have access to files, e-mail, and other services. This is called remote access.

■ **Run communications programs.** Servers can also be used to run communications programs, including specific applications such as e-mail, groupware, or intranets. These communications solutions are covered further in Chapter 6.

Benefits

A SERVER BRINGS A NEW DYNAMIC TO THE NETWORK, PROVIDING A CENTRAL resource for the entire network and offering additional benefits beyond a peer-to-peer network. In general, the advantages of running a server on your network are to:

■ **Bring different computers together.** If you have different computers on the network, they may not be able to talk to each other in a peer-to-peer environment. For example, one person may be running a Windows 95 machine, another Windows 3.1, and someone else may use a Macintosh. A server can act as the central translator to get them all to communicate, share resources, and even share files.

■ **Improve accessibility.** Peer-to-peer networks, those without a server, are fine for many situations. But one of the problems with a peer-to-peer network is that everything is located on individual computers. Servers help to remedy the problems of peer-to-peer file sharing by providing better, more organized access. Because the server is powered on all the time, it can always be accessed, unlike desktop computers. Because directory organization on the server is usually controlled by one person, it is easier to follow the structure. And since everything is in one place, it is easy to find the latest version of a file.

■ **Improve security.** Security is one of the key benefits of a server. Peer-to-peer operating systems allow users to set up passwords for access to their files and attached peripherals. That is fine if you want give someone access to your computer. You give them the password and they can get on your computer whenever they need to. But what happens when that person gives out that password? Anyone with the password can access your shared files and peripherals, whether they got the password from you or someone else.

Client/server operating systems have more advanced security features, such as user-level security for accessing resources on desktop computers or servers. User-level security lets you specify which users or groups can have access to your files or other resources through a pre-assigned account that the person uses to log on the server. After logging onto the server, these users have access to the resources they have been given access rights to. Servers also provide individual rights or privileges as well. So your assistant may have access to read, write, and copy files into a folder, but your clumsy coworker down the hall can only read files. This prevents your coworker from accidentally deleting the document you have worked on for the last week.

■ **Save money on software.** Client/server networks also facilitate networked application sharing. As mentioned previously, file servers can store applications used under a network license. Multiple users can access and use the applications as if they are located on their own computers. Network licenses are generally less expensive than purchasing separate applications for each computer. Application sharing should be done within reason. Word processors, spreadsheet applications, e-mail, clients, and other frequently used software programs are better suited for running on desktop computers. Other applications such as databases, accounting software, and manufacturing software are suited or even designed for running on servers.

By running some applications from a server, you not only save money with licensing, but you also save time because you only have to upgrade the server.

■ **Improve performance.** Because a server is shared by the entire network, it is generally more powerful than any other computer on the network and can be used for very specific functions that can benefit the entire network. By contrast, in a peer-to-peer network employees have to access an individual computer to use to a file, printer, or modem, which drags that computer's performance down. Servers, on the other hand, are designed for performance. So they can handle even a large number of people using them regularly.

■ **Perform backup.** A server often includes a way to back up data in case the server crashes, so you will always have a copy of your data if anything goes wrong. Users may back up critical data on the server, which is then backed up regularly to some type of storage media such as tape or CD-ROM. If the network goes down, the data is stored so that it can be retrieved.

Is It for You?

SERVERS CAN BE HIGHLY EFFECTIVE, BUT THEY CAN ALSO BE COMPLEX AND expensive. Many smaller networks start without a server and add one later on as their needs change or they grow. If you are just starting out and running a small network, you may want to try going without one for a while. However, the benefits of a server are many, so there may be no time like the present.

WHEN TO CONSIDER A SERVER
1. *You want to connect computers running different computer operating systems.* If you are running different operating systems, such as Windows 3.1, Windows 95, and Macintosh, then you need to run a server if you want to get them all to communicate over

the network. Even with a server, getting them to communicate can be as difficult as arbitrating a United Nations meeting.

2. *You are running computers with no peer-to-peer operating system.* Some computer operating systems such as Windows 3.11 don't have a built-in network operating system, so you probably need a server to get these computers on a network. You should probably consider upgrading your computers while you are at it.

3. *You have more than 10 computers.* A peer-to-peer network will become burdened if you have 10 to 15 individual computers on it. Imagine all these computers trying to access your hard drive at the same time.

4. *You have special applications that need to be shared across the network.* If you want to share applications over the network, especially database or accounting applications, using a server is the way to do it.

5. *You want to perform many different functions on the network.* If you want to share a printer and an Internet connection as well as run applications, you should probably consider a server. The more operations you want to have on the network, they more cost-effective it is to run them on the network.

Cautions

BEFORE GOING OUT AND CUTTING A CHECK FOR A SERVER FOR YOUR NETwork, you should be aware that servers are not for everyone. Servers are big, expensive, complex machines. They require time to manage and maintain. You should consider the darker side of life with a server.

ADDED COMPLEXITY

Servers have more of everything, including complexity. The network operating system on the server is complex, and the server itself interacts with many other computers and is accessed by many people. All of this spells out the potential for problems.

HIGHER COST

Servers are not as affordable as a desktop computer. They generally offer:

- More memory (RAM)
- Bigger hard disks (and room for more of them)
- More processors
- Data backup systems
- More slots for adding network, video, and other cards
- More room for expansion
- Redundant fans and power supplies
- Faster input and output

This is all good, because as your network grows—either in the number of users or the amount of time your current employees spend on the network—you don't want your server to become obsolete.

But this expandability comes at a price. While you can get a good desktop computer for around $1,000 today, a server costs well over $3,500 at the low end. Many better servers for small networks cost from $5,000 to $10,000 and more. Add the network operating system on top of that, as well as modems or other peripherals, and it can be a very expensive investment.

INCREASED NETWORK TRAFFIC

In a peer-to-peer network, everyone is an equal on the network. All of the data—often called traffic—on the network is pretty well distributed from computer to computer. But when you add a server on the network, it becomes the central source for much of the data. In other words, many computers are trying to access one big computer. Soon your network becomes a funnel, with a very tight bottleneck going to the server. This bottleneck may become apparent to network users and decrease the value of the server as a high-speed computer. If it is serious enough, it requires an investment in a faster network, usually Fast Ethernet or switched Ethernet.

PROLIFERATION

With some users, the lure of having a server on the network is too much. Some users start treating the server as if it were their own personal electronic junk drawer, putting all their files and applications on it. Others may find other uses for the server that it wasn't made for. Pretty soon the server becomes the black hole of the network, sucking in every piece of data until the server fills up. To counter this situation, limits can be placed on what individual users can access and how much they can put on the server. Some vigilant server monitoring can prevent too much abuse.

Also, don't load every software application on the file server and have all users running their applications over the network. This scenario is good for some applications, and you may think that you can save a lot of disk space by putting them on a server. But it will bog down the network and you won't be happy if the server ever goes down and no one can access any applications. Popular applications such as word processors and spreadsheets should reside on desktop computers.

SOFTWARE PIRACY

If you plan to run applications on your server for individuals to use over the network, remember that it is illegal to share among many users an application for which you have only one license. You must buy an application that has multiple seats, or licenses, to allow employees to use it over the network.

MANAGEMENT AND SECURITY

Because a server does so much, it quickly becomes the most important device on the network. This means that the server must be maintained regularly. Someone has to watch the server for disk space problems, hard drive failures, overheating, CPU utilization, fans and power supplies going out, and other problems. Adding a new user to the network is no longer a matter of simply connecting another computer to the network. It involves setting that user up for access rights and maintaining passwords and privileges. Servers also require regular maintenance to keep them running. That means scheduled backups, periodic checkups, deletion of old information, and repairing or removing corrupted files. These maintenance jobs can be done by someone in-house or by a networking consultant.

In addition, you need to protect the data that is on the server. Remember that your data is far more valuable than the server itself is. You can always replace the server, but you may never be able to replace the information stored on it. Keep the server locked in a safe, cool place. Make sure that you have redundant power supplies and fans, and hook the server to an uninterruptible power supply in case the power goes out. Also, make sure that you are backing up your data regularly and storing it off-site.

Network Appliances

IF YOU ARE FEELING OVERWHELMED WITH THE WHOLE CONCEPT OF SPENDING money for a full-blown server and only have one or two reasons for needing one, then take heart—there may be a server that fits your needs. There is a new class of products referred to by a number of names—network appliances, thin servers, or even microservers—that you might want to consider.

Whatever the name, these small products are designed for very focused operations and come bundled with everything for a small network with limited needs. They are called "thin" because, unlike "fat" servers that are general-purpose and run a "fat" operating system such as Windows NT or NetWare and perform many different functions, these healthier versions run a smaller, specialized operating system tuned to perform one or two functions.

Network appliances perform one or perhaps several similar functions, and they come with all the hardware and software that you need, integrated into one complete, self-contained package. Network appliances are used as intranet servers, e-mail servers, CD-ROM sharing servers, and even for network file storage. Multifunction network appliances handle several related functions, such as Internet access, e-mail, and website hosting. As combined hardware and software and with only several functions, they offer one big advantage: they are relatively easy to set up and maintain. Most are designed to be set up by those with little computer or networking experience. Most network appliances are under $2,000, with many selling for less than $1,000, so that they are much less than a server running on operating system like Windows NT.

However, one thing to remember is that network appliances are not expandable to do jobs beyond their original design. For example, if you buy a network appliance for a specific function such as e-mail, you probably won't be able to load a second function, such as network file storage, on it at a later time. Also, they often handle only a small group of users at a time; most will support 50 users or so, but the range varies by product function.

Although network appliances appear to be new, they really aren't. Print servers, which have been around for years and allow you to share printers on a network, are essentially the precursor to the network appliance: They are small, inexpensive, and handle one function: sharing printers on the network.

Getting Started

TO GET STARTED ON USING A SERVER ON YOUR NETWORK, THE FIRST THING that you must determine is what you want to use your server for. This chapter, along with Chapters 6 and 7 that follow, cover many of the applications that you can consider. Read through the examples to help get started.

Second, choose your network operating system. In general, there have been two options in the past: Microsoft's Windows NT Server and Novell's NetWare. Both are complex to set up. However, both also offer small-business versions that are somewhat easier to set up and include many applications to get your network started.

Third, find the server that fits your needs. Servers are large and powerful computers. Choosing the right features for a server can be tricky. The main inputs for determining your needs are to know 1) what applications you plan to run, 2) how many people you will have connecting to the server, and 3) what network operating system you will use. Options for memory, disk space, network connection, processors, and power depend entirely on these three factors. The job of deciding what your company needs and how to serve those needs is usually better left to a professional computer reseller or consultant. Many of them can build a custom server for you based on your needs.

However, there are also new network servers designed specifically for small businesses by large computer manufacturers such as Compaq Computer, Dell Computer, Gateway 2000, and Hewlett-Packard. These servers run preconfigured network operating systems made specifically for small business—for example, Microsoft's BackOffice Small Business Server or Novell's NetWare for Small Business. These packages essentially have everything you need to get started, including the network operating system, as well as software to share peripherals, connect to the Internet, use e-mail, and perform many other functions. They are generally less flexible than a custom-built server because they are designed for general-purpose use, but they are probably adequate for most needs. It still isn't easy to get these systems set up; they require a lot of work to configure everything. But if you have some patience, time (an entire Saturday, perhaps), and know-how, you can probably do it yourself.

Present needs shouldn't be your only concern. Servers are like houses—you should really plan to buy bigger than you currently need because you will grow into it. So think about what you might be doing in the future. You don't need to buy everything now, but the server has to be expandable enough for you to add on in the future. A good, expandable server will generally have space for more processors, more memory, bays for additional hard drives or other media, and it will also have extra slots in the back for networking, modem, and other cards. In computer lingo, this is called "scalability." Plan for tomorrow today by thinking about what applications or uses you may want to have later on.

Make sure that your server has as much performance as you can afford. Don't skimp on performance or it will come back to haunt you. That means making sure that you get a fast processor, a large cache, plenty of memory, and high-speed input and output. When evaluating different server options, find out about the warranty and support for the product as well. Almost all server vendors offer a good warranty; most offer a three-year warranty and some level of on-site service and toll-free technical support. The last thing you want is for the server to go down and find you have no one to turn to.

Those looking to run special applications should speak with a computer reseller that builds systems with custom specifications. There is no magic to this, but a reseller can design a system that has the features for the applications you are running. Direct manufacturers such as Dell and Gateway will also configure a custom server for your needs if you tell them what applications you are running and what the requirements are.

Depending on the number of employees on the network and what applications you are running, you may need a server dedicated to a single purpose. For example, if you plan on running groupware such as Lotus Notes for 50 people, you will probably need one server dedicated to that application only.

Whatever your needs and options, a network server can bring added benefits when networking your business. It will provide your company's employees with more tools than ever to share files and applications, access other resources, and even communicate better. Taking your sever to the next level to improve company communications is the topic of our next chapter.

CHAPTER 6

Getting Your Company Communicating

HAVE YOU EVER BEEN IN A MEETING IN YOUR COMPANY WHERE SOMEONE HAS said, "Well, if I had just received that information from so and so," or "No one informed me of that"? If your company is like most, it probably happens frequently. Internal communication is one of the biggest challenges facing companies today. Poor communication hurts company productivity, quality of service, coordination, and morale. One would like to think that this lack of communication is only the problem of large, multinational corporations, but all businesses face the same difficulties in keeping everyone communicating.

What is the technological solution to this problem? Open up your company's channels of communication across a network and transform your computer from a computational device that crunches numbers or creates graphics to a communications resource.

Communicating on a Network

APPLICATIONS AVAILABLE FOR INCREASING COMMUNICATION WITHIN YOUR company can improve the information flow and collaboration between your employees. Applications come in many different types, ranging from programs for publishing information to sending electronic messages to collaborating online. Because these applications involve sharing information with everyone on your network, they usually run on a central server, although some of them can run on a peer-to-peer network. There are many ways for your employees to interact with one another, but the three most popular options are electronic mail, groupware, and intranets.

LAN E-MAIL

LAN electronic mail, or e-mail, is the ability to send messages from one employee to another across the network. The concept is similar to regular mail, with everyone having an e-mail "address" that others send electronic letters to. E-mail is a great way to communicate with others, allowing you to send files as attachments that others can download to their computer. Sending attached files is the easiest and most popular way to share files over a network.

Let's take, for example, a manufacturing company that has grown to 25 employees and reached the point where employees are having a difficult time communicating easily with one another. There are increased complaints in meetings that information is not readily available, even though employees can share files on the network. The company president also notices many people having to walk around the building in order to talk to all individuals in the company and a lot of paper being wasted on intracompany memos.

The company decides to implement an e-mail system across its network. Since everyone in the front office has a computer, e-mail allows all employees to share information electronically, provide updates to information, and keep up to date on what is happening. Because it is network-based, e-mail cuts down on the daily paper shuffle of the office.

Most e-mail systems can also be used for Internet-based e-mail so that employees can also communicate with others outside the company, including other companies and individuals that have Internet access.

GROUPWARE

Groupware extends beyond sending electronic messages to others; it allows users to communicate, publish, collaborate, and share information. While most groupware applications run on very large installations, they can be scaled to smaller networks as well.

Groupware comes in many forms and includes many functions. It often includes the ability to send and receive electronic mail, publish documents, share personal calendars and schedules, set up meetings, and hold computer-based "discussions" in which users publish their information in a hierarchical forum in an open area for some or all employees to see. It can also include workflow management items such as task management, document routing, and calendar coordination. Products that fit into this category include Lotus Notes and Lotus Domino, Microsoft Exchange, and Novell's GroupWise. An example of a groupware application is shown in Figure 6-1.

Figure 6-1. *User Interface for Novell GroupWise*

Groupware works well in situations where more collaboration is needed beyond just sending information to others. It addresses the static and limited nature of e-mail. Electronic mail, for example, is great for letting everyone know that the sales team just landed that big new client. You can send out a message and you will probably get a few responses of congratulations back from some employees. However, if you want to hold an electronic discussion about how to win the next big client and have documents to route in the process, groupware may be a better forum. With groupware you can post a plan for everyone to read, set up a discussion group to get feedback or revisions on the plan, create a meeting on everyone's calendar to discuss next steps, assign tasks for individuals, and even track the project as it moves forward. Groupware is more dynamic and offers more ways to communicate. Groupware applications also require more proactive setup procedures than electronic mail. While products such as Lotus Notes come with many templates, they are designed to be customized to your needs. So if you want anything beyond the standard templates, someone at your company needs to learn how to customize the application or you need to turn to a groupware consultant.

An example where groupware is an effective application is in law firms. Law firms are paper-intensive offices, with a lot of information and interaction going on between workers. A groupware application on a local server allows attorneys to set up their cases on the server. Attorneys then post summaries about the cases, legal briefs, and research to the server. Others who are working on the case can review the legal briefs and post changes with comments, add additional research, and even post documents or comments on strategies for the cases. In addition, attorneys can coordinate calendars for meetings and even keep task lists for filing dates and other important deadlines. All of this information is kept together in one area where the attorneys can return to review and modify at any time. This solution provides a much greater level of interaction than e-mail, which allows users to send mail and attach information but has little organizational functionality.

INTRANETS

Intranets are the newest tool for internal communications. Intranets are analogous to running the Internet's graphical World Wide Web on your local area network, allowing you to publish information to the company in the form of a web page.

Intranets can be used for anything that you would normally publish for your employees. With an intranet, you can publish calendars, policies, company news, and even projects. If you are thinking that your company would never need an internal website, you may want to think again. Intranets are very compelling solutions because of their ease of use. An intranet's flexibility can also open up solutions you can't achieve with other products.

Let's say that your company has just produced policies on corporate travel. You have information on authorizations, use of calling cards, the company travel agent, hotel limits, and even a new expense spreadsheet for employees to use for reimbursements. Your normal process may be to print all of that information, take it to the copier, and make and distribute copies for everyone in the company who travels. You can also make a copy of the spreadsheet on a few floppy disks and hand out the packet and disk to each one of them. From that day on you will live a life of making additional copies for employees who lose the information or claim they never got it, for new employees, or whenever there are changes to policies.

The alternative is to post the information on an intranet. You type it up once, post it on your internal website, and give everyone the address. All employees have to do is look up the address with a web browser from their computer, just as they would with an Internet site, and read the information from the server over the network. They can also print or download the spreadsheet if they wish. Any time you need to make changes, you make it right on the website itself. There is no more confusion and no photocopies. An example of what your corporate travel site might look like is shown in Figure 6-2. As you can see, because it is an internal website, it doesn't have to be pretty, just functional.

Intranets can be set up for more than company policies. Users can publish their calendars, leave messages for each other, prepare information about competitors, and set up pages about projects where employees

Figure 6-2. *Company Information Posted on an Intranet*

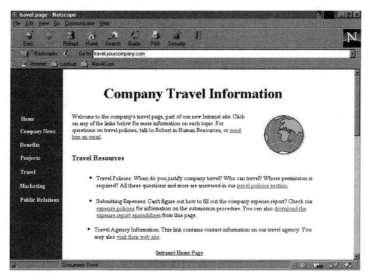

can post files and other information. You can even publish the company newsletter. Virtually any information that is valuable to the company's employees can go on an intranet site.

Designing and setting up an intranet site isn't too difficult. Most word processors, spreadsheets, and other applications can now save documents in the HyperText Markup Language (HTML), which is a code that web browsers read, so it is easy to design web pages. All you need is server space from which to run web server software and store the HTML documents you create. For small networks, intranets can also be used in a peer-to-peer network. (The next section contains details on communicating without a server.) Then each computer needs to be able to run the TCP/IP networking protocol and a web browser.

Intranets have other benefits over solutions such as groupware and e-mail. For one, intranets can be viewed by any computer that can run a web browser, including Windows, Macintosh, or other systems. Also, because intranets use web browsers such as Microsoft's Internet Explorer or Netscape's Navigator (which are free) to present information, there are no client software fees for each computer. Contrast that to e-mail and groupware, for which there are charges not only for the server software but also for the software that runs on each computer. And finally, because intranets work like the World Wide Web, users usually require less training on how to use the intranet compared with other solutions. Anyone who has ever surfed a website already knows how to navigate an intranet site.

Teamware

A new variation on intranets is also starting to appear called "teamware." Teamware is relatively new and can be used either on your local network or as a service on the Internet to improve company collaboration. Teamware combines the benefits of groupware with the simplicity of an intranet to form a virtual home base for employees. Some products, such as Netopia's Netopia Virtual Office, run on local computers and function like a computerized "inbox." Other teamware products that can be used over the Internet include Instinctive Technologies' eRoom, HotOffice Technologies' HotOffice, and Netscape's Virtual Office, which uses Netopia's software. These services allow you to dial up to the Internet and reach an employee's inbox, where you can use several different ways of communicating and collaborating, depending on which teamware package you use. Most allow you to send electronic messages, transfer files, chat online, and even make phone calls over the Internet. Teamware products generally have predefined functions, so they are not really flexible, but they are easier to set up than an intranet. They are great for people who travel or work away from the office because they can reach their "virtual office" anywhere through the Internet. More information on these types of teamware products is covered in Chapter 11 on communicating over the Internet.

There are similar "intranet in a box" packages that run on a server on your local area network and come with a set of teamware-like collaborative applications, giving every employee a separate working page that others can access. One such product is Intranetics97 from Intranetics that runs on a local server. The advantage of this type of intranet is that it comes with templates already, so your setup time is a lot less than designing an intranet from scratch.

Communicating Without a Server

WHILE MOST COMMUNICATIONS SOFTWARE IS DESIGNED TO RUN ON A SERVER, there are options for running some applications such as e-mail and even intranets without a server. This method can work well for smaller installations with a few computers. The great advantage of these types of programs is that they are usually free.

For e-mail within your company, you can use Microsoft Mail to set up mailboxes on any Windows 95, Windows 98, or Windows for Workgroup computer. Microsoft Mail uses one computer on the network as the central post office that stores messages for all other computers on the network. Likewise, if you want to set up an intranet but don't have a server, Microsoft's Personal Web Sharing is a free application that creates an Internet website on your desktop computer. Other users on your network can use a web browser, type in the address of your computer, and bring up your web page. You can use it for publishing all sorts of information, such as your personal calendar or projects you are working on, and posting files that others can download. These solutions are cost-effective for getting small networks communicating.

Benefits

WHETHER YOU ARE LOOKING FOR E-MAIL, INTRANET, OR GROUPWARE solutions, the obvious focus of these applications is to improve the way your employees communicate with one another. Benefits include better communication, improved coordination, and more efficient office operations.

BETTER COMMUNICATION

All of the applications mentioned so far improve the way information is disseminated to employees. As more information is provided to employees, it will help them make more informed decisions.

IMPROVED COORDINATION

Coordination means that employees are able to work together, whether in discussion groups or through e-mail, to talk about issues, make recommendations, and even make alterations to documents and send them to other employees.

MORE EFFICIENT OFFICE OPERATIONS

Among the benefits here are:

■ **Reduced paper flow.** While the ideal of the "paperless office" still hasn't come to pass and may never be realized, these networked applications tend to reduce the paper flow and paper costs.

■ **Electronic record keeping.** Communicating over the network allows you to keep a record of information without the paper chase. These applications are much easier to organize than that stack of paper on your desk, and you can maintain the records and sources long after you have thrown that pile of paper in the waste can.

Is It for You?

INDICATORS THAT YOU MAY NEED A NETWORK-BASED COMMUNICATION SOLUTION

■ You depend heavily on employee communication.

■ Employees regularly complain about communication flow.

■ There is an obvious company paper trail of memos and other documents.

■ Employees feel as if they're in too many meetings (don't they always feel that way?).

Cautions

WHILE ALL OF THESE NETWORK-BASED APPLICATIONS HELP IN IMPROVING office communication, there are some things that you should consider before implementing them for your company. Among the potential problems are cost, complexity, actual usage, and lack of privacy.

COST

You may already be wondering how much one of these solutions is going to set the company coffers back. It really depends on the solution. If you already have a server that can be used, you are part of the way there. Many applications require you to purchase software for the server as well as each client computer. Of course, some solutions, including peer-to-peer e-mail such as Microsoft Mail or an intranet with Personal Web Sharing, are free (I know, it has a nice sound to it.).

COMPLEXITY

With the exception of the peer-to-peer systems discussed, most of these systems are fairly complex to install and maintain. You will probably have to bring in a consultant to recommend what you need, help you install it, and possibly maintain it for you.

USE

As with all solutions shown, the success of any solution you implement will be determined by its use—how much and how well. Use will depend on two things: need and user comfort. The rule here is to determine true needs up-front and implement the appropriate solution. Then, training is paramount. There have been many times where a complex groupware system costing tens of thousands of dollars has gone unused because there was little or no user training involved. Even a simple intranet or e-mail system will be used more after some formal employee training.

SNOOPING

With all of the information flying around the office, the company executives might be tempted to snoop around and see what the employees are saying. This can easily be done, especially with electronic mail and groupware applications, which have settings that let an administrator see anything anyone has sent or published. Just to inform you, U.S. court cases have upheld the right of companies to monitor and read employees' e-mail that is sent with company equipment. Keeping personal opinions aside of whether this practice is right or wrong, here is one suggestion: If you are going to snoop through employees' messages for any reason, give your employees fair warning first. Issue a general statement about the company's reserved right to monitor information. Believe me, you don't want to be caught reading company e-mail by employees without having given them a warning beforehand. It will severely hurt morale.

Getting Started

INSTALLING AN APPLICATION TO IMPROVE COMMUNICATIONS WITHIN YOUR office takes some planning and an understanding of the actual communication flow among your employees, so that you know what you need.

Your first step should be deciding who is going to use the solution and why. Look at who is communicating (or should be communicating) in the company and the type of information that is flowing between them. It is important to understand what type of information is shared, because that will help determine the medium needed. Is it just short messages, or do employees need to collaborate on documents? Does the communication flow in one direction or both? Don't be afraid to ask employees how they communicate with others in the company. You need to understand the workflow of your company to know the communications medium you need.

Second, once you have identified the who and what, you need to consider the best medium for sharing that information. If your communications requirements revolve around being able to send simple messages, then e-mail is probably the solution. One indication of which solution should be implemented is how the information is currently distributed. For example, if your company already sends many paper memos, the alternative may be an e-mail system. If you have loads of documentation, policies, news, or other information to transmit to employees, an intranet may be the best solution. If you currently have many meetings where people need to coordinate information, make revisions, and give feedback, communication may be improved with a groupware system. If your communication extends to employees who frequently work outside the office, then possibly a teamware solution over the Internet could be most appropriate.

When looking at a network-based communications solution, don't forget to consider employees who may work outside company premises. If you have workers who regularly work from home or travel, you should read Chapter 7 on remote access. Also, if you have customers, suppliers, and others outside the company you communicate with on a regular basis, make sure that you consider them also. You may want to extend your communications solution so that it is Internet-based or at least make sure that it can connect to the Internet at a later time. Most e-mail applications today support the common Internet e-mail protocols, such as Post Office Protocol (POP3) and Internet Messaging Access Protocol (IMAP4) for the storage of e-mail and Simple Mail Transfer Protocol (SMTP) for transferring e-mail. If you are going with a groupware application, it should be able to run over a TCP/IP network and support web browser viewing in addition to whatever client software the vendor provides.

Remember that if you are buying a server for the first time as well as the communications software, you can use a small-business network operating system and get the communications software thrown in. Both Novell's NetWare for Small Business and Microsoft's BackOffice Small Business Server include their own e-mail/groupware software as part of the solution. NetWare for Small Business includes Novell's GroupWise messaging software, while Small Business Server includes Microsoft's popular Exchange Server. If either application meets your needs, this is a cost-effective way to get your solution in one tidy little package.

When it comes to the actual implementation of your solution, you may want to turn it over into the hands of a professional. With the complexity of servers, software, clients, and networking protocols—and, in the case of groupware, possible software customization—there are too many components that go into a solution for most people to feel comfortable doing it without some experience. Of course, intranet and teamware solutions can be easier to set up and can be done if you're willing to try. However, you must be willing to learn how to use an HTML editor (at least a simple one such as Microsoft Word) to create an intranet.

Improving company communications is one of the most valuable and cost-effective uses of a network. The benefits of improved communications within your company will be clearly evident. Within a short time of implementing a communications solution, you will wonder how your company ever got by without it. With the proper tools in place, you will see a dramatic improvement in employee collaboration, coordination, and productivity. Our next chapter covers how we can build upon those benefits and others by extending them to employees outside the company with remote access.

CHAPTER 7

Connecting With Remote Access

WITH YOUR NETWORK SET UP, YOU CAN SHARE FILES AND INFORMATION freely and experience big gains in productivity. And as your company's employees grow used to the ability to share files and e-mail back and forth, it will become an essential tool to your business. However, in today's business environment, much work is done outside the company, with employees traveling for sales meetings, training, and presentations. In addition, businesses have become more progressive in where and when work is done, offering employees the option of working at home, either as a lifestyle accommodation, a perk, or as a way to cut costs. Other employees put in extra hours from home in the evening and on weekends. Unfortunately, while much work is being done outside the walls of your company, your data and other information is still inside. That means employees need a way to access their information from remote locations.

What Is Remote Access?

REMOTE ACCESS IS THE LINK BETWEEN EMPLOYEES OUTSIDE THE COMPANY and the information and resources that reside on your network. It involves using a modem on a computer to connect to the network and access files, send and receive e-mail, print to local computers, and even access the Internet. A good remote access solution should allow employees to work outside the office and still do just about anything that employees sitting in the office can do.

There are two types of remote access: remote control and remote node.

■ **Remote control.** This solution allows users to dial into and connect directly to a computer (called the slave or host computer) from another computer (called the master computer) through a modem. It sounds fairly draconian. Then, using software such as Symantec's pcAnywhere or Netopia's Timbuktu, the user can control all of the mouse and keyboard functions of the host computer through the master computer. This is handy for accessing files and running applications from the slave computer (if your connection is fast enough). Remote control does not require a connection to the network. It can be done by dialing in directly to the PC, as shown in Figure 7-1.

Figure 7-1. *Remote Control*

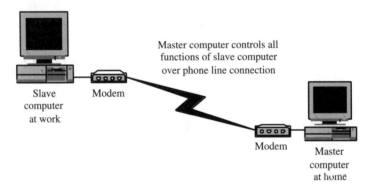

Master computer controls all
functions of slave computer
over phone line connection

Slave   Modem
computer
at work

Modem   Master
computer
at home

■ **Remote node.** This solution, which is the focus of most of this chapter, is set up so that users can dial into the network and their computer becomes another connection, or node, on the local network. Users connect directly to the network through a modem attached to a server on the network. They use a modem attached to their computer to dial into the server and gain access to networked files, printers, and programs such as e-mail and groupware.

One of the best uses of remote access is for keeping mobile workers in communication with the rest of the company while on the road. Some employees are often away from the office and out of touch with what is happening. Figure 7-2 shows a company's remote access connection using a client/server local area network. Employees regularly use e-mail on the local area network to communicate with one another, and the marketing department has recently put an intranet website on the server to allow employees to stay up to date on project schedules and even download presentations on products. The company has two salespeople who travel every week, and one salesperson who works out of his home on the East Coast. All three employees need to keep in touch with the vice president of sales and marketing through e-mail and access the intranet to stay abreast of new projects.

Figure 7-2. *Remote Access (Mobile Workers)*

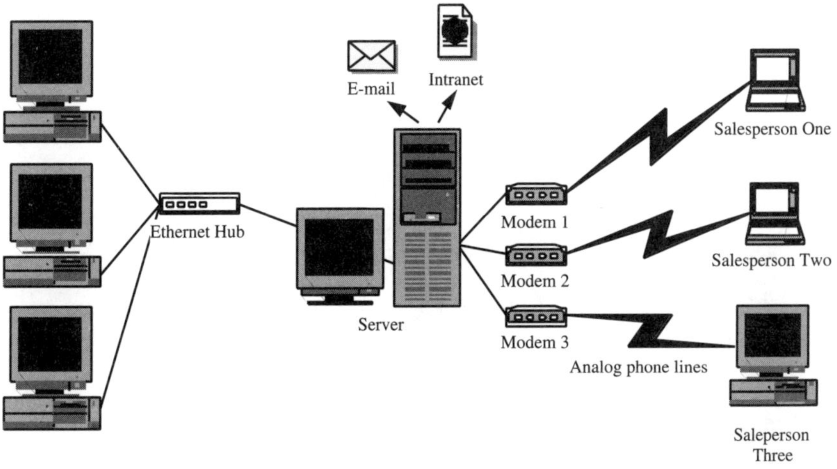

To keep the sales team connected, the company sets up a remote access connection through the network server. This is done by adding three analog modems with phone lines to the server. The network operating system that is already on the company's server can accommodate remote access (Microsoft's Windows NT and Novell's NetWare operating systems both have remote access capabilities built in), so the cost of setting up the system is nominal. The monthly fees are only the cost of the phone lines and any long-distance charges to dial in.

With a remote access connection to the server, all three salespeople can dial in to check e-mail and review schedules and marketing information from the intranet that helps them better serve their customers and stay in contact with the rest of the company.

The second environment where remote access is used is for home workers. Home workers include telecommuters, such as regional sales-people who may work out of their home in a different city or state and em-ployees who work at home full- or part-time during normal business hours. Home workers also include after-hours workers who work extra hours from home at night or on the weekends.

The example in Figure 7-3 shows a company that has offered several employees the ability to work from home a few days per week. One em-ployee, a documentation writer, works at home two days each week to avoid distractions in the office. Several other employees have also ex-pressed interest in working from home from time to time, either by taking home their notebook computers or using their own personal computers at home. However, although the company has a server, it is not able to ac-commodate a remote access connection.

Figure 7-3. *Telecommuter Access*

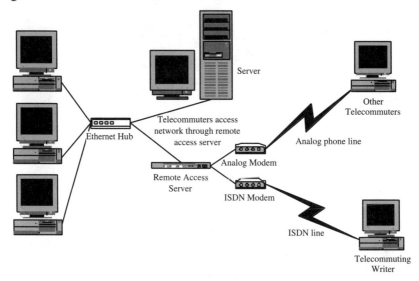

The company's needs can be accommodated with a standalone re-mote access server, which is a device that connects to the network and uses either analog modems or Integrated Services Digital Network (ISDN) terminal adapters for their connections. ISDN, which runs at 128 kilobits per second (Kbps), is many times faster than a regular analog mo-dem but requires a special digital phone line.

In this example, the work-at-home writer is the heavy user of the network and requires an ISDN solution to access large files on the server, so special digital lines are installed in her home and at work. The company also installs a regular analog phone line to the remote access server for the other telecommuters. Other workers use the analog line to access files and read their e-mail after hours. This solution allows the company to accommodate its workers' unique needs and benefits the company with employees working extra time after work hours.

VPN REMOTE ACCESS

A new type of remote access called Virtual Private Network (VPN) remote access is also available for users dialing in over long distances. VPNs allow remote users to connect to their network through the Internet. This is done by creating a "virtual" circuit from the computer to the company network; that is, the connection appears to be private to the users even though it runs across the public Internet. All data and information running across the connection are encrypted—scrambled—so that no one else can read them.

The main advantage of using a VPN for remote access is saving on long-distance phone charges. To show how, let's take our example of a company with three salespersons who need to dial in remotely for e-mail and Intranet access. Using the previous setup as shown in Figure 7-2, the salespersons incur long-distance charges when they dial in to the network. However, Figure 7-4 shows that by using a VPN connection the three salespersons can connect to the company network through the Internet with a secure connection and dispense with the long-distance charges. With their computers properly configured, all they do is make a local call to the Internet to access their company network. All data is then routed securely between their computers and the network through the Internet.

VPN remote access requires that the company network be connected directly to the Internet. This necessitates a router or server that connects to the Internet and supports VPN software. Additional network security in the form of a "firewall" between the network and the Internet is also required to prevent unwanted entry by others from the Internet. It also requires each computer to support VPN protocols such as Microsoft's Point-to-Point Tunneling Protocol (PPTP). Of course, each remote user also needs access to the Internet in whatever location they are. VPN remote access is still in its infancy but will become a very important solution in the future for businesses of all sizes.

Figure 7-4. *VPN Remote Access*

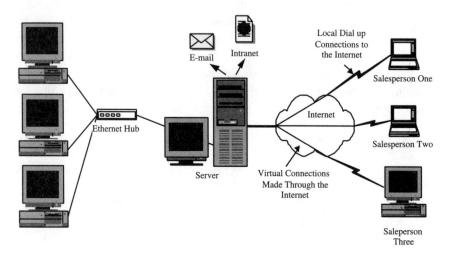

Benefits

REMOTE ACCESS PROVIDES ALL OF THE BENEFITS OF CONNECTING TO THE local area network to those workers who are out of the office some or all of the time—namely, improved communications, productivity, and resource sharing. What they can't access or use on the network is usually only limited by the speed of their dialup connection to the network. It is a vital solution for keeping traveling employees in touch.

Using remote access for telecommuting can bring additional benefits as well. If some employees work outside the office a majority of the time, your company can save money on the costs of maintaining an office for them. Many companies have found that having employees work from home improves their productivity. This is often attributed to less frequent interruptions, distractions, and meetings. In addition, telecommuters often work longer hours than other workers, using the time saved on commuting to get more done. However, results vary from person to person and company to company, so it is best to try it out on an experimental basis and judge the results yourself. In addition, telecommuting can also be an advantage when trying to hire and keep good employees who may see it as a perk.

Is It for You?

When to Consider Remote Access

■ You should consider remote access if you have workers who regularly work outside the office and could benefit from accessing resources on the local area network.

■ You should also look into a remote access solution if you can benefit from starting a company telecommuting program to improve productivity, lower costs of working facilities, or provide an added benefit to attract new employees or retain current employees.

Cautions

While remote access can help a company expand its network, increase employee productivity, and improve communications, there are some concerns related to setting up a remote access solution. Remote access can affect many areas of your company, from network security to human resources and management.

Security

Making your remote access solution secure should be your number-one concern. Remote access opens up your network to let employees dial in. It can also potentially allow other unauthorized users to dial in and access your network and everything on it. When you are considering a remote access server or remote access software to load on a server, make sure that it has adequate security to prevent unwanted users from accessing your network. After that, the best way to keep anyone from getting into your network is to ensure that your employees choose good passwords, change them often, and never give them out to anyone. Mobile employees should protect their notebook computers to deter theft and set up their dial-in access software so that they have to type in the password every time they call in.

Long-Distance Charges

If you plan on using remote access to keep traveling employees connected, make sure that long-distance charges don't skyrocket. Many remote users get involved in their work or read e-mail and forget how long their computer has been connected over a long-distance line. Since most mobile users will connect from a hotel room, it can become very costly to connect. Some ways to get around this is to bill the long-distance charges to a company calling card or get an 800 number at your office to dial into. Also, since reading e-mail online (i.e., while remaining connected) is one of the biggest time killers, choose an e-mail application that allows users to connect and download all e-mail and then read their mail while disconnected. Finally, a VPN remote access solution can also save on long-distance costs by using the Internet.

TELECOMMUTING ABUSES

Telecommuting can be a wonderful thing and is usually a win-win situation for the employee and the company. However, there are times when employees will take advantage of the opportunity and spend their time doing things other than work. The temptation can be too much for some workers, who use the time to spend with family, run errands, clean their house, or watch their favorite soap opera. The best way to take care of this is to establish telecommuting policies on what is expected of employees. (Some ideas for setting policies are discussed in the final section on "Getting Started.")

EQUIPMENT USE

Equipment costs can run beyond what you would normally expect. For example, if you have employees working at home, do they use their own personal computer or one that the company purchases? You need to decide what, if any, equipment you will supply at home, including office furniture, fax machines, printers, and analog or ISDN lines. Most small companies find it is too cost-prohibitive to provide employees with all the equipment necessary to set up an at-home office, unless the employee spends a majority of time working at home.

Getting Started

MANY OF TODAY'S REMOTE ACCESS SERVERS CAN BE FAIRLY SIMPLE TO INSTALL and maintain and can be set up in a few hours. For some, remote access can be established without the help of an expert. However, careful attention should be paid to the security of the system to make sure that you are not opening up your network to anyone who wants to dial in. After you have decided which employees in the company can benefit from a remote access connection, you will want to take the following actions.

Recommended Course of Action

1. *Decide how users will dial in.* For full remote access to files, e-mail, printers, and other network functions, you basically have two options. You can either set up an existing network server with the modems and software, or you can purchase a standalone remote access server. A remote access server is a small device that connects to your network and has a number of modems connected for dial-in access by your remote users. Whichever option you choose, make sure that you have enough connections for at least several people to connect at the same time. The general rule is to have at least one connection for every five telecommuting or mobile employees that are outside the office at a given time. So, if you have up to 10 employees out of the office that can dial in, your solution should include at least two modem connections into the server. A better ratio may be necessary for more frequent connections or to prevent employees from becoming frustrated if they try dialing in but find the line is busy. Setting up a remote access connection through an existing network server can be an intimidating process, but it is still within the limits of an individual, provided you have some patience and pay attention to the security of the network. It is a much more economical option if you already have a server. All you need to supply are modems; the software is already built into NetWare and Windows NT.

2. *Decide on your connection type.* When looking at connections you can choose from analog or ISDN modems. Analog is cheaper and easier to install, but the speed of the connection tops out at around 50 Kbps. ISDN is much faster, around 128 Kbps, but you will pay more for it, depending on where you live. You also need an ISDN line into the company and one in the home of each worker who will use it. However, ISDN is a great option for employees transferring large files and doing other intensive work over the network. If employees just need access to e-mail and the ability to download a few files from time to time, then an analog

connection will do just fine. If your solution is for road warriors who travel a lot, analog is your only choice since most hotels don't have ISDN lines. Others choices, such as higher-speed cable modems and ADSL (Asymmetrical Digital Subscriber Line) connections, are available in a limited number of areas.

3. *Make sure that you have the proper software and protocols.* If you are running Windows on the client side (i.e., the computer that dials up), you will likely use Windows Dial-Up Networking, which is Microsoft's remote access software. If you are running a server as your remote access connection, you will need dial-up software (although both NetWare and Windows NT include it). If you plan on using a standalone remote access server, then the software is built in, but you need the right protocols as well. Most dial-up solutions use Point-to-Point Protocol (PPP) for the connection.

4. *Consider security for your network.* If you have not caught on to the security issues of remote access yet, this is your last chance. Remember to use a remote access server that at least uses Password Authentication Protocol (PAP) and Challenge Handshake Authentication Protocol (CHAP) for password protection. Callback is a great feature that provides extra security by disconnecting the call generated by the remote worker and calling the user back at a predetermined number. It is only available when you know ahead of time the number you will be calling from, such as with a telecommuter.

5. *Set policies for any telecommuters.* Avoiding abuse may be your first concern when you think about letting your employees work at home. For example, you may want to clearly spell out to telecommuting employees that they are to put in a full eight-hour workday and that they need to check in for phone and e-mail messages at least every two hours.

Determining what jobs and personalities are best suited to telecommuting before getting started is just as important as making sure workers aren't idly sitting around. Jobs that work best for telecommuting are mostly information-based. Obviously there are some jobs, such as the receptionist, that are not appropriate for working at home. Likewise, managers should be limited to only occasional telecommuting. As for personalities, that should be left up to management to review on a case-by-case basis. Generally workers who are project- and goal-oriented and are moderately social are the best personalities. If you don't have to watch over the person at work, you probably don't have to worry about their work ethic at home.

If employees use company equipment at home, you may want to have them sign fixed-asset agreements before you send them home with a bunch of equipment. That way you make sure what goes out of the office building eventually comes back by tracking what each employee has at home. These are only some of the considerations for policies. If you need more help, there are plenty of places to turn to for help on telecommuting polices, including several books on telecommuting and even technology and human resources consultants who can help you draft some simple written policies.

Make sure that management is comfortable with the telecommuting program your company establishes. If managers allow telecommuting but are continually suspicious of their employees' work ethic, employees will sense the distrust and resent it. Training may be important for both sides to ensure that everyone feels comfortable with the program.

As a final point, make your telecommuting program voluntary. Some employees may not want to telecommute, for whatever reason. Don't force them into it. If you have access to the Internet, one of the best sites to learn more about telecommuting is Gil Gordon's telecommuting site (www.gilgordon.com).

Remote access is a critical tool in our fast-paced, mobile business community. If used properly, it can become an essential part of helping your company to communicate with employees when they are outside the office and to make them more productive and informed.

CHAPTER 8

Planning Your LAN

By NOW YOU HAVE ALREADY STARTED TO SEE ALL OF THE ADVANTAGES OF A local area network (LAN) and have a good idea of how a LAN would most benefit your company. Without a doubt, you can hardly contain your excitement and are ready to run down to your local computer store, open up the company checkbook, and buy an entire network with every possible bell and whistle. Money is no object, right? Yeah, right.

Unless your company is different from the rest of the business world, it has limitations. Most limits come in the form of time and money, but you should also consider other factors, such as what the company's employees can handle learning and using at one time or what applications can run on their computers. You will certainly not use all of the solutions we have discussed, but you have to know at least where to start and what to focus on. It is important to set your priorities and know where you are going in order to reach your objectives.

While a network is a worthwhile tool, it will meet your needs only if it is well planned, well implemented, and well used. Whether you have someone to help you design and implement your network or you want to do it yourself, you should put your plan on paper and formalize the solutions that will best help your business and can reasonably be done within your limitations. One of the worst things that you can do is to jump ahead and start spending money before you have planned out what you need and what you can afford.

The purpose of this chapter is to help you prioritize your options and decide how to start implementing your company's LAN. You will also learn about sources for getting advice on your network and where to purchase LAN products, as well as information on how to choose a network consultant. Do-it-yourselfers who are interested in saving a few dollars will also find information that will help you get started on building a LAN on your own.

Your Network Notebook

BEFORE WE MOVE ON, IT IS A GOOD TIME TO INTRODUCE YOU TO YOUR WORKING project: your network notebook. You are probably used to planning in your business; many companies develop yearly company and marketing plans. The notebook is designed to be your plan for using networking technology to help your business. When it is complete, your notebook will include information about your company's computers and your networking needs. If you wish, you can create complete sections in your notebook, such as Networking Plans, Financial Budgeting and Justification, Inventory, Training, and Contacts (for phone numbers of your local computer reseller, customer support lines, and your favorite takeout restaurant). You may even find additional information or sections that you wish to have in your binder that haven't been included in this book. Feel free to change your network notebook to fit your needs. The objective is to get you to think about what you need and to write those needs down. Of course, you don't have to call it the network notebook. Come up with a better name for it—maybe "Master Communications Plan for Company XYZ."

You should use a three-ring binder for your plan so that you can move things around as needed. The best way to build your plan is to do it in a word-processing program on your computer. Any word processor such as Microsoft Word will do just fine and will allow you to easily make changes. Appendix A of this book contains some basic templates to work from. Feel free to copy and use them, or re-create them on your own computer to use.

When it is finished, your networking plan should have everything needed to show what you want to do and why. If you decide to let someone else implement the network, you will be able to show them a document that explains exactly what you want to do. If you build the network yourself, the plan will be your own guide to make sure that you stay on track. Now, let's get started creating your network notebook with the first section: a plan for a local area network.

STEP ONE: TAKING INVENTORY

The first step of the LAN planning stage is taking stock of what you currently have: computers, printers, whatever can be shared on a network. Before you determine where you want to go, you need to know where you are.

For now, taking inventory of the computers means just putting down the basics: who's using the computer and what operating system it is running. You will also want a list of peripherals that are connected to each computer, such as printers, removable media drives, CD-ROMs, and even scanners. You may not be able to, or even want to, share all of these peripheral devices on the network, but it is worthwhile to know they are there. An example of a basic inventory list is in Table 8-1. (Form A-1 in Appendix A is a blank form you can copy and use.) If you can, it is best to have a more advanced inventory listing of each computer. Why? Whoever buys all of the necessary network components needs to have a good idea of what they have to work with. Information such as processor speed, hard drive space, the amount of memory, and the type and number of expansion slots are very beneficial to know in order to determine if any computers you plan to connect to the network need additional components to run on the network. However, this is not for the faint of heart; you need to know your way around your operating system to get all of the information. If you are running Windows 95 or Windows 98, most of this information can be found under the System settings in your Windows Control Panel. Form A-2 in Appendix A shows a complete inventory list.

Table 8-1. *Sample Inventory List*

Computer User	Computer Processor	Computer Operating System	Available Expansion Slots	Attached Peripherals
Mary	486-33 MHz	Windows 3.11	One ISA slot	Inkjet printer
Vince	Pentium 133 MHz	Windows 95	Two PCI slots	Laser printer, Iomega Zip drive
Chuck	Pentium II 266 MHz	Windows 98	Three PCI slots	Iomega Jaz drive
John	Pentium 75 MHz	Windows 95	One PCI slot	None

While it may seem inconvenient to find all of this information, it can help you in two ways. First, all computers are not created equal. For example, you want Mary on the network, but she is only running Windows 3.11, which can't be connected to the network without a server or upgrading the computer to Windows 95. Second, you now have a good idea of what can be shared on the network.

STEP TWO: PLANNING FOR YOUR NEEDS

The next step in planning for your local area network is to decide which networking tools will best help your company. This step involves thinking about your work environment. What are our most important work processes? What equipment do you already have and can share? Who communicates with whom? Take some time to review the solutions outlined in previous chapters. Of course, a basic network is the place to start. Having the infrastructure together to connect all of the computers in a peer-to-peer or client/server network will give you basic file sharing and the foundation to share other resources such as printers. Your general observations will help you determine what else you need.

So grab another sheet of paper. Or, if you are writing your plan in a word-processing program, hit the Enter key a few times and type the heading "LAN Needs." You may want to include descriptions of what you want to accomplish now, as well as what you hope to do in the future and separate the two. You don't have to be too specific, just some highlights will do. Remember to include a justification as well. Table 8-2 shows a good format; you can also use Form A-4 in Appendix A as your guide.

By including both your needs and the justification for them, you check yourself by having actually thought through your decision to install a network. You also have a foundation for creating a financial justification for the network. Chapter 16 shows you how to financially justify your network.

STEP THREE: DECIDING WHO NEEDS NETWORKED RESOURCES

Now that you have taken inventory and have decided what you want to do on the network, the final step of planning your local area network is to match up what you want to do with the users on the network. So take a third sheet of paper, or hit the Enter key a few times, and type or write "network resources" at the top. This will be your guide to make sure that the right resources are going to the right employees.

Not everyone will need or should have access to everything. For example, you may want to add a color printer on the network, but you may

Table 8-2. *Sample Network Plan*

Need	Priority	Time Frame	Justification
File Sharing	One	This month	We need a basic network to do file sharing from computer to computer. We are always exchanging files between computers. Using floppy disks for file transfers takes too long, and now we are running into problems getting larger files on floppy disks.
Share Chuck's Laser Printer	One	This month	Since Chuck got the new laser printer, everyone has been using it. We don't want to buy a laser printer for everyone else, but they keep kicking Chuck off his computer to get to his printer. Sharing it on the network would save a lot of time, and Chuck would be more productive.
Share Vince's Zip Drive	One	This month	We want to create backup copies of some of our more important files. Using the Zip drive on Vince's machine would save us from having to buy extra drives for everyone.
Local E-Mail	Two	Within six months	We have taken out half the rain forest with the paper we use for office memos. Also, marketing has been complaining that it doesn't get timely updates on what is happening from Engineering. Both departments think they can communicate better with e-mail. It would help us to communicate better as a company, cut down on paper, and reduce all the meetings we have been having.
Share Customer Database	Two	Six to nine months	Sales has had a hard time getting the customer database synchronized because everyone in the department runs database programs on different machines. We need a simpler way for everyone to share the same information and update it so everyone can see it. Putting it on the network would give everyone access to the same information at the same time.
Remote Access to LAN	Three	Nine months to one year	Sales reps claim that they don't know what is going on when reps are on the road. Our marketing people claim that they can never get in touch with sales because they are always out of the office. A remote access connection to the network will keep sales informed with e-mail and file sharing. Remote access will also help the two people working at home to dial in periodically to check for messages.

not want everyone to use it. To show who has access to what, use a matrix that shows the users on the network on the horizontal axis and your priorities on the vertical axis. Table 8-3 shows a simple matrix (based on Form A-5 in Appendix A) that you can use in deciding whether or not your various users get access to network resources.

Table 8-3. *Network Resources Matrix*

Resource	Priority	Mary	Vince	Chuck	John
File Sharing	One	Yes	Yes	Yes	Yes
Share Chuck's Printer	One	Yes	Yes	Yes	Yes
Share Zip Drive	One	Yes			Yes
LAN E-Mail	Two	Yes	Yes	Yes	Yes
Share Database	Two		Yes	Yes	
Remote Access	Three			Yes	Yes
Internet E-Mail	Three	Yes	Yes	Yes	Yes
Share Database Software	Three	Yes	Yes		Yes

Obviously this matrix can become quite large depending on the number of users and the number of solutions you plan to implement. However, you can also see just how difficult it would be to remember all of this if you are planning on building your own network. It would be equally difficult to relate all this information to someone else without a list of exactly what you want to do.

That's it! With the three components you've just created, you now have a basic plan in place describing what you expect to do with a local area network. Anyone reading your plan should have a pretty good idea of what you want out of your network.

Finding Help

INEVITABLY, MOST COMPANIES AT SOME POINT IN TIME WILL TURN TO A professional for help with their network. Because many of your company's processes and communications will eventually be based on your network, it is important that you choose a partner you trust so that you can be sure your network fulfills your present and future needs.

If you are looking for help with installing your network, you won't find a lack of alternatives. People all around you are willing to provide advice, from your brother-in-law to a bona fide network specialist. If your brother-in-law is a networking specialist, then you've lucked out. If not, the information presented in this section may help you with the process. Different sources of help—consultants, resellers, and moonlighters—are outlined later in this chapter, but for now any one of these sources is generically referred to as a "network consultant."

Before we go into the different sources of help, let's address the different types of support you can seek from a professional network consultant. Your options generally fall into four basic areas: assessment and recommendation, installation, training, and management and maintenance. You may want assistance with any one or several of these stages or all of them:

■ **Assessment and recommendation.** Stage one involves understanding your needs and making recommendations of specific solutions that best fit your needs. This stage should start with one or more meetings with your network consultants until they have a good understanding of your company's processes and how technology can best address your company's needs, and it should end with a formal proposal of the solution, including an itemization of the costs involved.

For this process to run smoothly, you need to be open with your consultants and expect them to be open with you. Sometimes there is a certain fear or awe that occurs when working with someone who understands technology. Don't let that happen to you. If you do, you are subject to their advice and their mercy. To be an effective partner, you must be willing to explain to your consultant how you want to better leverage your computers and improve the company. Swallow your pride and ask questions when you don't understand the consultant's recommendations or comments. This initial consultation should be free—don't let anyone charge you a fee at this stage. If the consultant wants to charge you, find someone else.

■ **Installation.** The next stage is the actual implementation of a solution. At this point your consultant's expertise becomes most apparent. It is also where they will spend most of their time and your money for the equipment and time to implement the network. This can take anywhere from a few hours to a few days, depending on the complexity of the solution. As a small business, you should try to get the installation done over a weekend or at night to minimize disruption to your business.

■ **Training.** The third stage is providing training for your company on how to use the network. Again, the need for training depends on the complexity of the network. If it is a peer-to-peer network, you probably don't need much training at all. If you are running a server with complex applications, then you should be willing to spend some time and money making sure that your employees feel comfortable using their new tools. Not all consultants offer training. If they don't, other training options are discussed in Chapter 15.

■ **Management and maintenance.** The final area where consultants may play a role is in the management and maintenance of your network. All networks need at least some supervision and maintenance to ensure that they continue to run properly. Peer-to-peer networks may need some tweaks from time to time, while more complex networks can require daily monitoring.

If there is no one within the company to manage and maintain the network, you may contract with your consultant to do it for you. Many consultants will undertake this work with a service agreement. As part of the agreement you pay them a set amount of money per month (usually at a discount from their standard hourly rate) or prepay for a determined number of hours for them to maintain your network periodically. In addition, when there is a problem with the network the consultant will come over at a minute's notice to assess and fix the problem. Of course, if you are willing to work on it yourself, or if your network is so simple that it doesn't need maintenance, you may not need any regular maintenance help. In this scenario you call your consultant only when there is a major problem and pay the standard rate for help.

Sources of Help

Professional networking consultants come in all different shapes, sizes, and levels of ability. The general classifications of professionals to choose from include consultants, resellers, and moonlighters.

Consultants
Consultants deal mostly with providing the service of advice and di-

rection. They don't usually sell networking products themselves, but they may sell a few specialized products that relate to their area of expertise. Consultants are best used when they have a specialization, such as database expertise or design of Internet websites. However, since their real business is selling advice, not products, they probably won't offer the best prices for equipment. Some will even buy from a retail store and mark the price up to you. Working with consultants may be an advantage if they consult on a project without selling you the hardware. If that is the case, save yourself a few dollars and buy the products yourself, then let the consultant install them.

Resellers

The term *reseller* means different things to different people. For the sake of this discussion, we'll define resellers as companies or individuals that make money from selling both products and their service. Services include those outlined previously (e.g., doing assessments and recommendations, installations, training, and network maintenance). Resellers are also known as value-added resellers (VARs) and dealers. Many resellers are generalists who sell just about anything related to a computer.

Some resellers cater to specific industries or professions, specializing in products for law firms, accounting firms, or desktop publishing businesses. Others focus specifically on networking, although they will often sell other products too. While they are very knowledgeable, most network resellers work with large companies. They may look at smaller businesses as too much effort for too little payback, or they may try to cram big-business solutions into your company. Most generalist resellers have enough technical knowledge about networking to be able to help you set up a network and troubleshoot when you have a problem.

Moonlighters

Moonlighters carry a regular day job, usually as a network manager in a larger company, but work on the side on individual projects to earn a few extra dollars. Moonlighters range in knowledge, skill, and cost, but they can help specify and install your network. For a small fee, many moonlighters are even willing to come out to the company for regular network maintenance. Moonlighters may save you some money by buying the products for you, with or without a small markup, or they will give you a laundry list of what they need and have you purchase it, so you can save any added costs.

Moonlighters are easy to find. Many corporate network managers moonlight. Just ask your corporate friends about their network managers. You are likely to find a good one who does some work on the side. The downside to moonlighters is that there is no guarantee they will be there when you need them. If your moonlighting consultant has a day job and your network goes down, you have to be willing to wait until after business hours for him to come in and look at it.

CHOOSING A GOOD RESOURCE

With so many options, it may seem difficult to find the help that best fits your needs. How do you tell one consultant, reseller, or moonlighter from another? Like any other professional situation, you want to find someone who has enough experience to assist you in assessing your networking needs and recommending solutions. The best time to do this is during the initial recommendation stage. You should bring in several candidates, give them your requirements, and have each of them give you recommendations and a cost estimate. It is the best way to keep them honest. Beyond that, here are some things you should ask about when looking for in a good technology partner.

WHAT TO CONSIDER WHEN SHOPPING FOR A CONSULTANT OR RESELLER

■ **Certifications.** The only things more prevalent than acronyms in the computer industry are certifications. Certifications designate that networking professionals have passed an examination of their knowledge on a certain topic or product. Unfortunately, there is no single professional certification to distinguish a good networking professional from a bad one. Many major networking vendors offer some sort of certification program, but they range in significance. The most relevant certifications are from Microsoft Corp. and Novell Inc., the two networking software giants. Their products are often the most complex part of the network, so they have set up programs to qualify people who know their products well. These programs are the next best thing to a universal certification. Table 8-4 shows the different certifications from both companies and explains what they really mean. Many of these certifications include significant training on general networking, as well as on specific products from each vendor. You may want to find a Certified Novell Engineer (CNE) to help if your small-business network runs NetWare; a Microsoft Certified

Table 8-4. *Professional Networking Certifications*

Certification	Requirements	What It Means
Microsoft Certified Product Specialist (MCPS)	One exam for each product	Certified knowledge of one or more Microsoft product, including at least one operating system
Microsoft Certified Solution Developer (MCSD)	Four exams	Qualified developers for designing custom business solutions using Microsoft products
Microsoft Certified Systems Engineer (MCSE)	Six exams	Certified to plan, implement, maintain, and support information systems in a range of computing environments
Microsoft Certified Systems Engineer + Internet (MCSE+Internet)	Nine exams	Same as MCSE but also certifies ability to work on internet and intranet solutions
Certified Novell Administrator (CNA)	One course and exam	Certified to administer for NetWare and other Novell products
Novell's Certified Internet Professional (CIP)	Five courses and five exams	Certified in five targeted areas of Internet website development and management
Certified Novell Engineer (CNE)	Seven courses and seven exams	Qualified to support Novell products; certification considered very reputable; about 50% of curriculum is generic
Master CNE	CNE plus specialization testing	A step above CNE; includes specialized knowledge in a specific advanced skill area

Systems Engineer (MCSE) is a good counterpart if you are running Windows NT.

■ **Price.** When deciding the best channel for purchasing products, it is easy to get caught up in the pricing game. Price can vary significantly from one reseller to another, based on the resellers' desire to make money, how much product they have to purchase, and what discounts or rebates they get. Your best strategy is to shop around with a number of resellers for the best deal. Don't be afraid to talk to several resellers and get a few quotes.

Remember, though, that price isn't everything. Don't let a reseller specify cheap products to get the bid. When choosing equipment, go with established companies you can trust. Saving a few dollars today may cost you more in the long run with repairs and replacement.

■ **Terms/conditions.** Some resellers are willing to offer you special terms for financing your equipment, or they may even lease the equipment to you. You should consider either of these options if your budget doesn't exactly meet your needs.

■ **Location.** Location, location, location is important in real estate. It is also more important than you think for your reseller. First, resellers are busy sorts, and they don't want to travel all over the place to service customers. Believe it or not, some even charge by the hour for travel time to your office (usually at a reduced rate). So find a reseller who is close by; otherwise, when you have a service call, they may already have a bill for you by the time they show up at the door.

Second, if you live out in the middle of nowhere and Bob's Computers is the only place in town, you may discover that his pricing reflects the lack of competition. If that is the case, you may want to purchase your networking products from a mail-order catalog that offers more competitive pricing and let someone else do the installation.

■ **Installation time.** If you are going to have a reseller install your network, see if the work can be done at night or over the weekend. It could save you some headaches and keep your employees productive.

■ **Training.** Depending on what kind of network you install, you may want to see what your reseller has to offer in the way of training. A reseller may be willing to throw training time in for little or no cost to sweeten the deal.

■ **Support/management.** Recommending and installing the network is only the beginning. Depending on the complexity, you may want to have your reseller or someone else periodically manage the network, keep it tuned up, troubleshoot problems, and be available for emergencies, such as when someone drops a monster-size convenience-store drink on the server. Check with your potential networking consultant and see what their rates and availability are for a maintenance contract or emergency service. You don't want to find out that your consultant can't come out immediately at the time there is a problem.

■ **Networking experience.** The networking business is so vast that some consultants may have focused on some other area for so long that they haven't done anything new recently. If they start talking to you about the last ARCNET network they installed, run away quickly. They have been out of the business too long.

■ **Small-business experience.** While it isn't necessary, it is preferable that the consultant that you work with has small-business experience. It is helpful when the reseller already has an idea of what to expect and how to cater to the specific needs of a small business. In addition, if you are the only small business the reseller is working with, and there is the choice between coming out and servicing you or the big, multimillion-dollar company down the street, you may end up the loser.

■ **Solution experience.** If you are installing your network around a specific, critical solution, you may need to find a reseller that has experience with the specific solution you are looking for. Some resellers specialize in setting up groupware applications, Internet websites, remote access, accounting or inventory software, or other solutions. When looking for a reseller for a specific application, ask about their experience with your particular problem before you let them recommend and implement a solution. Servers, communications packages, remote access, and specialized software solutions require experience and familiarity. Make sure your reseller has done it before.

Once you have found a consultant or reseller and entered into a relationship with them, you will find that there is a lot of flexibility in how you can work together. Make sure that you set parameters defining what you need and what you can afford. In other words, go in with your plan. If you need to improve employee communication, tell the consultant who the employees are, what you want to accomplish, and why. Don't leave a situation open so that the consultant has free reign.

Purchasing Strategies

IF YOU PLAN ON WORKING WITH A COMPUTER RESELLER, YOU HAVE PROBABLY accepted the fact that you'll sacrifice price for the sake of convenience, service, and support. However, that doesn't mean that you need to be raked over the coals and pay the highest price for your equipment just because you want a little help setting it up. The following are some ideas on how to get the best deal even when you are working with a professional:

■ **The computer and networking market is competitive—take advantage of it.** Shop around for price, and pit bidders against one another. This strategy can be particularly effective in the reseller market, where prices are more flexible and there is some margin to play with. Get several quotes in writing and don't feel bad about shopping around. In fact, when you start working with a reseller, tell them that you will be going to other resellers and get them to give you a competitive bid up-front. Then hit the phone book and start comparing prices. Make sure that you position yourself as a company that has a future. A reseller doesn't want to work with a company that is going nowhere.

■ **Get your reseller to differentiate with service.** Of course you want the best price you can get, but what happens if a reseller won't budge? Try to get them to sweeten the deal with a service bonus. Ask them to throw in a few months of technical support on that new server or the new network to get the deal. They may look at it as an opportunity to keep you on those lucrative service contracts in the future and jump at the chance.

■ **Go to your PC vendor.** As effective as it is to play the field, it may be advantageous to work with your current PC reseller. If you have bought a number of computers from a reseller, you may be able to leverage that business to get a good deal on your networking equipment also. One other benefit is that as you purchase new PCs, you can get the reseller to install network adapters in the PCs for you and configure them, too.

■ **Use a consultant.** A final strategy is to use an independent consultant instead of a reseller. If you want to save a few dollars on products, but still need a professional to help you through the installation, you may be able to find a consultant or moonlighter who will advise you on what you need, let you buy the equipment, and then come in and install it for you. You can save the money by purchasing from mail order or retail yourself and still get the benefits of a knowledgeable network professional.

Designing Your Own Network

LET'S SAY THAT YOU ARE AN INDEPENDENT PERSON. YOU STILL CHANGE THE oil in your car. You taught yourself how to play the piano. You enjoy doing home repairs. Or maybe you just don't want to spend the money on having someone else install a network for you. If any of these describe you, then you may be able to rise above the masses that pay someone $100 per hour to string some cabling and install a few adapters.

The design and installation of a network can be done by mere mortals, especially if you start out with a simple peer-to-peer network. Setting up a network is within the scope of anyone who has some knowledge about computers and isn't afraid to open up a computer and install a network adapter. Of course, the more difficult the network, the more time, patience, and technical support you will need. If you want to try installing a network yourself, you have only a few key decisions to make: What you are sharing and who shares it? What network standard and topology will you choose? And finally, which network operating system are you running? These decisions are described in Chapter 4.

The decision to run a server is based entirely on your needs. If your network is small enough, you only plan to do file and printer sharing, and your computers are all running a peer-to-peer operating system (Windows 95 or 98), you can get by without a server. However, if you want to run more advanced applications or have more computers, you will need a server. If you do need a server, look into some of the small-business servers mentioned in Chapter 5.

After you have made the big decisions, everything will begin to fall into place. However, to make sure things run smoothly, here are some other things you should consider as you plan your network.

PLANNING CONSIDERATIONS

1. *Since you are planning your own network, make sure that you leave some room to grow.* For example, if you are connecting five computers, buy an eight-port hub so you have a few extra ports for the future. When choosing network adapters, buy 10/100 cards that run at both Ethernet and Fast Ethernet speeds. Also make sure that you use Category 5 cabling, the best grade available, for your network. The last thing that you ever want to replace or repair is the cable after it is in the walls. Paying a little more today for these features will be much easier than having to change everything down the road.

2. *Take small steps to get your network running.* Get one thing running and let it run for a while before moving on. Build a basic network this week. Add a print server next week. Set up your server next month. By spacing out the work, you'll prevent being overwhelmed. This strategy will also allow you to solve any problems with what you are working on more easily before moving on to the next step.

3. *Diagram your network.* After you have an adequate plan for your network, design it on paper. Use some graph paper and plot out your company's floor plan. Show each office and computer, and draw what your network connections will look like.

One great way to diagram your network is on a computer because you can change things around as needed. One of the best products on the market for diagramming networks is Visio from Visio Corporation. Visio Professional has a module specifically for diagramming networks. It is the program used for most of the network diagrams in this book.

4. *Build a laundry list of components based on your diagram, so you know exactly what you need.* Use your inventory list to determine what network adapters, hubs, and other equipment you need.

5. *Ask everyone you can find for advice.* Ask the person at the computer store, your friend down the street who knows a lot about computers, your mother-in-law. Show them your plan and your diagram and ask for their feedback and recommendations. Most will be willing to give it. Who knows, someone may even feel sorry for you and offer to help.

6. *Realize that installing cable is half the headache.* Stringing the cable all over the building, through ceilings, walls, and floors, is a pain. Then there is the cutting and crimping and putting on those little connectors. It is awful. Unless all of the computers are in the same room, have a professional install the cabling. Your network diagram will be important at this stage, so if you thought you could get away without drawing it on paper, think again.

7. *Read a good how-to book on networks.* Okay, so read another good book after this one. There are several books out there that can guide you through the nuts and bolts of setting up a network, telling you just about anything that a professional knows. Pick up several and read through them. Particularly helpful are books that give in-depth information on the networking operating system you plan to use.

8. *Do the work during off-hours.* Don't try to install your network during work hours. The last thing you want to do is disrupt normal work time by taking employees' computers apart and trying to get them networked. You'll end up with half the company peering over your shoulder and wondering what you're doing, wasting productive time.

Purchasing Options

IF YOU DECIDE TO SAVE A FEW DOLLARS AND BUILD YOUR OWN NETWORK OR have someone else besides a reseller do it for you, you need to decide on where to purchase your networking products to get the best price. Your options include:

■ **Direct from manufacturer.** Unlike purchasing computers from some manufacturers, you probably won't be able to buy networking products directly from the manufacturer. Many companies that sell networking products, such as 3Com, Intel, and Microsoft, are large, multinational corporations selling thousands of products to thousands of people. With few exceptions, networking vendors simply do not have the resources to sell products direct, and when they do, it is only to large, established corporate accounts that purchase complex products that require a lot of support to understand and set up.

However, computers and servers can be purchased direct from companies such as Dell Computer, Gateway, or Micron with network adapters already installed and configured. Servers may also be purchased preconfigured with software such as Novell's NetWare for Small Business or Microsoft's BackOffice Small Business Server. These are great options if you want to set up a server yourself but don't have a lot of expertise.

■ **Retail channels.** Retail computer stores are a good place to buy computers and software. They offer a good selection and decent prices. To keep up with the times, many computer retail stores now sell network adapters, hubs, and cabling. The advantage of buying these products from a retail store is good pricing. In addition, the product is visible and tangible on the store's shelves, so you can pick it up and look at it. Sometimes it helps to be able to see the product when making a decision. The other nice things about retail are that stores usually have return policies, and you know that they will probably still be in business if anything goes wrong.

However, if you are looking for a place to find knowledgeable people that can help you determine your needs and even pick the right product, look elsewhere. Remember that the person that is selling you a network adapter just sold a computer game, a new video card, and a printer today, and these same salespeople may have been selling shoes last month at the store down the street. Some retail salespeople will know something about networking, but many have never even seen an actual network. The lesson here is that if you buy networking components from retail outlets, do your homework first.

■ **Catalogs.** Catalog resellers are nationwide direct-mail suppliers. They are generally the best source for pricing. They sell lots of product and they sell it cheap. They usually get the product to you the next day. Some are fairly competent at recommending solutions because they often receive regular training on the products and their employee turnover is somewhat less than retail. Obviously, their weakness is support and service. They will not fly out and install the product for you or fix it, but they will take it back if there is a problem.

When it comes to mail-order catalogs, their offerings and expertise are as diverse as anything you will find. Catalog resellers deal with networking products in different ways. Some focus on the network connection and are knowledgeable about networking products. Others treat networking as an afterthought and are not very knowledgeable.

Don't be afraid to shop around from one catalog to another. They all have 800 numbers, so call around and get the best price. Once you have purchased from a catalog company, prepare for the deluge of catalogs that will start hitting your mailbox every month.

■ **Resellers.** Because of the diverse types of resellers, it is difficult to generalize on their attributes. Whether you are shopping around to install your network yourself or have someone else do it, resellers are not generally going to give you the best price. If you want someone to decide what you need, install it, and manage it once it is up and running, resellers are your best option. In addition, there will be some things that may be hard to find anywhere else. If you run into such a product, a reseller can special order just about anything that you need.

As you can see, there are many options for setting up and installing your network. With a good plan and, if necessary, a good partner, you can be well on your way to building a more productive and efficient business. If, after reading this chapter, you feel confident that a LAN is appropriate for your company, then set your plan and forge ahead into the world of wired businesses.

Small Business Guide to Wide Area Networks

CHAPTER 9

Wide Area Network Essentials

LOCAL AREA NETWORKS ARE THE CORE OF NETWORKING AND COMMUNICA-tions. They drive communications and the sharing of computers and re-sources within a relatively short distance of each other, usually several hundred feet at most. But what if your business extends beyond one loca-tion? If your network only works in one building or site, all is well. But if your business extends to several sites, you may want a network that con-nects all computers at all locations.

Perhaps you run several retail stores within a city, with computer net-works in each store to handle sales, inventory, and accounting information. Or you may have several professional offices in a region, state, or even across the country, each with its own Local Area Network (LAN). If you need to share information between these distant sites, you obviously can't run your own cable from one location to the other; that would require get-ting permission from multiple businesses, cities, and states, among others, to dig and lay cabling between each site. It is a process that would cost far too much effort, coordination, and money to be practical. So there must be a way to get multiple Local Area Networks to communicate even though they are physically distant. That is where Wide Area Networks come in.

Characteristics of Wide Area Networks

WHEREAS A LAN RUNS WITHIN A BUILDING OR CLOSE DISTANCES, A WIDE Area Network (WAN) runs distances of up to thousands of miles. WANs use the public telephone system to connect multiple LANs that are physically distant from each other.

Wide area networks are not for everyone. First of all, WANs are designed to connect multiple Local Area Networks in separate offices or sites in different locations. If you don't run multiple offices or sites, there is no need for a WAN. In addition, WANs do not connect a home or mobile computer to an office LAN; that is called remote access and is discussed in Chapter 7.

The second reason that Wide Area Networks aren't for everyone is that they are expensive and complex. Because you cannot just string your own cabling from one side of town to another, you must use a public network, such as the phone company's, to make the connection for you. This can cost you from hundreds to thousands of dollars per month, depending on the distance and speed. WAN equipment is also very expensive, generally costing several thousand dollars or more to get started. And because the equipment is highly complex, it requires specialists, such as someone from the telephone company or a consultant, to set it up. You can just imagine how much that costs.

However, even with all of the potential complications and expense, WANs can be a valuable asset to businesses of all sizes. Often the integration of disparate information and other resources cannot be accomplished without a wide area connection.

There are several characteristics that distinguish a Wide Area Network from a Local Area Network. In general, Wide Area Networks have the following characteristics:

- *WANs extend beyond a single building or premises.* WANs are used in geographical areas that are greater than the distance obtainable with a LAN, usually several thousand feet or more. Some WANs for corporations can connect sites across the world.
- *WANs connect multiple LANs.* Wide area networks connect two or more Local Area Networks together.
- *WANs use a public infrastructure to link different sites.* Because of the expense and difficulty in running cable from site to site, WANs use the telephone company's infrastructure.
- *WANs cost a monthly fee.* Because Wide Area Networks use the public telephone network, you are charged a monthly fee for using the telephone company's service. The costs range widely depending on your needs.

■ *WANs are slower than LANs.* Wide area network speeds generally run from the low end of 33.6 Kbps (least expensive) to the high end of 1.5 Mbps (more expensive), although they can go faster. As a speed reference, Ethernet LANs run at 10 Mbps. That means some of the fastest WANs operate at only 15 percent of the speed of the slowest LANs. If you use Fast Ethernet at 100 Mbps, it is only 1.5 percent of the speed. Obviously, with those restrictions you can't do the same things over a WAN as you can a LAN.

■ *WANs require more security and complexity.* Because they operate over a public telephone network, WANs must be more secure than a Local Area Network so that no one has access to your data. In addition, WANs are more complex than LANs, especially when it comes to knowing what to send over the WAN and making sure that the data being sent is accurate.

WAN Benefits

WIDE AREA NETWORKS ARE AN EXTENSION OF THE LOCAL AREA NETWORK, so their benefits are similar. They include sharing files; communicating with other employees through e-mail and other applications; running intranets; and sharing common data such as customer databases, accounting information, and other financial resources.

For example, let's assume that your company has several retail outlets scattered across a city. Each store has a point-of-purchase system that is run on a computer. Rather than managing a separate accounting system on each computer, you want to automate the process of logging and tracking sales in each store with one accounting package on a computer server in your main office. Because the data is sensitive, you may want to have a secure method to transmit the information from the retail stores to the computer server in the main office. Or you may have several offices spread across a city, state, or the country that need to share video, voice calls, or other services across a network. If so, you may need a Wide Area Network connection to facilitate the flow of information from one source to another.

Is It for You?

AS STATED EARLIER, WIDE AREA NETWORKS ARE NOT FOR EVERYONE. However, here are some general rules to keep in mind.

113

When to Consider Implementing a WAN

1. *You have more than one office or location that is a workplace.* (This does not include mobile workers or employees working out of their home.)

2. *Each workplace or site has a Local Area Network.* Wide area networks are generally used to connect multiple LANs. If you only have a single computer, when dialing in, that computer is usually considered a remote access connection to the network.

3. *You regularly need to communicate information between locations.* The need for frequent, timely transmittal of information is an important reason for implementing WANs. Frequent communication means that you need to communicate at least once a day between your sites.

4. *Your information needs to be secure.* Important communications or financial transactions are the type of data that should go over a WAN rather than the Internet. The exception is if you use a VPN for secure Internet transmissions (which is explained later in this chapter). Transmitting less sensitive information, such as e-mail, between several offices can be done over the Internet much more cost-effectively than with a WAN.

Table 9-1. *Wide Area Network Options*

Technology	Connection Type	Speed	Possible simultaneous connections	Cost	Recommendation
Analog	Dial up	33.6 Kbps to 56 Kbps	One	Low	For periodic communications
ISDN (Basic Rate Interface)	Dial up	128 Kbps	One or two	Moderate	For periodic communications
Frame Relay	Dedicated (full-time)	Up to 1.5 Mbps	Multiple	High	Good for regular traffic; can handle multiple sites and "bursty" traffic
Leased Line	Dedicated (full-time)	Up to 1.5 Mbps	One	High	For constant, heavy traffic between two offices

WAN Technologies

THERE ARE SEVERAL DIFFERENT CONNECTION OPTIONS FOR WIDE AREA Networks. Each offers different trade-offs in speed and cost. Which connection option is right for you depends on your needs. Table 9-1 summarizes each option discussed below.

LEASED LINE

A leased line is a full-time, 24-hour-a-day connection between two dedicated points; thus it is often referred to as a dedicated line. It is always available, whether you are using it or not, and you pay for that luxury. Leased lines should only be used when the communications between two offices is very frequent and heavy.

Leased lines are fast and expensive. The cost of a dedicated line depends on the distance and speed of the connection. It can cost thousands of dollars or even hundreds of thousands of dollars per year. Leased lines are point-to-point connections, meaning they only connect from point A to point B. The most common leased line is called a T1 line, and it is available at a speed of 1.5 Mbps, which is fast by WAN standards. Faster T3 lines operate at 45 Mbps, but they are far beyond the needs and budgets of most businesses. Leased lines are also available as fractional T1 lines— that is, you can contract to use only a fraction of a line, such as a 128, 256, or 512 Kbps channel, for less money. With leased lines, the speed you buy is the speed you get, anytime, day or night.

The example in Figure 9-1 shows how a law firm uses a leased line or dedicated connection. In this example, the firm has two offices within a city. The firm keeps an extensive electronic database of reference material on a server in one office that is maintained by the firm's administrative staff. The material is referenced daily by attorneys in both offices. In addition, attorneys at both offices regularly work together on cases. In the past, the attorneys would often travel across the city to meet and collaborate. To be more efficient with the attorneys' time, the firm has set up a video conferencing center in each office that allows lawyers to view each other and the documents they are discussing through video monitors.

Obviously, with the need for constant flow of data and a video conferencing center established between the two offices, there is a need for a high-bandwidth solution between the two offices. The firm uses a T1 line that runs at 1.5 Mbps between the two offices. This solution gives the

Figure 9-1. *Leased Line WAN*

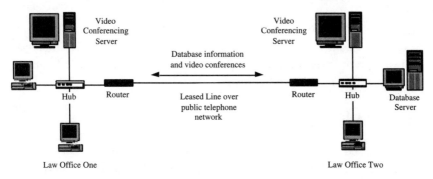

lawyers the full-time connection they need and enough speed to get their work done. Because it is dedicated, it is a great technology for sending video, voice, and data.

SWITCHED CONNECTIONS

Switched connections have become a popular option for WANs. Like leased lines, the cost of switched connections is based on speed and distance. There are two types of switched networks: frame relay and X.25 (pronounced "X dot twenty-five"). Frame relay is far more popular, but ultimately your choice of service depends on what your telecommunications provider offers as much as which solution is better for your company. Switched connections like Frame Relay are often referred to as leased lines because they use a line like a T-1 or fractional T-1 between the company network and the switched service provider (usually the telephone company).

Unlike a leased line, which only goes from one point to another, one of the big advantages of a switched connection is that it connects to multiple locations at the same time. Although you only have one dedicated line going into the public network (the telephone company's network), you are able to connect with many different sites. Frame relay is generally available in speeds as low as 56 Kbps and as fast as 1.5 Mbps. Because of its speed, frame relay can be used for many applications, including voice, video, and data.

The importance of a switched network such as frame relay is illustrated in this example of a law firm with four offices in Boston, New York,

Philadelphia, and Baltimore. While the firm's networking needs are similar to the example in Figure 9-1, the law firm has an additional consideration of trying to connect four offices. Multiple offices make leased line connections, which are dedicated lines between two points, a very expensive option. Why? To use a leased line in this scenario the firm would have to pay for a line from each office *to every other office*, as shown in Figure 9-2. That means that the firm would have to purchase six dedicated leased lines and 12 pieces of equipment (often called Customer Premises Equipment, or CPE) in order to communicate among all the offices.

Figure 9-2. *Leased Lines With Multiple Offices*

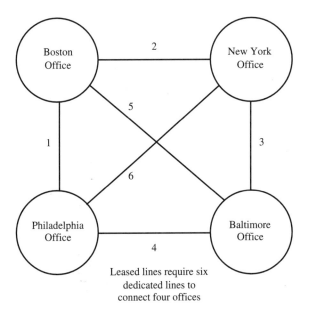

Leased lines require six
dedicated lines to
connect four offices

A better solution in this case is to use frame relay. Because frame relay can connect to multiple sources simultaneously, the firm only needs four connections, shown in Figure 9-3. In this scenario all of the sites connect into the frame relay "cloud" that represents the telephone company's backbone. Switched connections provide the high-speed connection needed, but for less money than separate dedicated leased lines.

The other advantage of frame relay is its "bursty" capability, which refers to its ability to handle sporadic larger amounts of data. Usually, when you buy a frame relay connection, you are given a Committed Information Rate (CIR). A CIR is the minimum bandwidth you are guaranteed, although your actual bandwidth at any time may be higher, depending on who else is sharing your connection. For example, let's say your CIR is 56 Kbps, but you may at times require connections as fast as 256 Kbps. That means that you can always get at least 56 Kbps, but if no other organizations are using their bandwidth, you can get that full 256 Kbps speed all to yourself. But look out, if you have bandwidth-intensive applications such as video that need that full 256 Kbps and some other organization sharing the connection is using all of their bandwidth you will only get your guaranteed 56 Kbps. Without this bursting feature, you would be required to pay for the full 256 Kbps of bandwidth all the time even though you only need 56 Kbps most of the time.

Figure 9-3. *Multiple Offices Using Frame Relay*

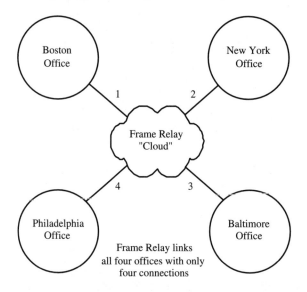

DIAL-UP LINES

A dial-up line is the least expensive and slowest type of Wide Area Network connection you can use. Dial-up lines stay idle, or disconnected, until they are used. They are less expensive because you only call up the network through the telephone system and establish a connection when you are ready to send information. Then the dial-up line transmits all the information and disconnects. Dial-up connections come in two basic types: analog and Integrated Services Digital Network (ISDN).

Analog dial-up connections use modems such as those in or plugged into your computer. An analog connection dials up through a standard phone line to make the connection. It is every bit as slow as your computer's modem, so it isn't recommended for networks that regularly send a lot of information. The maximum rate you could really expect from an analog connection is 56 Kbps (which really amounts to 53 Kbps with the limit set by the Federal Communications Commission).

Analog dial-up connections can only link two locations together at a time. So if you have multiple offices, once your network dials up to connect to another office, it can only connect to that one office until the connection is finished. The only way around it is to buy more equipment to dial into multiple offices at the same time. Analog lines are fine for small amounts of data, infrequent transmissions, or transmissions that are done after-hours. Their main advantage is that they are usually far less expensive than the alternatives.

ISDN is the other type of dial-up connection. Like an analog modem, ISDN dials up and generally only connects to one site at a time, although it can possibly connect to two sites at the same time. However, unlike analog phone lines, which use plain old telephone lines, ISDN is digital and uses special digital phone lines.

But ISDN has a great advantage over analog modems—speed. It runs at speeds of up to 128 Kbps, compared to 33.6 Kbps or 56 Kbps for analog modems. In addition, ISDN dials and connects much faster than analog phone modems.

However, as you would expect, ISDN is more expensive. Users are usually billed on a per-minute basis, similar to a cellular phone call. That means that you will be paying extra for each minute that you are connected. Depending on what you are sending and how often you do it, the charges can add up. ISDN is also not readily available in all areas.

An example of an analog dial-up connection is shown in Figure 9-4. The sporting goods chain in this example has three retail stores in the same city. The company has a Local Area Network in each store that connects several computer systems used as cash registers in each store. The company also has a central office where all accounting, marketing, sales, and purchasing activities are located. The company has a problem with tracking inventory from each store. Current reports come in weekly from each store, but they show up too late to track sales trends and allow the company buyer to react to the week's inventory changes. As a result, the company regularly loses sales on some items that do better than expected and sell out. The company also has excess inventory on several items that it expected to sell well but did not. In both cases, the company could have reacted better to inventory levels if it had more frequently updated information.

Figure 9-4. *Dial-Up WAN*

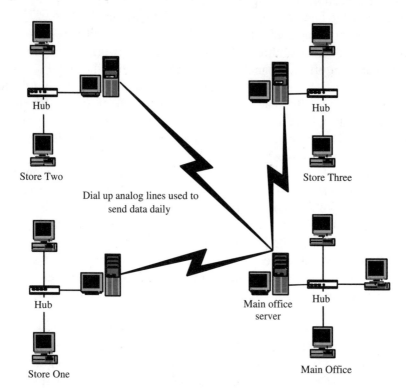

To improve the inventory control situation, the company decides to connect the three stores with the central office through a Wide Area Network. With a connection from each store's server to the main office, the company ties in the accounting and inventory software from each store to the central site's accounting server. At the end of each day, the stores send data on the day's sales and inventory levels to the central site, where it is downloaded to the server. Both the purchasing and sales managers can then review the previous day's sales in the morning each day and decide what changes need to be made to current orders.

Because the data between the retail stores is only sent once a day after-hours, an analog connection is an adequate solution. Each server on the network is equipped with a modem and a normal analog phone line.

DSL

A potential new technology on the block for Wide Area Networks is Digital Subscriber Line (DSL). DSL comes in many flavors, ranging from relatively slow speeds to absolutely blazing fast. It is still not available in all areas, but where it is, it is generally cheaper than a leased line or frame relay. Some forms of DSL, such as ADSL, may be not suited for a WAN connection because it is an *asymmetrical* technology (that's an engineer's way of saying that the speed in one direction is faster than the speed in the other direction). Others services such as SDSL are *symmetrical* and would work well for a Wide Area Network. Check with your local telephone company for DSL service options and availability.

VIRTUAL PRIVATE NETWORKS

Virtual private networking is a new technique for Wide Area Networks. A virtual private network (VPN) uses a public network—the Internet—to connect multiple LANs together with a secure connection. VPNs do this with two important technologies: tunneling and encryption. First, a VPN creates a "virtual" circuit between the two sites through the Internet. The VPN then uses tunneling to encapsulate the data into the protocol (language) of the Internet—TCP/IP—so that it can be easily transported. Encryption scrambles the information sent so that only the intended recipient can descramble and read it.

Using the Internet for a WAN connection saves money because the company only pays for the connection from their building to their Internet Service Provider (ISP), which is the company that provides Internet access, and from the ISP to the company site at the other end. Thus you pay for only a short distance for your WAN—from the Internet Service Provider to the company location on both sides. Since distance is a factor in the cost of the Wide Area Network, a VPN can cost significantly less than a similar connection using the phone company's traditional backbone the entire way. Virtual Private Networks use the same connection technologies as other Wide Area Networks, including leased and switched lines and dial-up analog and ISDN modems. Another benefit of a VPN is that you can use your connection for your WAN and to connect to the Internet, so you can save costs of having separate connections to each.

Figure 9-5 shows another possible scenario for a law firm using a Wide Area Network. The firm in this example has offices in New York and Washington, D.C., and it needs to transmit information several times a day between offices in order to consolidate information on client billings and coordinate client projects between law offices, which all come out of the Washington, D.C., office. Although the law firm uses the Internet frequently for research and communications with clients and between offices, it has been wary of sending sensitive client and financial information over the Internet for security reasons. It has also investigated setting up a WAN solution between the two offices using frame relay. However, the distance of the connection has made it too expensive for the firm to consider.

Figure 9-5. *Virtual Private Network*

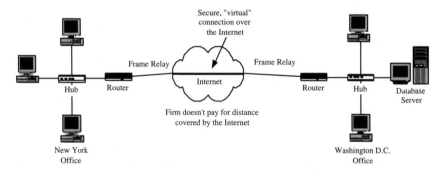

The firm finds an alternative to either solution with a Virtual Private Network. By using a VPN connection through the Internet, the law firm is ensured transmission of data between sites without the expense of a long-distance connection. With the VPN, the firm only pays for connections from their offices to the Internet (the connection to their Internet Service Provider). They don't pay for the distance the data travels over the Internet. In addition, both offices are able to use their connections to the Internet for web surfing and sending e-mail over the Internet to clients.

Equipment

THE EQUIPMENT USED FOR WIDE AREA NETWORKS DEPENDS ON THE IMPLE-
mentation. The range of possible solutions is so varied that a discussion
with your WAN provider will be necessary to determine what you need.

GENERAL EQUIPMENT YOU WILL PROBABLY NEED

■ **Router.** Routers are used for analog, ISDN, leased line, or frame relay
WANs. Routers are important for a Wide Area Network because they use
network addresses and forward "packets" of information based on location. Therefore a router will only send information across the WAN when
it is intended for someone at another location. This is helpful because
everything on your LAN can't make it across that small WAN connection,
so the router limits the traffic only to that which is necessary.

Routers connect directly to your network and have connections on
the other end for whatever communication technology they use. If they
are using analog or ISDN, often the connection is built in. If frame relay
or a leased line is used, a DSU/CSU device (see description below) is connected to the other side to make the connection from the router to the
Wide Area Network. Alternatively, connections may also be made between two servers that have the necessary equipment and router software
installed in them.

■ **FRAD.** A frame relay assembler/disassembler (FRAD) is a device that
can be used in place of a router to connect to a frame relay connection
through a DSU/CSU. FRADs take the data coming from your local segment and format it to run across the frame relay connection. A multiport
FRAD will connect multiple devices to a DSU/CSU.

■ **DSU/CSU.** This piece of equipment wins the longest acronym award.
DSU/CSU stands for digital service unit/channel service unit. (Not surprisingly, it is often referred to as a CSU/DSU as well.) A DSU/CSU connects the router or FRAD to the WAN line, much like a modem, except
that this device is digital.

Getting Started

INSTALLING A WIDE AREA NETWORKING SOLUTION REQUIRES THE HELP OF A
professional who understands the complexity of the situation and is familiar with the available solutions. Your options are limited only by the

number of service providers in your area. Most areas have at least several options: long-distance carriers (e.g., Sprint, MCI, and AT&T) and Local Exchange Carriers (LECs) such as the Baby Bells and others. LECs include U.S. West, Southwestern Bell, and Pacific Bell.

Your best bet in finding the right option for you is to call all the service providers in your area. Every one of the providers will have a sales desk. Let them know what it is you are looking for and ask them to give you a bid. Most can tell you almost immediately what is available and what they recommend. They should all be able to provide the equipment and even set it up for you. If you feel uncomfortable working directly with a telecommunications company, you can probably find a computer reseller or consultant to work with you. They can be helpful in determining your needs and specifying and installing equipment. However, find one that is very experienced with WANs—this is a very specialized area of networking that few resellers have a command of.

When calling the providers in your area, you will want to give them specific information on what you are looking for. In general, your telecommunications provider will want to know about the following:

■ **Number of sites.** The number of sites that are communicating over the Wide Area Network will make a big difference in the decision of what type of WAN to put in. If two sites are communicating with each other, a leased line may be an option because it goes from point to point and can only connect two points together. However, if multiple sites are communicating with each other, frame relay is a better option.

■ **Distance.** Distance will play a large role in the solution you use. Remember that most leased services are billed according to speed and distance. If you are using frame relay or a dedicated line, the longer the distance of your WAN, the more expensive it will be.

Distance will also have a bearing on the price quotes you receive from different providers. Telephone services are divided up into local access and transport areas (LATAs). Local phone companies provide service within LATAs. Long-distance carriers such as AT&T, Sprint, and MCI provide service in the long-distance areas between LATAs. As a general rule, if your WAN stays within one LATA, local exchange carriers such as U.S. West and Pacific Bell will be less expensive. However, if your WAN goes across one or more of these local transport areas, the big long-distance carriers may be less expensive. Of course, the only way you can really tell is by having both types of providers bid on your solution.

■ **Type of communications.** This refers to the amount and frequency of communications between sites. Your provider will want to know how much data is sent and how often. The amount of traffic that will be sent between locations is a big determinant of the type of connection that you will need. Heavy traffic can quickly overwhelm an analog line, while sending e-mail across a T1 leased line is a waste of money.

In general, if your company requires a connection for more than four hours a day, you should consider a dedicated or switched connection. If your needs are less than four hours connection time per day, you may be able to get by with a dial-up connection between sites.

If you go with a solution such as an analog or ISDN connection, the speed that you get for your connection is fixed, based upon your needs. If you decide on a frame relay connection, your provider will often recommend a solution based on a Committed Information Rate (CIR), which is the minimum bandwidth the telecommunications company guarantees that you will have at any given time. If you go with frame relay, make sure you ask what your CIR is.

One of the limiting factors in your solution may be the availability of services. Not all services are available in all areas. Some telecommunications companies have invested more heavily in one type of connection technology than another, so they may not have exactly what you need. Or they may have what you need, but it may be priced out of your reach.

Implementing a Wide Area Network requires a lot of planning and coordination. If you feel that you need a Wide Area Network, then your business is more sophisticated than most. It is best to try to summarize your needs for a Wide Area Network before you sit down with a telecommunications provider. Understand your needs: the different company sites that you wish to connect together, and what type of data will be transmitted, how much, and how often. Then, let the telecommunications providers in your area bid on what they think best fulfills your needs for a Wide Area Network. If you think a Virtual Private Network may fit your needs, you may want to contact your local computer reseller or Internet Service Provider.

For years, Wide Area Networks were only in the domain of large companies with many locations and very deep pockets. But, like most networking technologies, there are applications for small businesses with the need. If your company has clearly identified its needs, there may be a solution for you.

125

Small Business Guide to the Internet

CHAPTER 10

Internet Essentials

THE INTERNET IS THE HOTTEST TOPIC IN NETWORKING TODAY. WITHOUT A doubt, you have seen it and heard about it all around you. It probably seems as if you can't get away from it, but you may not want to. The Internet may be the most important business tool you can find, helping you to expand your business, reach more customers, communicate with suppliers, and even lower your operating costs.

Internet Components

WHEN SOMEONE TALKS ABOUT THE INTERNET, MOST PEOPLE IMMEDIATELY think of the World Wide Web, which is its graphical extension. But there is really much more to the Internet than surfing to your favorite website. The Internet has many important features and components that can be very useful.

World Wide Web

The World Wide Web is the most popular part of the Internet. It is the graphic portion of the Internet that allows users to "surf" from location to location as easily as pointing and clicking with a mouse. It is used by companies, individuals, nonprofit organizations, universities, and governments to create their own websites and publish information.

The World Wide Web is made possible with a programming language called HyperText Markup Language (HTML), which allows web documents to be displayed on virtually any computer with software called a web browser. With the ability to include active graphics and even mini-applications (called Applets), through Sun Microsystems' Java and Microsoft's ActiveX technology, websites have become even more useful and interesting.

INTERNET E-MAIL

Electronic mail, or e-mail, is an extremely popular component of the Internet. In fact, it is by far the most popular use of the Internet. It provides users with inexpensive, simple communications and a fast medium for sending messages and other documents to customers and suppliers. E-mail is growing in popularity and is one of the best ways to send and receive business correspondence. With no postage required and almost instant delivery, e-mail is a great alternative to "snail mail," the Internet's term for the postal system. E-mail also gives you the ability to "attach" files, so you can send an e-mail and attach a word processing, video, picture, or other data file across the Internet almost instantly.

FTP

File Transfer Protocol (FTP) is a standard used to send and receive files through the Internet. This may not sound exciting, but it is extremely useful for transferring large files. While it may seem as if all transmissions can be handled by sending e-mail attachments, FTP allows larger files to be transferred and does it faster and more reliably than e-mail. Like sending e-mail with file attachments, FTP saves money over postage or fax charges.

GOPHER

Gopher is a term used to describe a way of navigating through information in a list format on the Internet. It presents information in a readable format by using hierarchical lists that allow you to navigate using a Gopher client. The Gopher function of the Internet has seen its more popular days in terms of general use, having been supplanted by the World Wide Web. However, it is still a great way to find information on the Internet.

USENET/NEWSGROUPS

Usenet, which stands for User Network, is the final major component of the Internet that is made up of newsgroups. Usenet gives Internet users the forum to meet and converse with others about specific topics of mutual interest. It is all done in a posted format, meaning that you can read through an individual's comments and others' replies as they are posted to an electronic bulletin board. Figure 10-1 shows the user interface of a typical Usenet group.

Figure 10-1. *Usenet (Newsgroup) Discussion*

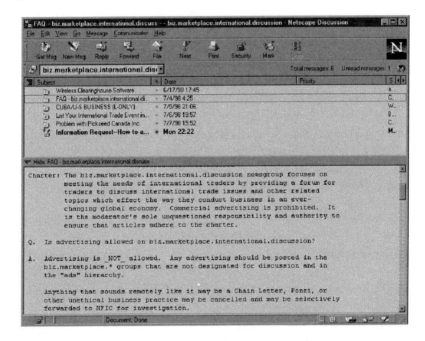

You can find a newsgroup about almost any topic. Some have no direct business application, but many are appropriate for business use. Whether you want information on new computer technology, traveling to Bolivia, direct marketing, expanding internationally, or biochemistry, you will find Usenet groups on any and all of these topics. In fact, there are somewhere between 25,000 and 30,000 newsgroups currently on the Internet.

History of the Internet

THIS IS JUST ENOUGH INFORMATION ON THE HISTORY OF THE INTERNET FOR you to bore the pants off people at parties. (You can feel free to skip this section and move on if you aren't concerned with the past but only want to know the future potential of the Internet.) With all of the hype about the Internet over the past few years, it is hard to believe that it has its origins in the 1960s. Yet this vast, public forum had its humble beginnings with an attempt to build a strong, reliable network that would facilitate government communications across a wide area. Like many inventions, the Internet was a product of military technology; its genesis was a network known as ARPANET, which was designed to link various military installations to allow them to communicate. Because it was set up for military use and, of course, the military designs things for war, the Internet has an interesting characteristic: It is designed so that there is no point of failure, no weak spot vulnerable to attack, and no controlling center. If a segment of the Internet were taken out, the information would still find a way to its destination.

The Internet eventually started to grow beyond its military roots into an effective way for academia at universities to communicate and share information. ARPANET eventually became a connection between colleges and universities, while MILNET became the continuation of the Defense Department's network. Advances were made along the way, adding e-mail capabilities, a unique addressing system, and the language of the Internet, the Transmission Control Protocol/Internet Protocol. It was the late 1980s when the National Science Foundation created NSFNet, composed of several supercomputing centers that formed the backbone of the Internet.

But it wasn't until the 1990s that the Internet really evolved into the network it is today. In 1990, ARPANET ceased to exist. In that same year the first commercial company to provide access to the Internet came into existence. The following year, the World Wide Web and web browsers were created, paving the way for individuals and companies to create graphical pages and others to access them, then surf from location to location by clicking on graphics and words that link to other web pages or websites.

The Internet has grown so fast since then that no one really knows how big it is, only that it is big. Estimates on the number of users, connected computers, and websites vary, but almost everyone can agree that they are all growing rapidly. Most people who are familiar with the Internet expect that it will continue to grow in the future.

Who Controls the Internet?

NO ONE REALLY CONTROLS THE INTERNET. THERE ARE NO GOVERNMENT bodies that control its growth, content (with some exceptions for decency), or direction. It is as free and open as those who use it. However, the National Science Foundation still controls the registration process for domains (i.e., unique addresses). Network Solutions, Inc. (NSI), a private company, is the exclusive contractor of domains. This is about to change, pending government legislation, so that others will be able to license Internet domains also. (Domains are explained in depth later in the chapter.)

NSI uses an organization called InterNIC, which was created in 1993, to sell the rights to the user-friendly names, called domain names, which are used on the Internet to navigate the World Wide Web. In exchange for its services in helping you find and register a name, InterNIC charges a setup and yearly maintenance fee for the domain name.

How Does the Internet Work?

THE INTERNET IS A COMPLEX AND DISORGANIZED STRUCTURE OF INDIVIDUAL computers and networks connected together. It is designed to be a durable, lasting network solution where everyone is equal. There are no central servers or supercomputers that run the Internet; instead it is highly distributed. This was done by design. Because the military created the Internet for reliable communications under any circumstances, it is built so that no one thing is running it. Therefore no one thing can go down and bring the entire Internet down with it.

There are many different types of computers and networks on the Internet that serve different functions. However, the one common feature between all of the devices connected to the Internet is that they all speak a common language, or protocol, called Transmission Control Protocol/ Internet Protocol (TCP/IP). TCP/IP (pronounced by spelling it out letter by letter) was developed by the Department of Defense to interconnect different types of networks. The TCP part provides for the transportation of information, making sure that the information you send arrives at its destination. The IP part ensures that the information gets to a specific destination by providing the address. The Internet Protocol address is comprised of a series of four numbers separated by periods or "dots." For example, an address for a computer on the Internet may be 254.168.54.100. Any requests for information made to that address are sent to that particular computer. It is analogous to a phone number for that computer.

Computers on the Internet are connected together by routers. Routers are designed to forward packets of information to a specific destination. They use the IP addressing described previously to narrow in on a destination, find it, and deliver the information. Again, it is analogous to dialing a telephone number, where a country code lets me narrow the number down to a specific country; the area code lets me narrow it down a geographic region; the prefix (or next three numbers) lets me narrow it further within that area; and the suffix (or last four numbers) lets me find a specific business or residence. Although IP addressing isn't set up on a geographic basis, routers do much the same work by passing the information along and using the address to find the most efficient path to reach its final destination.

Connecting the Dots:
Domains, URLs, and Hyperlinks

THE WORLD WIDE WEB HAS A UNIQUE STRUCTURE TO FACILITATE THE WAY we locate and navigate through information. As mentioned previously, all computers on the Internet are identified by an IP address. Imagine what it would be like trying to remember four sets of three numbers for the address of every site you want to visit on the Internet. It would be like remembering the phone number of every place you ever want to call. For some of us it is hard enough remembering our own phone numbers.

To facilitate a way to get to places easily, a naming system was designed in the 1980s to make it easy for users to identify addresses on the Internet. You may have seen the addresses of the Internet set up as www.anybusiness.com, or someone's e-mail address written as Bob@any business.com. The main part of the address—"anybusiness.com"—is known as the domain. Internet domains allow you to use names instead of numbers to get around on the Web (i.e., it is the difference between typing in www.intel.com, instead of 192.246.100.42). A particular address is also known as a Uniform Resource Locator, or URL (which is pronounced letter by letter). When you want someone's URL, just ask, "What's your web address?" or "What's your URL?"

At the end of a domain name, after the final period, is the top-level domain (TLD) name, which indicates the type of organization it is. TLDs include designations for businesses, nonprofit organizations, educational institutions, and other organizations. A list of current and proposed additional TLDs is included in Table 10-1. Endings differ for other countries also. For example, .au is for domains in Australia and .uk is for those in the United Kingdom.

Hyperlinks, also known as links, are the underlined, highlighted words or special graphics embedded into web pages that allow you to navigate quickly on the World Wide Web. You move from one web page to the next by clicking on a hyperlink with your mouse. It is an ingenious way of allowing web surfers to navigate the web with a mouse, making the Internet easy enough for anyone to use.

Table 10-1. *Top-Level Domains*

Current Top-Level Domains	Organization Type
.com	Commercial
.edu	Education
.gov	Government
.org	Not-for-profit
.net	Internet Service Providers
.mil	Military
Proposed Additional Top-Level Domains	Organization Type
.arts	Arts and entertainment
.firm	Businesses
.info	Information services
.rec	Recreation
.store	Online stores
.web	Web-related activites

Internet Servers

SERVERS ARE THE WHERE INFORMATION IS STORED ON THE INTERNET. THEY are high-powered computers that run special software and give users the ability to use different types of Internet services. Servers can perform specific functions, such as holding graphical HTML pages that you access with your web browser when you surf the World Wide Web. They can also hold files that you upload or download through FTP, or servers are also used to send, receive, and store Internet e-mail for an entire network of users.

Internet Service Providers

AN INTERNET SERVICE PROVIDER, ALSO KNOWN AS AN ISP, IS YOUR GATEWAY to the Internet and all of its resources. An Internet Service Provider has a direct or indirect connection to the Internet. ISPs provide you with a connection to the Internet through their network. ISPs lease access to the Internet through a very fast connection that ultimately leads to an Internet Point of Presence (POP) or access point, and then let you use their connection for a fee. Internet Service Providers come in all different shapes and sizes. Chapter 14 explains the different types of Internet Service Providers and how to choose a good one.

Connection Types

THERE ARE TWO WAYS FOR MOST BUSINESSES TO CONNECT TO THE Internet—from an individual computer or through a networked connection. Which is the best method depends on how you are using the Internet, how often you access it, and how many users you have.

Individual connections to the Internet are made from a single computer that dials into the Internet and connects only for the duration needed. This type of connection is exactly the same as those used by individuals who connect from home. As shown in Figure 10-2, you may have one or many individual computers connecting to the Internet, but each one requires a modem, a phone line, and an account with an ISP. The advantage of individual connections is that they are inexpensive and easy to set up. They use slower connections such as analog modems, but some can be used with higher-speed ISDN, ADSL, or cable modems.

Figure 10-2. *Individual Dial-Up Accounts*

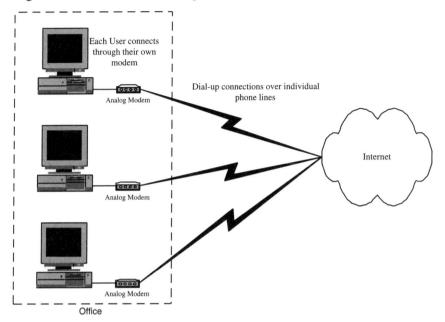

The downside to individual dial-up connections is that they become incrementally more expensive with every user that you add to the network. Adding a user means purchasing an additional account, extra phone line, and possibly even an additional modem. After a while, all those individual costs start to add up.

The alternative to individual accounts is to set up an Internet connection through a router or server attached to the Local Area Network. Instead of connecting with a modem, all users send and receive data to the Internet through the network. Figure 10-3 shows a networked connection to the Internet.

Networked connections are usually faster than individual connections and use either a dial-up technology such as ISDN or a dedicated frame relay connection that is up 24 hours a day. Although higher-speed network connections may seem expensive as you price them out, they are often less expensive than buying a number of individual accounts. Networked connections are generally more difficult to set up than individual connections.

Figure 10-3. *Networked Internet Connection*

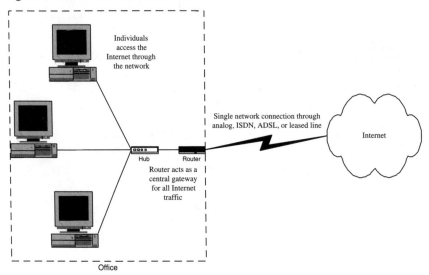

CONNECTION TECHNOLOGIES

When looking for a connection technology to the Internet, you have three basic options to choose from: analog modems, ISDN, or dedicated line such as frame relay. Each has its own trade-offs in speed, cost, and ease of use.

Analog Modems

If you have ever used the modem in your personal computer, then you are probably familiar with analog modems. They are the staple of connectivity for most computers and are often used for dialing up to the Internet from an individual computer. The advantage of using an analog modem is that it is inexpensive and uses ordinary telephone lines.

While analog modems are used most often for individual computer connections, they can also be used for a networked Internet connection. There are several routers on the market that support an analog modem connection, including products made by Intel Corp. and 3Com.

Older modems range in speed from 28.8 to 33.6 Kbps, but newer modems have a top speed of 56 Kbps, although current FCC regulations actually limit the speed to only 53 Kbps. (The actual speed will be closer to 24 Kbps to 50 Kbps.) Any modem that is more than a few years old is probably slower than 28.8 Kbps and is too slow to handle the heavy graphics of the World Wide Web.

Until recently, there have been two competing and incompatible standards for 56 Kbps modems—the x2 standard from 3Com/U.S. Robotics, and K56Flex from Lucent Technologies and Rockwell. However, a new, unified standard for 56 Kbps modems has recently been agreed upon called V.90. If you plan to buy any new modems for Internet connections, make sure that they support the new V.90 standard.

ISDN

ISDN stands for Integrated Services Digital Network. While ISDN has been around for nearly two decades and is extremely popular in Europe, it has only recently started to take off in the United States over the past two years.

ISDN is a digital technology, just like most of the telephone companies' infrastructure (they convert telephone lines to analog before they reach your home or office). Because it is digital, it has some benefits over analog modems—namely, faster dial up and less distortion. The most common type of ISDN is called Basic Rate Interface (BRI). BRI ISDN connects using two channels, called B channels, each of which runs at speeds of up to 64 Kbps each and carry all of the data. BRI ISDN also has a third channel, called a D channel, that carries other signals. In all, BRI ISDN goes as fast as 128 Kbps, or almost three times faster than most analog modems. For limited needs, one 64 Kbps B channel can be used.

ISDN is usually fast enough for most network connections to the Internet. Using a router that supports ISDN, the network has a connection that can dial in to the Internet almost instantly and then disconnect when no longer in use. ISDN can also be used for individual computer connections.

Unfortunately, ISDN is not available everywhere. Some telephone companies can easily support your need for ISDN, while others barely know how to spell it. In addition, ISDN pricing varies widely by area. Many telephone companies charge a monthly fee and then charge by the minute for connection time. Most Internet Service Providers also charge extra for an ISDN connection. Those charges can add up to a large monthly bill.

Dedicated Lines

The fastest option for a connection to the Internet is through a dedicated line such as a T1 line or a frame relay. The difference between these

139

options and the analog and ISDN solutions previously described is that dedicated connections are up 24 hours per day, 7 days per week. Dedicated connections are always made between your local area network to the Internet Service Provider.

Dedicated lines range in speed from 56 or 64 Kbps and up to T1 line speeds, with many increments in between. A full T1 line is around 1.5 Mbps. However, with high speed comes a hefty price tag. Expect to pay at least several hundred dollars per month for a dedicated line.

The other downside to dedicated lines is that your network is connected full-time to the Internet. While there are many security solutions, such as firewalls, to decrease your security risk, a dedicated connection makes it easier for others to hack their way on to your network and even the individual computers connected to it from the Internet

Connections of the Future

While you have basically three choices for connecting to the Internet today, you can rest assured that executives at high tech companies, telephone providers, and even cable TV companies (that's right, the companies that bring you the Cartoon Network and QVC) are going without sleep at night trying to figure out how to get you a faster connection to the Internet and get your money in their coffers. There are essentially three competing technologies beginning deployment in the U.S.A.—DSL, cable modems, and wireless—that may one day be the best way to get you connected to the Internet. While they are technologies of the future, they are already being tested or commercially launched in many areas and one or more may be available in your region.

EMERGING INTERNET ACCESS TECHNOLOGIES

■ **Digital Subscriber Line (DSL).** This is a promising technology for Internet access. DSL is a digital technology like ISDN. But unlike ISDN, DSL uses your existing copper phone wire. Also, DSL can use the same lines for phone calls and Internet access at the same time by using different frequencies on the phone line.

Asymmetrical Digital Subscriber Line (ADSL) is the version that will most likely be used by businesses and individuals for Internet access. Full-speed ADSL runs at speeds up to 8 Mbps. A variation called ADSL G.lite (pronounced g-dot-lite) will run at slower speeds and have half the calories and fat of the regular version, so to speak. Even the slowest versions of ADSL are at least twice as fast as ISDN. ADSL is asymmetrical, which means that the line's upload speed is usually slower than its download speed. So, for example, you may get 1.5 Mbps access to download (i.e., receive) information from the Internet, but only 64 Kbps to upload (i.e., transmit) information over the network. This is usually fine since you will download more information than you upload. Other versions of DSL will run at even faster speeds in the future.

DSL has been tested in several markets for the past few years and is just starting to roll out in many areas. Most phone companies are jumping at the chance to begin offering DSL service to their customers. In addition, DSL has support from many of the biggest names in the computer industry, including Cisco Systems, Compaq Computer, Intel Corp., Microsoft Corp., and 3Com.

■ **Cable modems.** Cable modems can only be described as fast, fast, fast. These superfast connections have download speeds of up to 30 Mbps. However, cable modems generally have shared bandwidth. That is, everyone who gets on a segment shares the same 30 Mbps. The more people on, the less bandwidth each person gets.

Cable modems have already been deployed in many areas. One major cable modem supplier, @Home, claims to have about 100,000 subscribers and now has a business service called (surprisingly) @Work. Time Warner, which supplies the RoadRunner cable modem, also claims a high number of cable modem connections in use. While most cable modems are used as individual connections today, cable will be used as a network connection in the future. New products allow cable modems to be connected to a router to give entire networks Internet access through the cable modem.

The big downfall with cable modems is that many are under the domain of cable companies. Are you ready to put all of your data and communications in the hands of the company that can't keep your cable TV up and running? Cable companies have much to learn about customer service and reliability before they win the hearts of business customers.

The other problem that cable modems have is with cabling. Most of the existing coaxial cable infrastructure is made for one-way communications—from the cable company to you. Cable modems require two-way communications for Internet access, so much of the existing cable infrastructure needs to be replaced. In addition, if your company is like most others, you don't have cable access to your building. It will be a while before cable modems are available for your business location. For now, you may be better off leaving cable modems for home Internet access.

■ **Wireless.** The third new technology for Internet access is wireless. It is by far the most promising because it isn't limited by the cabling infrastructure. But of all the Internet connection options, it is also the one that will take longest to become pervasive. Wireless download speeds are around 50 Mbps, almost twice as fast as some cable modems. Wireless will eventually be offered as either a networked or an individual connection. However, wireless is expensive and still has limited availability. Unless you are one of the lucky ones that has wireless Internet access in your area, don't hold your breath waiting for it.

As you can see, there are several different decisions to make on how to connect to the Internet, including networked or individual connections and which technology to use. Your selection depends on many factors, especially what options are available in your area. Before deciding on a type of Internet connection, you need to have a good understanding of what you want to do on the Internet. Chapters 11, 12, and 13 will help you wade through your options. Then, after deciding what you want to do on the Internet, Chapter 14 will help you decide which connection is right for you.

Internet, Round Two

BY NOW YOU MAY HAVE HEARD OF INTERNET2. IF YOU HAVE, IT MAY BE confusing if you aren't even on the first Internet yet. Internet2 is a working project of major universities and computer and telecommunications companies, including Cisco Systems, IBM Corp., and AT&T. Internet2 is designed from the ground up to be what the Internet should have been had someone carefully planned it, rather than it evolving with a life of its own into the free and open network we know today.

Internet2's main objective is to increase the speed of the network to support gigabit-per-second or megafast speeds. That will allow for more applications that can't run on the pokey old first Internet. It was kicked off in 1998—but don't worry, Internet2 won't be ready for anyone but academics and developers for quite a few years. In the meantime, use the first (and for now only) Internet. If you are interested in learning more about Internet2's progress, visit www.internet2.edu.

The Internet is a great opportunity for businesses of almost any size and type. There are so many possibilities that the options to tap and leverage its resources are almost endless. If you believe the Internet may be an option for helping your business, then review the following three chapters. They will help you understand how the Internet can help you improve communications with customers and suppliers, research important information, reach new customers through the World Wide Web, and even open a new channel to sell your products or services.

CHAPTER 11

Communicating and Researching Through the Internet

WHEN YOU THINK ABOUT ALL OF THE WAYS THAT YOU CAN COMMUNICATE with the outside world, the methods are as diverse as the businesses that use them. In an average day your company probably uses a number of methods, including fax machines, telephones, voice mail, the postal service, and overnight package services to share information with customers, potential customers, suppliers, partners, and investors. But are these methods always the most cost-effective or efficient ways to communicate? In the past there were few cost-effective alternatives, but with the Internet as a powerful communications tool, that may no longer be the case.

And what about accessing information? Your company probably thrives on information for all areas of the business. Where do you turn for information on markets, competitors, finances, or running your business? We now live in the information age, with a plethora of information available all on millions of topics. In spite of that, we often have problems finding and accessing exactly the information we need. By leveraging the power and information on the Internet, you can access valuable information that will help your business in many ways. All you need is to know where to look.

This chapter discusses how the Internet can be used as a communication and research tool for your business. It will show you how to use the

Internet to improve communications with anyone outside your company. In addition, you will learn how the Internet can be used as a tool for searching and retrieving valuable information for your business.

Communicating Through the Internet

THE INTERNET IS ONE OF THE MOST COST-EFFECTIVE, EFFICIENT, AND EASIEST ways to communicate with the outside world. By using the Internet you can keep in contact with suppliers, customers, and employees through e-mail, file transfers, Internet telephone calls, video conferencing, group discussions and collaborative software, and even faxing. These applications cost far less than traditional methods of communication.

Potential Ways to Communicate Over the Internet

■ **E-mail.** E-mail is by far the most popular Internet application. Internet e-mail, like LAN e-mail, can be used to send text messages, documents, and other attachments. Internet e-mail is one of the fastest and most cost-effective tools available to businesses.

■ **Virtual office/teamware.** Virtual office applications, also known as teamware, are a new form of groupware. A virtual office is generally much simpler to set up and use than those bulky, expensive groupware applications that run on a local network. While some teamware applications run on Local Area Networks, many use the Internet to give users the ability to publish Internet-like graphical documents, send and receive e-mail, set up discussion groups, and even publish calendars. Everything is read through a web browser, so there is a simple, common interface that works with any type of computer. Teamware is generally set up as an independent service on the Internet and users pay a monthly service to use it. Users access the service by going to a specific site on the Web and logging onto their personal area. While there, they are able to receive e-mail, messages, and documents left for them by others, as well as hold real-time chats with others.

Popular products in this category include HotOffice Technologies' HotOffice, Netopia's Netopia Virtual Office, Netscape's Virtual Office (which uses Netopia's technology), and Instinctive Technologies' eRoom. An example of a teamware product is shown in Figure 11-1.

Figure 11-1. *A Teamware Application*

Teamware is the perfect product, for example, for an investment consulting company with four employees that operate out of a small office. The four employee-owners are often on the road looking at potential investments. Because of their individual travel schedules, the four rarely sit down together to discuss their findings at the same time. In fact, the employees frequently lose track of where the others are traveling and find it difficult to keep up with the others' schedules.

To improve communications and keep each member of the firm in contact, the company invests in a virtual office presence on the Internet. The virtual office allows each employee to set up project files, post information and files, hold discussions on various topics, and even publish calendars for others to read. Using individual access accounts, the four dial into the Internet and share information with the others from most locations throughout the country and even internationally.

■ **FTP.** Do you regularly share documents or other computer files with others outside of the company? Then setting up a server to do file transfers over the Internet using File Transfer Protocol (FTP) may be a great way to go.

Figure 11-2 shows an example of how an FTP site operates. In this example, a company that collects and tabulates market research data has customers spread over a large geographic area. The company receives data from market researchers and tabulates the information in a readable format. The company constantly faces tight deadlines and quick turn-around times to meet demand. Often a day or more is lost in the process on overnight shipping of files to get rush jobs through.

Figure 11-2. *FTP Server*

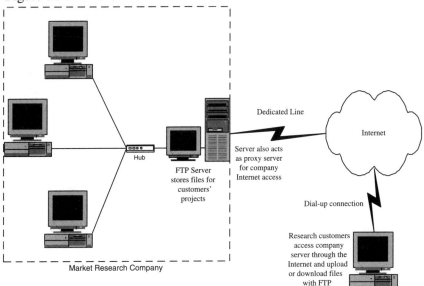

To become more competitive and increase reaction and turnaround time, the company sets up an FTP site with Internet access on its Local Area Network through a dedicated connection. With a server connected to the Internet, the company's clients can now transfer data files through the Internet to the company's server. The company now receives files in minutes rather than overnight, helping employees to better meet their customers' needs. In addition, finished projects can also be posted by the company in special, secure folders that clients are able to access and download files from, saving even more time.

■ **Internet fax.** Is your monthly long-distance bill for faxing getting out of control? If so, Internet fax could be the solution for you. Internet fax, also

147

known as IP faxing, is designed to help companies cut down on their long-distance bills by using the Internet to send and receive faxes. This is particularly helpful for companies that frequently do business internationally, but may also help companies that spend a lot on domestic long-distance faxing.

Internet faxing can be done any one of three different ways: through an individual PC, an IP fax server on the network, or through a device that connects to your standard fax machine. No matter the method, the fax being sent is converted to a format to send over the Internet. The fax is actually transmitted over the Internet by way of an Internet Service Provider to a fax server near the fax's destination. The local fax server then dials the fax number through a local call and completes the transmission of the fax.

Figure 11-3 shows how IP faxing works for sending a fax from New York to Portland, Oregon. As the fax is sent, the fax server on the network in New York checks its destination. Realizing that the fax goes to the 503 area code, which is a long-distance call, the fax server forwards the fax through the Internet to a fax server in the Portland area. The local fax server in Portland makes a local call to the destination fax machine in Portland and completes the transmission of the fax. That process saves the long-distance charges normally incurred from New York to Portland. Of

Figure 11-3. *IP Faxing*

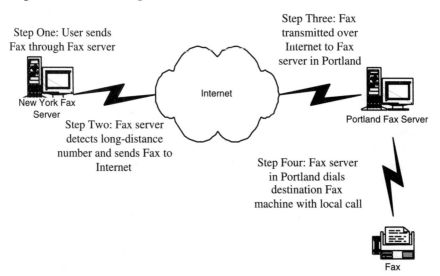

Table 11-1. *Internet Fax Options*

Company	Product Name	URL
AT&T	AT&T Worldnet Enhanced Fax Service	www.att.com
Comfax	Comfax	www.comfax.com
Digital Serve	FaxSav	www.digitalserve.com
FaxAway	FaxAway	www.faxaway.com
JFAX	JFAX Send	www.jfax.com
PSINet	InternetPaper	www.psi.com
UUNet	UUFAX	www.uunet.com

course, Internet Service Providers that support this feature charge for it, but it is usually a flat rate per fax that is less than the telephone charges. For large corporations, IP faxing is done through the Internet with their own local fax servers set up in areas where they sent and receive many faxes. Smaller companies with lower fax volumes can't justify the cost of their own fax servers in each location they fax to. But don't worry: Several large national and multinational Internet Service Providers have set up faxing capabilities as part of their Internet services, providing the fax servers in many local areas for you to use. Table 11-1 lists several leading providers of Internet fax services.

■ **Voice and video.** Voice and video transmissions over the Internet are still in their infancy. They both have great potential, allowing users to hear and/or view each other over the Internet for free. Internet phone applications allow users to dial into someone's computer and literally talk for free over the Internet through the computer. Likewise, video conferencing over the Internet provides a means for real-time collaboration without incurring long-distance charges. However, sending voice and video over the Internet still has its limitations in terms of speed, quality, and reliability. Both applications will improve over time and become a cost-effective tool for small businesses. Someday you may be making all of your long-distance calls over the Internet.

Benefits

OF COURSE, THESE INTERNET TOOLS HELP YOU IMPROVE YOUR COMMUNICA-
tions with others outside your company. But there are distinct advantages
of the using the Internet as a communications tool.

COST

One of the great things about using the Internet for communications
is that the incremental costs for usage is very low. Unlike regular mail and
long-distance telephone phone calls, Internet e-mail does not have a
charge for usage. It doesn't matter if you use e-mail two times a month or
two hundred times; you pay the same amount of money for your account.
Calculate the savings if you could cut your company's long-distance bill
by even 10 percent by using e-mail instead of phone calls. You can see
how quickly those savings can add up. Collaborative applications such as
teamware can often save the cost of many long-distance phone calls because all discussions, files transfers, messages, and even scheduling can
be done over the Internet.

SPEED

A decade ago, overnight-delivery services kicked businesses into
high gear. Virtually anything could be sent overnight to anywhere in the
world. Now the bar has been raised again as businesses work in Internet
time. Messages, files, and more can be sent and received almost instantly
from anywhere in the world to anywhere in the world. The Internet allows
people to send and receive documents almost instantaneously. Even under
heavy use, most e-mails and file transfers usually happen in minutes, not
hours or days. In addition, many communications—such as collaborating
on an application running on several computers simultaneously, or even
chat and discussion sessions—can be done in real time.

UNIVERSALITY

The Internet is now almost a requisite tool for business communications. If you want to keep up with your competitors and stay in touch with
your clients, the Internet is one of the best ways to do it. It is reaching the
point where doing business without the Internet will seem as foreign as
doing business without a telephone.

Is It for You?

USING THE INTERNET FOR COMMUNICATIONS CAN WORK FOR JUST ABOUT ANY company. Review the list that follows to see if your company has some of the attributes for Internet communications.

WHEN TO CONSIDER INTERNET COMMUNICATIONS

1. You have customers, suppliers, or employees outside the office that you communicate with on a regular basis. If you communicate with others daily or weekly, much of that communication can be done quicker and more cost-effectively on the Internet.
2. You have a number of customers or suppliers requesting your e-mail address. Responding to customer demand is always a nice thing to consider. If your customers and suppliers are already on the Internet, you could improve communication flow dramatically by getting your company on the Net also.
3. You spend a lot of money on postage and long-distance charges. E-mail, file transfers, and Internet faxing can be an effective way to reduce these costs.

Cautions

OF COURSE, THERE ARE SOME CAUTIONS TO CONSIDER BEFORE JUMPING INTO Internet communications. They are small and shouldn't prevent most companies from starting to transition at least some of their communications to the Internet, but they require some consideration nonetheless.

SPEED

The speed of communications over the Internet is fast and near-instantaneous at times, but it isn't foolproof. E-mail may arrive in seconds or hours. Once in a while it may take days if there is a problem. And even when messages do arrive, people don't always check for them immediately. In addition, faxing over the Internet is generally slower than faxing over phone lines, so it is not for urgent deliveries. More immediate communications may need to go by another route. Voice calls and video conferencing over the Internet are also subject to potential delays. Under heavy Internet traffic, the delays between sending and receiving a voice call can make you think the other person is on Jupiter.

SECURITY

Obviously, opening up your computers and your network to the Internet brings an added dimension to security concerns. Transferring files to and from your computers increases the chance of computer viruses infiltrating your company's computers. In addition, there is the risk that communicating across a public network, such as the Internet, increases the chances of your information getting into the wrong hands.

However, the security risk of the Internet should be put into proper perspective. Your level of security should be no less than it is through other public forums, including your cellular phone service. There are also excellent security products such as Secure/Multipurpose Internet Mail Extensions (S/MIME) and Pretty Good Privacy (PGP), along with digital certificates for secure e-mail and Secure Socket Layer (SSL) technology for communications with web servers. In addition, when downloading files from the Internet, antivirus software is critical. Chapter 15 covers additional information on Internet security protocols.

Getting Started

YOUR FIRST STEP IN PROVIDING COMPANY INTERNET COMMUNICATIONS IS TO decide what you need and with whom you will communicate. Like our discussion on internal communications in Chapter 6, this involves observing your own company's processes and understanding what can be improved upon. Look at whom you communicate with and what type of information is passed on. Also, observe what employees, suppliers, or customers are complaining about—that is often a good source of information.

Second, match those observed needs to a solution. Do your suppliers complain that they don't get information soon enough? An e-mail connection may be the right solution. If you have employees that travel often, a teamware solution might be appropriate. If your company sends and receives a lot of information or spends heavily on mailing documents, then you might need an FTP server. If your fax bill is sky high, it is time to consider an IP faxing option.

Third, discuss your needs and options with an Internet Service Provider (ISP). An ISP will be able to show you what solutions are available. Make sure that you check around with a number of providers. Keep in mind as you are looking at solutions that not all communications can or should be transferred to the Internet.

Fourth, depending on your other Internet needs, determine your connection type. Your ISP will be able to help you in this area. Your two options are either through individual modems or through a network connection. Which one you need, and how fast your Internet connection needs to be, depends what you will do across the connection. A discussion of how to choose an ISP and Internet connection type is in Chapter 14.

If you are looking at e-mail as a solution, you are not alone. Most companies on the Internet use e-mail. E-mail clients (i.e., software programs that run on your computer) are almost ubiquitous and inexpensive. Many e-mail clients, such as Eudora Lite, Netscape Mail, or Microsoft's Outlook Express, are free. If you only have a few e-mail accounts, you can get away with each employee dialing up to the Internet and getting their own mail. If you have more users, you should consider an e-mail server that supports IMAP or POP3 for incoming mail and SMTP for outgoing mail. (See Chapter 6 for information on servers and Internet e-mail protocols.) The server should have an Internet connection to send and receive e-mail for your entire network. If you already have LAN-based e-mail software, you will want to check whether it has options to work on the Internet as well. Of course, whether you use individual or network connections, your computers need to be set up for TCP/IP, the networking protocol of the Internet.

Teamware packages are generally stored on third-party servers on the Internet for a small monthly fee. You will need to sign up with a third party such as HotOffice or Netscape's Virtual Office to use their services. Others products, such as Netopia Virtual Office or eRoom, run from your network but can be used over the Internet; eRoom is also offered by some service providers.

For some teamware services, you may not need to look any further than your own web browser. Both Netscape's and Microsoft's web browsers come with applications for whiteboards, chats, application sharing, file transfers, and even phone calls over the Internet. If they are not part of the browser, many of these applications can be used as "plug ins" that are used in the browsers.

FTP and IP faxing servers are best left to your Internet Service Provider to handle for you. Go with a provider that already has the equipment in place and can offer you its service and expertise in setting up a solution for you.

No matter what solution fits your needs the best, you will find that using the Internet for your communications can be one of the most cost-effective moves you can make.

Internet Research

LIKE OTHER COMPANIES, YOU RELY ON INFORMATION FOR ALL AREAS OF YOUR business. Yet time and financial constraints may limit your access to information. You may not have either the money or time to dedicate someone to supplying you with essential information to help run your business. But that information is as crucial to you and your company's decisions as it is to a Fortune 500 company, and while there may be restrictions on what you can obtain, not knowing where or how to access it should not the barrier.

WWW Resources

WITH AN INTERNET CONNECTION IN PLACE, YOU HAVE A HUGE INFORMATION source for your business on a variety of topics. In particular, the World Wide Web (WWW) component of the Internet is a vast source of information presented in a graphical format that is easily accessible. Undeniably, there is a lot of garbage on the Internet, but there is also a lot of beneficial information out there that can be easily found and used with little or no expense. By using the Internet's World Wide Web, you can become more informed and make better decisions. All you need to know is where and how to find the right information.

Using the Internet for research and information is simple and cost-effective. In addition, it is easy to use bookmarks in your web browser to mark areas that you want to go back to anytime you need information. All you need is a connection to the Internet and a web browser such as Netscape Navigator or Microsoft's Internet Explorer.

What Type of Information?

THE INTERNET IS A VAST SUPPLY OF INFORMATION JUST WAITING TO BE TAPPED and used. While it is impossible to categorize it all, here are some examples of some of the things you can find on the Internet that may help your company:

■ **Competitive intelligence.** Interested in how your competitors are doing?

If they have a website, you can probably get a pretty good idea. If your competitor has a website, scour it. Search through product information, annual reports, press releases, even job openings to see what types of employees the competition is hiring. It is amazing what some companies are willing to put on their websites.

You can probably find information on your competitors on other sites as well, notably industry sites, trade publications, and government and financial sites. If it is a public company, you can search investment websites as a start. Also, read the online versions of local newspapers from where your competitor is located for stories on the company.

■ **Marketing data.** The Internet is a great source for researching markets. You may find market data and demographics reports in government websites, analysis of industries on industry-sponsored websites, or even data in financial reports or marketing websites.

■ **Financial data.** Financial data is one of the most prevalent areas of information on the Internet, including data on individual stocks, companies, national economic data, and current exchange rates.

■ **Business/legal information.** The World Wide Web also has a vast collection of business and legal information, including information on such topics as tax laws, how to export your goods, and how to file for a patent or trademark. Information in this area is provided by companies, government agencies, and even individuals who have been through the pain of assembling information and are nice enough to share it with others.

■ **Other information.** Just about anything else you are interested in finding is on the World Wide Web. Whether you want to find information on combustion engines or how to get a reasonably priced hotel room for your next trip to New York, the information is available. Also, you will find thousands of websites with tips for entrepreneurs on every aspect of running a business. You can also find other valuable information, such as individual or company phone numbers and addresses. So next time, instead of dialing 1-411 to look up a phone number, look it up on the Internet and save yourself some money.

Research Tools

SOME WEBSITES ARE BETTER SOURCES OF INFORMATION THAN OTHERS, AND what is best for the information you need depends on what you are looking for. Some good places to get started are listed here:

Table 11-2. *Government Websites*

Name	Site	Description
Census Bureau	www.census.gov	Demographic information
Department of Commerce	www.doc.gov	Information on a variety of commerce topics
Department of Labor	www.dol.gov	Covers labor and workforce issues
FedNet	www.fednet.net	Monitors congressional activities
FedStats	www.fedstats.gov	Statistics from 60 government organizations
FedWorld	www.fedworld.gov	Search government databases
Internal Revenue Service	www.irs.gov	Tax information galore
Minority Business Development Agency	www.mbda.gov	Information to help minority-owned businesses
Small Business Information	www.sba.gov	Help for small businesses
Stat-USA	www.stat-usa.gov	Economic, business, and trade information
U.S. Patent and Trademark Office	www.uspto.gov	Information on patents and trademarks
The Zipper	www.voxpop/org:80/zipper/	Finds congressional representatives by zip code

■ **Government websites.** The federal government is one of the best sources for information on a vast number of topics, including economic and demographic information, statistical data, and even information on how to better run your business. Most of the information available from the federal government is free; however, there are some sites that, if you can believe it, charge a fee. Table 11-2 lists some of the best government sites for small businesses. Also, check state government websites for local information. ■ **Business/financial sites.** Investment companies are often good information sources on industries and companies. If you are looking to enter a

Table 11-3. *Investment and Business Websites*

Name	Site	Description	Cost
ABCompass	www.abcompass.com	Monitors many company websites. Notifies of new postings	Free
BizWeb	www.bizweb.com	Information on 26,000 companies	Free
CompaniesOnline	www.companiesonline.com	Information on more than 100,000 companies	Free
Corporate Financials Online	www.cfonews.com	Just what it says— financials and more	Free
Edgar Online	www.edgar-online.com	Commissioned by SEC to hold all filings of public companies	Paid
Industry.net	www.industry.net	Listings of companies	Free/Paid
Japan Company Record	www.japancompanyrecord.com	Financial information on Japanese companies	Free
Market Guide	www.marketguide.com/mgi	Company financial information	Free
Public Register's Annual Report Service	www.prars.com	Free company reports	Free
Thomas Register of American Manufacturers	www.thomasregister.com	Web version of the famous register of manufacturers and suppliers	Free
U.S. Chamber of Commerce	www.uschamber.com	Assistance for businesses	Free
Wall Street Journal Online	www.wsj.com	Financial and company information	Free
Bloomberg website	www.bloomberg.com	Financial and investment information	Paid

particular market, find a competitor's weakness, or identify a potential business partner, you should visit several financial websites. Some of the best business and financial websites are listed in Table 11-3.

■ **Search engines.** Search engines are websites that help you look up topics or categories and lead you to the websites most likely to contain the information you are looking for. Search engines are unique repositories that use "spiders" or "robots" that search the Internet for information and catalog it in vast databases for you to access. With hundreds of millions of documents on the Internet, it's important that someone keep tabs on what is available.

Search engines use keywords to find the information you want. For example, you could go to a search engine such as Yahoo! (www.yahoo.com) and type in "small business networking." The site would come back with a series of links for sites with information on networks for small businesses. Most likely the links would lead you to some of the vendors of networking products as well as some sites that contain information on how to get started networking a small business.

Some search engines such as Lycos (www.lycos.com) support natural language queries. These let you search for information by asking questions as you normally speak. For example, if you wish to know the population of Buffalo, you could type, "What is the population of Buffalo, New York?" into Lycos' search window. The search engine will then come back with web sites that will likely answer your question.

Search engines are the best places to start any search on the Internet. Table 11-4 shows a listing of the top search engines on the Internet.

■ **Reference sites.** There are thousands of reference materials on the Internet. Do you want to know what a particular network acronym means? How about translating a word from English to Italian? Looking for a good quote for your next speech? How about finding the phone number of a potential client? The reference sites in Table 11-5 are some good places for getting started.

■ **Small-business sites.** There are literally thousands of sites on the Internet dedicated to small businesses. Whether you are looking for tax and financial information or how to write a business plan, there are plenty of places to turn. Many of these sites are owned by companies trying to lure you in, but don't be put off by the blatant marketing effort. Many are quite useful. Some of the top small-business Internet sites are shown in Table 11-6.

Table 11-4. *Popular Search Engines*

Search Engine	Site
AltaVista	www.altavista.com
Excite	www.excite.com
Hotbot	www.hotbot.com
Infoseek	www.infoseek.com
Lycos	www.lycos.com
Northern Light	www.northernlight.com
Snap	www.snap.com
Yahoo!	www.yahoo.com

■ **Subscription services.** Some websites are paid information services that you can use to search for particular information. Hoover's Online, for example, provides information on thousands of companies throughout the world. For a monthly fee you can access the information as much as you want to do research on company financial, strategic, and marketing information.

Others, such as Lexus/Nexus and other traditional database and research services, are also on the Internet. An Internet subscription to one of these services may or may not be any cheaper than a traditional subscription (i.e., on CD-ROM or in print), but the online versions are easier to access. It almost seems sacrilegious to pay for anything on the Internet, but many of these companies offer good services with a depth of information that may be difficult to find elsewhere. A list of top for-a-fee services on the Internet is in Table 11-7.

■ **Industry experts.** There are many industry experts that offer their consulting services for a particular market or topic. Oftentimes these experts will have their own website, offering their services to anyone who is willing to pay the money. But their websites are also valuable information on their area of expertise and can lead you to the information you need. Your best bet in finding some of these experts is to search for your topic through one of the popular search engines.

■ **Newsgroups.** We have talked a lot about World Wide Web sites for research, but don't forget another essential component of the Internet: Usenet or newsgroups. With as many as 30,000 different newsgroups available, there is likely to be one for your needs. Tapping into news-

(text continues on page 162)

159

Table 11-5. *Reference Websites*

Name	Site	Description
Acronym Finder	www.mtnds.com/af/	Decipher any acronym
Bartlett Familiar Quotations	www.columbia.edu/acis/ bartleby/bartlett/	Find a quote for next inspirational speech
BigBook	www.bigbook.com	Yellow pages
Britannica Internet Guide	www.ebig.com	Reference of Internet sites; search by topic
Findout	www.findout.com	Ask any question— answers first 100 per day
Four11	www.four11.com	White pages
InfoSpace	www.infospace.com	News, public records, international and government information, and much more
LookSmart	www.looksmart.com	Information on 20,000 subjects
My Reference Desk	www.refdesk.com	Dictionaries, maps, libraries, and statistics
Newsbot	www.newsbot.com	Online clipping service
Nolo Press's Legal Encyclopedia	www.nolo.com	Legal reference
Switchboard	www.switchboard.com	People and business directory
Tracerlock	www.peacefire.org/ tracerlock	Finds information on new websites; e-mails information to registered users
A Web of Online Dictionaries	www.bucknell.edu/ ~rbeard/diction.html	Dictionaries and other reference material
WhoWhere?	www.whowhere.com	Finds people and e-mail addresses
ZipFind	www.link-usa.com/ zipcode	Finds zip codes

Table 11-6. *Small Business Websites*

Name	Site	Description
American Express Small Business Exchange	www.americanexpress.com/ smallbusiness/	Information on starting and managing a business, as well as reports for international markets.
America's Business Funding Directory	www.businessfinance.com /index.shtml	Find funding for your business
BizProWeb	www.bizproweb.com	Business newsgroups. with links to other sites.
Inc. Online	www.inc.com	Online version of magazine.
NAFTAnet Small Business Information	www.nafta.net/smallbiz.htm	Help for businesses expanding to international markets.
National Federation of Independent Businesses	www.nfibonline.com	The voice of small business on the Web
Quicken.com Small Business	www.quicken.com/ small_business	Legal, tax, management, payroll, and technical information.
SEC Small Business Information	www.sec.gov/smbus1.htm	Information on securities and raising capital.
Small Business Administration	www.sba.gov	Government help for your business.
SmallOffice.com	www.smalloffice.com	Technical information for small businesses.
Visa Small Business Site	www.visa.com/cgi-bin/vee/ fb/smbiz/main.html	Variety of information to help small businesses.
The Venture Capital Marketplace	www.v-capital.com	Hook up with venture capital firms online.

Table 11-7. *Paid Internet Services*

Name	Site	Description
Biz@dvantage	www.biz.n2k.com	Dun and Bradstreet service with information ranging from companies to patents. Cost varies.
Dow Jones Interactive	Bisdowjones.com	Business news service, clipping service, research and other information. Pay per use or flat corporate rate.
Electric Library	www.elibrary.com	Databases of publications, transcripts, new services, government data, and other references. Cost: $9.95 per month.
Ewatch	www.ewatch.com	Online news clipping service. Cost: $295 per month.
Gov.Research Center	grc.ntis.gov	Databases of government research and technical information.
Hoovers Online	www.hoovers.com	Financial and other information on thousands of companies in the U.S. and abroad. Cost: $12.95 per month.
Lexis Nexis	www.lexis-nexis.com	Varied business, legal, and government research.
Paperchase	www.paperchase.com	Medical databases. Cost: $19.95 per month.
Profound	www.profound.com	Market research.
TheStreet.Com	www.thestreet.com	Financial information. Articles written daily. Cost: $9.95 per month.

groups will give you an information source like none other. Feel free to ask opinions and even ask for help in finding other sources of information. Newsgroups can be accessed through your ISP's news server. You can also access discussion groups on the World Wide Web through Deja News at www.dejanews.com.

Cautions

THE WORLD WIDE WEB CAN BE A GREAT SOURCE OF INFORMATION FOR YOUR company, but it can also be a great waste of time for your employees. Web surfing can be comparable to watching television, and it is just as habit forming. If you think that the Web is too much of a temptation, you can limit who goes online or even use a blocking program to prevent users from going to particular websites.

Blocking programs (sometimes also called filtering programs) prevent users from visiting online sites that are distractions or that contain material you don't want them to see, including sports information, games, pornography, employment listings, or other time wasters. The software works either by blocking specific website addresses or blocking sites containing keywords such as "sex" or "football." Both methods have their advantages and are worth investigating if you want to curb online excesses.

Getting Started

LIKE INTERNET COMMUNICATIONS, SEARCHING THE WORLD WIDE WEB FOR research first requires an Internet connection with an ISP. You will also require a way to connect to the Internet, either through a modem on your computer, or through a network connection such as a router. Your choice of the best ISP and connection type depends on a number of factors, which are discussed at length in Chapter 14.

Your ISP will provide you with everything that you need to connect to the Internet, including the necessary software and help to set up your connection. Once you are online, the Internet is an open source of information for you to tap into. Try using some of the websites listed in this chapter to help you to get started, or begin with a search engine to find the information specific to your needs.

The Internet has been, and will continue to be, an important tool for businesses of all sizes. With some of these tools in hand, you will be able to use your Internet connection for communications as well as make your business better informed. The next step from here is to investigate how having your own website on the Internet can help you gain new customers and keep the ones you have. That is the topic of our next chapter.

CHAPTER 12

Your Company on the World Wide Web

IF YOUR COMPANY IS LIKE MANY OTHER BUSINESSES, YOU HAVE TWO BIG concerns: selling more of what you sell and keeping your costs low. Focusing on both of these issues helps your company to make a profit. However, it isn't always as easy as that. Selling more means getting your product or service out in front of more people, which costs money. And in today's competitive marketplace, reducing expenses is not always easy. However, for some small businesses, there is a solution to help with both needs: an Internet website.

Web Publishing

PUBLISHING ON THE WORLD WIDE WEB IS FAST BECOMING AN IMPORTANT medium for all types of businesses. Setting up a website is one of the best and most affordable ways to give your company a marketing presence and get the news out that you exist. It involves designing a website with graphical and text-based HyperText Markup Language (HTML) documents and setting it up on a server that is connected to the Internet. A web server can either be located at your Internet Service Provider or at your company. The website then becomes your electronic document and can be used for a variety of purposes: showing your company's wares, providing helpful information, and supporting current customers. Let's say, for example, that your company, Kilts 'R' Us, does a great local business selling Scottish kilts in Denver, Colorado. Sales are up, and men's kilts are the fashion rage around the city. But your customer base is only as big as Denver and its surrounding area. So why not show those same kilts to people in Salt Lake City, New York, and Buenos Aires through a website? With a website, your business has no geographic limits; it can be your first step toward becoming a global business. People dial up the Internet with their computers, surf to your site, and—voila!—Internet users from around the world can see your cool Scottish kilts from anywhere (see Figure 12-1).

Figure 12-1. *Company Website*

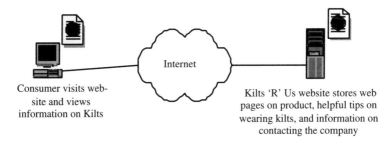

Consumer visits web-
site and views
information on Kilts

Internet

Kilts 'R' Us website stores web
pages on product, helpful tips on
wearing kilts, and information on
contacting the company

Benefits

THERE ARE MANY BENEFITS TO PUBLISHING A WEBSITE ON THE INTERNET. When most people think about an Internet site, they think about getting their name out in front new people, so they treat the Internet as a way to advertise their company's products or services. But the Internet can be more than that. For example, the Internet can help your company:

■ **Generate awareness.** A website may help your company generate awareness and sell more goods or services. Whether or not you actually sell over the Internet, the Internet lets you reach a potentially new customer base. As you might expect, Internet surfers tend to be better educated and more affluent than average consumers, since they have the money to buy personal computers and the extra time to use them. Selling to these affluent web surfers over the Internet, known as electronic commerce, is covered later in Chapter 13.

Not only can you reach new, more affluent customers, but a website will also allow you to reach out further geographically. Your website is as accessible to someone around the world as it is to someone around the block.

Not only does a web presence give you a new avenue to reach customers, it also gives your customers a way to check out your company in a non-intimidating way. Many people dislike calling a company for product or service information, only to be given the third degree by a salesperson. With a website, those potential customers can get information on their own terms.

■ **Reduce costs.** The Internet can also help you decrease your costs of servicing new and current customers. Say, for example, that you have a group of three inside sales representatives who do nothing but service phone calls for product literature, and you need to hire two more to keep up with customer interest. Instead of hiring two new salespeople, put your product information on your website. Then put your World Wide Web address on everything you print. Soon, people will be flocking to your website to read about your new product and get information on their own, and you won't have to hire those two new employees. You can even set up a section for people to register on your website so that you can still get their names for sales leads.

Or, for example, you find that your customer support calls are through the roof on your new product and you need to find a way to trim the cost of supporting those calls. You can supplement your phone support by setting up a website with product information that customers can access over the Internet. Some customers with Internet access will go to your website for information instead of calling your company, saving you both employee time and telephone charges. Using your website in this manner can help you reduce costs to the point of paying for the website itself.

■ **Improve customer service.** A website may also be used to improve customer support. Websites are often used to help customers find the product they want, troubleshoot problems, contact the company, or even find tips for how to do something better. And the information is available to customers 24 hours a day, 7 days a week. Many customers love the fact that they can view information on a website at any time, even in the middle of the night. Imagine the cost of paying a staff to work 24 hours a day.

Many companies put product or service information, troubleshooting or helpful tips, and answers to frequently asked questions on their website so that customers and potential customers can access information without calling the company.

■ **Improve the company image.** Whether you are American Express or the corner flower shop, you have a corporate image. Depending on the type of business you are in, an Internet website may be able to help yours. More technically savvy consumers have come to expect that businesses have a website. Now, of course, there are exceptions to this rule. If your company is the local engine repair shop, you may not have anyone looking for you on the World Wide Web. But for many, a website is a sign of legitimacy and often consumers, suppliers, and others will want to do research on your company before they do business with you. A website can help you build that image and even make you look larger than you are.

Is It for You?

WEBSITES CAN HELP MOST BUSINESSES BUILD A BETTER MARKETING PRESENCE, service their customers, and even cut their costs. To determine whether or not an Internet website is right for you, first ask yourself some questions about certain aspects of business. Consider the following:

■ **Your product/service.** Is your product or service well positioned and differentiated? Is it something that stands out in the crowd? If what you do is something that many others do, and you don't have a good point of differentiation, then a website may not be right for you. In fact, what are you doing in business?

■ **The Internet audience.** Do the types of customers you target also fit the profile of consumers on the Internet? If so, is there a special benefit for them in finding you there?

■ **Sales reach.** The Internet is a worldwide phenomenon; if your product or service isn't, it may not be right for the Internet. Businesses that usually require face-to-face contact, such as a doctor's office or engine-repair shop, often aren't well suited for an Internet website.

■ **Information distribution.** Do you have any expenses that could be cut back by using a website? Expenses that could be cut back include inbound long-distance calls, product literature, postage, and faxing costs. The Internet makes information distribution easier—just put it out there and people come and find it.

Cautions

THE FIRST WORD OF CAUTION IN DEVELOPING AN INTERNET WEBSITE IS TO make sure that you have a reason to do it. If you are just putting a website out there because everyone else you know has one, then stop and rethink the situation. This may sound obvious, but it happens. Putting up a site without any real content or purpose will do nothing for your company and will not attract anyone to your site. Websites that are ill-conceived raise additional concerns.

LOST IN SPACE

While the opportunities for creating and publishing your own website are endless, remember that you are just one in a million websites on the Internet. With so many websites, it is very easy to get lost in the crowd. Therefore, it is important to find ways to get people to your website after it is up and running. That means taking the time to promote it.

BORING SITES

The Internet has moved from a medium of boring, static text to a virtual Las Vegas, where professional web designers put as much style as content on their websites. Graphics, videos, sound, and smart design techniques adorn the most popular sites. In addition, the content is important. For example, if you go to a mortgage company website, you may find information on calculating mortgage payments and how much a potential buyer can afford for a house. Make sure that the information you put out is valuable, visually appealing, and changes often enough to get potential customers to come back.

OPENNESS

For many companies, a word of warning is in order about what they publish on the Internet. Remember, the Internet is a public forum. Don't publish information that you normally wouldn't disclose to the public in other forms. Too many companies are willing to publish far more than they should. Is it any wonder that one of the biggest uses of the Internet is checking out the competition? If you wouldn't feel comfortable publishing the information in a brochure and giving it to your competitors, then don't put it on your website.

Getting Started

WHEN BUILDING A WEBSITE, THERE ARE SOME THINGS THAT YOU SHOULD keep in mind to make your site attractive to your potential or current customers. Here some steps to get you started.

RECOMMENDED COURSE OF ACTION

1. *Set a strategy.* Don't just put up a website because it's the thing to do. Make sure that you have a plan that explains why you have a website and refer to it often. Your goal may be to cut down on support calls, increase your geographic reach, or improve your company's image, but each of these objectives can lead you down different paths on how to build your website.

   Your website strategy should automatically help you determine the type of information you put on your website. Set the content of your site based on your goals. If your goal is to sell your products or services, you will want to have heavy focus on product information. If you want to attract investors, your site will reflect the stability and viability of your company and market. If you want to decrease customer or sales support costs, then you will want to include more information about what you sell or a large section on troubleshooting tips.

   One thing you should do is get on the Internet and look around at some other companies' sites, especially those in the same business as your company. Study what their strategy is and what they emphasize.

2. *Design the site.* The design step includes creating content, graphics, and programming the site in HTML code. Designing and creating your website is easier than ever, but if you want it to look professional, hire a professional to do it. Hiring a good, creative designer can make the difference between a bad site and a good site. Not only should you hire a good designer, but the right designer—someone who can cater the site to your company's needs and image.

3. *Host the site.* One of the big decisions you will need to make in setting up your company website will be where to locate the site, either with an Internet Service Provider or on a server at your company.

Hosting your website at your company involves a lot of expense, both in setup and maintenance. If you expect a significant amount of traffic to your website, you will need a separate, dedicated server to host your site. Most web servers run Windows NT or a UNIX operating system, so they are not easy to set up. You will also need a high-speed, dedicated connection to the Internet, such as a frame relay or T1 connection that is up 24 hours a day, 7 days a week. This solution is expensive to set up and maintain. In addition, a dedicated connection to your network potentially leaves you open to security threats from the outside. If you have a dedicated connection, you will want a firewall between the connection and the rest of your network to protect it from outside access through the Internet.

By contrast, hosting your site with an Internet Service Provider can be cost-effective to set up and maintain. ISPs lease space on one of their servers to your company for hosting a website. For a monthly fee, they maintain the site on their server at their location. To the outside world, your site still looks as if it is residing on your own company server. The advantage is that the ISP will usually run a faster server and have a much faster connection to the Internet than you would.

Using an Internet Service Provider to host the website is the choice that most small businesses make. This saves the initial costs of purchasing a server, software, and a high-speed connection to your business. The hosting service, which can run from under fifty to several hundred dollars per month, is usually less than the cost of just the dedicated connection you would need for your own server. In addition, all of the maintenance of the server is on the shoulders of the ISP.

An alternative to hosting your site on an ISP's server is collocation. Collocation basically means that you own the server, but you keep it at your ISP. Your own dedicated server for your site can increase its speed and allow you to customize the server. But with collocation you don't need an expensive dedicated connection to the Internet.

4. *Promote your website.* Getting a website up and running is only half the battle. With so many sites on the Internet, you can easily spend thousands of dollars creating the world's best website, only for it to get lost in the crowd.

These are only some of the considerations in getting your business up and running on the World Wide Web. Chapter 14 will help you in selecting an ISP, hiring a website designer, and promoting your website.

Website Alternatives

YOU MAY WANT TO GIVE YOUR COMPANY A PRESENCE ON THE INTERNET, BUT are not ready to commit to the resources required to design, set up, and host a website. If not, there are alternatives to actually publishing your own website.

Many sites offer companies the opportunity to get their name in cyberspace without actually publishing a full website. These sites may offer the service for free as a way to lure people to their website, or their business may be as a directory service for others to find specific information. For example, both American Express and *Inc. Magazine* offer a place on their websites for small businesses to set up a small home page that lists a business description and contact information. Others, such as CitySearch, provide detailed information for people looking for a specific business locally or nationwide. These types of websites often charge a fee for posting a single web page. However, they act as a sort of Internet yellow pages and may offer you a presence on the Internet with less hassle and cost than building and managing your own website. My advice is to use these resources in addition to your website. Use them and link them to your own website to draw people to it. On their own, these options provide limited benefits, but they are better than having no web presence at all.

Having a presence on the Internet's World Wide Web is a great step for many businesses. If planned and implemented properly, a website can bring your company immediate benefits by increasing your exposure to more potential customers and reducing costs. Of course, the natural progression after posting your own website is to look to selling your products or services over the Internet. That is the topic of our next chapter.

CHAPTER 13

Selling on the Internet

ONCE YOU HAVE A WEBSITE THAT SHOWS YOUR PRODUCTS ON THE WORLD Wide Web, the next natural thought that should come to your mind is, "How do I make money from this?" It only makes sense. If customers take the time to find and look at your website and they like what you have, why stop there? Electronic commerce doesn't. With an electronic commerce site you can let those casual browsers act on their impulses and buy right over the Internet.

What Is Electronic Commerce?

SIMPLY PUT, ELECTRONIC COMMERCE IS A FINANCIAL TRANSACTION FOR A product or service over a network. Typically this means over the Internet. Electronic commerce, often known as e-commerce, is becoming big business. Companies such as Dell Computer have turned electronic commerce into a large portion of their business. Other companies, such as Amazon.com and CDnow, Inc., were created for and transact all of their sales through the Internet. An example of Dell's electronic commerce site is shown in Figure 13-1.

Electronic commerce is broken out into two areas:

■ **Web-based shopping** (or consumer electronic commerce). Consumer electronic commerce is the selling of goods and services directly to individual customers. Examples include sales of software, music, computers, and even airline tickets or insurance.

Figure 13-1. *Dell Computer's E-Commerce Website*

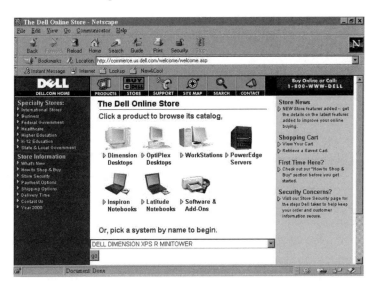

Reproduced by permission of Dell Computer Corporation. Copyright 1999 Dell Computer Corporation.

■ **Business-to-business electronic commerce.** Business-to-business e-commerce involves transactions between two companies. This type of e-commerce is actually the larger portion of the electronic commerce market. The precursor to this type of transaction is Electronic Data Interchange (EDI). EDI has a strong presence in the corporate and government world, where many transactions are done electronically on a daily basis. In the future, this type of business will be done by companies being able to access other companies' websites to order products, view inventory levels, check orders, and make manual or automatic purchases of materials.

The bulk of this section covers consumer electronic commerce, although business-to-business electronic commerce will include many of the same issues.

E-commerce has yet to fulfill its potential. Only a fraction of businesses have implemented an e-commerce strategy, and many have not been successful at it yet. However, there are enough success stories for e-commerce to show that it can be a successful source of revenue for the right companies.

Electronic commerce is transacted through World Wide Web sites that look basically the same as any other website on the Internet. However, there are many complexities beyond a normal website on the Internet to incorporate many different functions, such as ordering, security, credit authorization, order tracking, and payment systems.

An e-commerce website should include these four components:

1. *An electronic storefront.* This is essentially a website that lets you show your wares over the Internet. Often it is called an online catalog and is generally organized so users can browse your site looking at descriptions of what you are selling.

2. *A virtual shopping cart.* Customers need some way to choose and order and goods and services. Customers select items and store them in their virtual cart until they are ready to check out.

3. *One or more secure payment methods.* Customers may pay in any number of ways, including with a credit card or a variety of other electronic payment methods. Whatever method is used, payments are made electronically without any physical transfer of money. When using credit cards, the card's numbers are encrypted and sent electronically across the Internet to a transaction server, and the buyer's credit is then checked and the amount charged to the card. Other payment options have various methods of transferring funds.

4. *Integration with other "back office" services.* This is an optional component and includes the automation of order fulfillment, billing, manufacturing, shipping, inventory management, and even supplier ordering processes. This integration from the customer all the way through to suppliers entails a high level of sophistication and is generally known as electronic business. Sophisticated sites can take and fulfill orders very efficiently without human intervention, automating a company's entire process from the beginning to the end of the value chain. The goal of e-business is to make sales as cost-effective as possible.

There are some great examples of electronic commerce sites that are successful in operation and, for the most part, in profitability. Dell Computer (www.dell.com) has a great site where you can build your own custom computer and purchase it over the Internet. Dell now sells millions of dollars in computers over the Internet daily. Others, including

Figure 13-2. *Electronic Commerce*

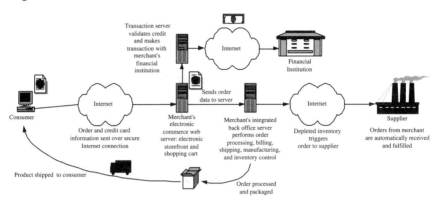

Travelocity (www.travelocity.com) and bookseller Amazon.com (www.amazon.com), are actually start-up companies that base their entire business on sales through the Internet.

An example of how electronic commerce works is shown in Figure 13-2. In this example, a clothing merchant implements an electronic commerce website to broaden its sales beyond its local area. A customer views the online catalog (i.e., electronic storefront) and finds the products she wants. She then submits her purchase via a secure web browser along with her encrypted credit card number over a secure Internet connection. The transaction is sent to the transaction server, which then transmits the credit card information to the merchant's financial institution for verification. The financial verification is made and the transaction is automatically completed and credited to the merchant. The web server then sends the customer order information to the merchant's back office server. Then, as part of the company's electronic business solution, the manufacturing server receives the customer order information into its database and generates the order. The order is then integrated into the merchant's order-fulfillment software where it is processed. Integrated shipping software even prepares the bill of lading with database information on the product's shipping weight and distance. The merchant's shipping software registers the product and it is picked up by the shipping company that begins to track the package shipment. The customer can now check the product's shipping status at any time over the Internet. The only time anyone physically intervenes with the process is to package and deliver the product.

As orders accumulate, the server tracks inventory and sales history and generates manufacturing orders for more clothing. It even creates purchase orders for the merchant's main supplier, which are sent over the Internet to the supplier's business-to-business electronic commerce server.

Of course, some goods can be electronically distributed. For example, software and music can be downloaded from the Internet after the customer pays for it.

Benefits

AS YOU CAN IMAGINE, IT WILL BE QUITE SOME TIME BEFORE MOST COMPANIES have implemented an electronic business process as automated and efficient as the one described in the previous example. But visionaries look forward to a business world with no boundaries, where people can buy and sell anywhere in the world without having to set up complicated or expensive offices, and where products are available to anyone, anywhere from superefficient companies that automate their processes. For those of us who are a little more grounded in today's world, the benefits of e-commerce relate to:

■ **Distribution.** If you are in a business where you must use a middleman or a distributor to resell your products, this may be the opportunity for you to build a new channel and sell without the middleman taking a cut. This is often referred to as disintermediation.

■ **Broader market reach.** E-commerce can give you a geographic reach beyond anything your company could normally handle with limited resources. Normal geographic expansion often requires additional salespersons, distributors, and money. But with an e-commerce site you can sell over the Internet to anyone in the world with (hopefully) lower costs.

■ **Affluent target customers.** Don't forget that Internet users tend to be more educated and more affluent than their non-web-surfing friends. With electronic commerce you can reach a new customer base with new products.

■ **Efficiency.** Many e-business solutions integrate credit verification, accounting, inventory, purchasing, and manufacturing processes into their electronic commerce solution. Taking advantage of some of these abilities can take your business a long way toward efficiency.

In addition to benefits to you, electronic commerce solutions can bring some big benefits to your customers. E-commerce generally offers customers the convenience of shopping at any time and any place, better pricing (sometimes) than they would get elsewhere, and better selection and options to buy what they want, when they want.

Is It for You?

BEFORE YOU POST YOUR ONLINE SHINGLE, THERE ARE SOME QUESTIONS THAT you should ask yourself to determine if selling your product over the Internet is right for your company.

First, how strong is your current distribution channel? How do you currently distribute your products? If you already sell direct, then selling over the Internet may work for you. However, if you rely heavily on distributors to buy products from you and resell them to the end user, an e-commerce site may potentially damage these relationships. Of course, the upside is the possibility of squeezing out the middleman and making more money and/or selling at a lower price.

Second, how unique is your product or service? To be successful, your product needs to be right for Internet sales. Products that sell well are computer software, music and books, electronics, and consumer services such as insurance, airline tickets, and financial services. The better branded your product is, the better chance it has to sell. If you have no brand recognition, it will be difficult to get people to know you exist.

Specialty products do well on the Internet also. If you have something that is interesting and not available everywhere (e.g., Maine lobsters, Russian music, or Scottish kilts), then your chances of finding a market on the Internet are much better than if you are selling something that is available anywhere.

Cautions

ELECTRONIC COMMERCE IS NO LESS COMPLEX THAN SETTING UP A NEW RETAIL store or distribution channel; it takes as much time and effort. If you are not staying up at night worrying about your e-commerce site, you are not taking it seriously enough. If you need some help, here are some things you should worry about.

HIGH EXPECTATIONS

One of the problems today with e-commerce today is that it is over-hyped. Almost every business that looks into setting up an e-commerce site does so with great expectations of how well its online venture will succeed. Keep your expectations realistic for what electronic commerce can do for your company.

SECURITY

The fear of the lack of security is the greatest issue facing electronic commerce. Admittedly, the threat of a security breach is there for both consumers and merchants. Despite the best security and encryption methods, there is always a possibility that any transaction can be intercepted or any server hacked into. But the threat is far less than the fear. People who use their credit cards to buy dinner at a local restaurant or give their credit card information over a cordless phone face a higher risk of having their number stolen than someone who transmits this information over the Internet using proper security precautions.

Nonetheless, measures must be set in order to protect yourself and your customers. If you don't, your potential customers will not be willing to risk a purchase on your website. That means that you must ensure that transactions are secure and the data on your server is safe. Secure transactions mean *you must use* encryption software. Eventually financial transactions may be handled by alternative electronic payment systems (emerging online payment systems are discussed later in this chapter in the section "Getting Started."

SELLING DIRECT

Selling direct to end users over the Internet may sound like a great way to expand your business and cut out the middleman, but unless you already sell direct it could be more headache than it's worth. Do you already have a system to handle the incoming orders for individuals buying direct? Consider whether present systems (e.g., payment, order fulfillment, and shipping) can handle a large number of small orders. Also, consider your relationships with current distributors and how it will affect them.

ACTIVE INVOLVEMENT

Electronic commerce puts you on the front line for selling your products. You are in charge of marketing your products, keeping up your electronic storefront, fulfilling orders in a timely manner, and living up to the needs and expectations of your customers. If you can't dedicate someone to do this work at least part-time, or aren't willing to pay an outside company to do it, then you shouldn't make the commitment.

DIFFERENTIATION

Your product or service needs to be something unique or sell at a substantial discount in order to entice people to buy online. You really need something to differentiate yourself. This is a business principle that can't be overemphasized.

Getting Started

THERE IS NO SINGLE, BEST PROCESS FOR SETTING UP AN E-COMMERCE website. There are so many options for a full solution that you are best off working with a professional consultant or ISP who will explain your options and help you decide what is best for your needs. The effort of setting up and maintaining an electronic commerce website can range from the very simple to the very difficult—and very expensive. You can spend as little as a few hundred dollars for a simple e-commerce site, or as much as hundreds of thousands of dollars for a complete e-business solution that is integrated with financial, inventory, manufacturing, and distribution systems.

When just starting out, you may want to consider some less expensive alternatives to a full-blown electronic commerce solution. Purchasing a server, web software, electronic commerce software, security software, and high-speed Internet connection can cost tens of thousands of dollars. Then there are fees for web design, server setup, payment systems, and more. You will be better off paying a monthly fee to let someone else host and mange your site for you and avoid the up-front costs until you know you can make money over the Internet.

Several sites on the Internet allow you to build your own solution as part of a larger group of other stores. These sites make it easy to set up your site by providing all the hardware, as well as the ordering and payment methods. Some solutions, such as Internet Mall or iCat's Commerce Online, let you sell your products in an online mall with other vendors and products. These solutions can cost less than $50 per month. If you have less than 10 items you can set up a site with iCat for free. Another company dedicated to hosting is ViaWeb (now owned by Internet giant Yahoo!). The advantage of these services is that they are relatively easy to set up, they let you get in on the ground level with very little cost, and they require little to no management. Most also include templates that allow you to put up a site with little web experience. The downside is that some of these options do not allow you to set up your own domain (www.yourcompany.com), so you miss out on the professional polish that you can get with your own cyberstore. Also, most on-line malls only allow for manual retrieval of orders by connecting to the service and downloading orders. The downside to virtual malls is that they have not lived up to their expectations. Many have failed to pull in the traffic needed and are too focused on just selling products, without providing the other benefits of a full website that build customer's confidence and trust in your company.

A second path to e-commerce is through hosting your site with an Internet Service Provider. At a national level there are several places you can turn to, or you can look for a local provider. AT&T, PSINet, UUNet, AOL, CompuServe, BBN Planet, and others offer electronic commerce hosting as part of their services. Almost any of these hosting services will be far less expensive than hosting a full e-commerce site yourself, and they offer the flexibility to build a full website that is customized to your needs. These types of sites usually require extensive development work, but many of these ISPs offer the software and even provide or recommend services to develop a website.

If you already have a website, you may not want to start from scratch with a new web hosting service to sell products. Internet Mall's OrderEasy lets you link your existing site to a secure transaction server for customers to buy products. Users go from your web page on your server to another server with the click of a button to make secure transactions without ever knowing that they are leaving your site.

As your needs grow, you may eventually want to move the site to your own location and integrate it as a more important part of your strategy. This gives you more control over your site and more integration into those back office applications that make your processes run smoother. Many server manufacturers now sell servers specifically for websites, and intermediate users should look at software including iCat's Electronic Commerce Suite, Lotus' Domino.Merchant, Microsoft's Site Server Commerce Edition, or Oracle's Internet Commerce Server, to name just a few. All of these products offer functions including store building, catalog management, order processing, and payment systems. Any of these applications, or the dozens of others like them, requires someone experienced in web design and hosting to get the system up and running. Of course, if you don't have anyone with web development experience, you should look to a professional designer to build your site.

Taking advantage of a full e-business solution means being able to integrate into back office functions such as billing, inventory management, and manufacturing. Some of the applications mentioned previously have the ability to integrate into these services. Others, such as Pandesic's e-business solution, include everything to integrate shipping, inventory management, collections, accounting and financial reporting, and even returns processing. E-business solutions require a huge commitment of time and money and help from a professional consultant.

No matter which solution you go with, there are several things that need to be in place to help ensure your cyberselling success.

HOW TO SELL ONLINE SUCCESSFULLY

1. *Ensure security.* Security is the number-one concern of consumers buying on the Internet. You need to allay your customers' fears by staying up with the latest security technology. Today, the main standard for secure transactions over the Internet is Secure Sockets Layer (SSL), which uses encryption to scramble financial information such as credit card numbers. This virtually ensures that no one will be able to intercept transactions from the Internet and decipher users' credit card numbers. A new encryption technology called Secure Electronic Transactions (SET) is a standard developed by MasterCard and Visa for credit card transactions. One of these two security systems must be in place. You won't ever be able to give a 100 percent guarantee that all transactions are safe, but you'll keep people from turning away from your website for fear of security if you use these technologies. Alternative methods of payment can be put into place, but they will not likely be as popular as using encrypted credit card numbers except with diehard Internet shoppers.

181

The transaction is itself is only part of the security concern. You must also be able to protect servers that contain information on customer names, credit card numbers, and other vital information. Intercepting a random financial transaction is a hit for a hacker. Breaking into a server with hundreds or thousands of names and credit card numbers is a gold mine. The best way to protect yourself is by having a secure firewall to prevent anyone from hacking into your server from the outside, as well as physically securing the server so that no one pulls out its hard drive and walks away with your customers' credit card numbers. One advantage of SET technology is that credit card information is stored at the merchant's financial institution, and not the merchant's server, so there is no chance of having the data stolen from your premises. If you don't feel that you can handle a secure server, then host your site with an Internet Service Provider that can.

2. *Determine payment methods.* By far the most popular way of paying over the Internet is by using encrypted credit card numbers. Encryption is done by scrambling buyers' credit card numbers and then decrypting them on your server. Both SSL and SET protocols encrypt credit card data. However, there are several alternatives for making payments over the Internet. Electronic payment systems that go by names such as electronic cash (e-cash) and digital cash allow merchants to debit money from customers' bank accounts. The advantage to this type of payment scheme is that users are not sending credit card numbers across the Internet.

Electronic wallets store credit card information and digital IDs on users' hard drives. Any time users make a purchase their computer sends the encrypted credit card information to the e-store for payment. Their credit card bills them as it would for any other transaction. Of course, each of these payment systems also includes the ability to validate credit before authorizing the purchase.

Someday, payments may come in the form of a smart card. The smart card acts as a debit card and can be inserted into a card reader next to the computer to pay for a transaction and even be recharged through a cyber ATM. Examples of different forms of electronic payment are shown in Table 13-1.

The common theme among all of these payment methods is security. Whatever you choose, make sure that it is very secure and widely used. Remember that the more payment types you sup-

Table 13-1. *Electronic Payment Systems*

Payment Type	Description	Example Product	Company
Credit Card Encryption	Credit card authorization and encryption of credit card numbers	OM-Transact	Open Market Inc.
Electronic Cash/ Digital Cash	Uses electronic bank accounts to transfer numeric digital money	eCash	DigiCash
Electronic Wallets	Stores credit card information and digital certificates on computer; can use multiple payment types and store receipts of transactions	VWallet	VeriFone
Micropayments	Handles very small transactions between $.25 and $10	CyberCoin	CyberCash Inc.
Smart Cards	Electronically "charged" cards are used in connected smartcard readers (i.e., hardware add-on)	SmartGATE	V-One Inc.

port, the less likely you will lose a customer who prefers paying a certain way. Also, make sure that you include an old-fashion 800 number for those who don't want to pay over the Internet at all.

3. *Set pricing.* Consumers are shopping on the Internet not only for convenience, but also for price. Keep a balance between luring Internet shoppers with good pricing and going too low so that you hurt your other business.

4. *Promote your site.* Promotion is the key to being discovered in the crowd. You need to promote yourself all over the web and help people find you online, or else you become one website among millions. Chapter 14 explains many ways to promote your website and get people to visit.

5. *Build repeat business.* If you have the type of product that people may buy repeatedly, keep them coming back. Build your site so

that it attracts customers to come back often. Use discount offers or even helpful tips on how to use the product better. Many sites now use custom marketing that makes special offers according to customer habits or interests. For an example, search for a certain book at Amazon.com and you will be shown custom screens that offer other books under the same topic.

But when building an electronic storefront, remember to keep the organization simple. Even though it is online, it is still a retail store. You want to make your products easy to find, the descriptions clear, and the site simple enough for browsers to navigate and find what they want.

Building an online presence can be a big boost to any business. The effective use of a site on the World Wide Web can help most companies reach new potential customers, cut support costs, and improve the company's image. By extending your web presence to include electronic transactions, you can significantly increase sales and decrease the costs of finding customers and selling to them, and you may even improve your own internal processes.

CHAPTER 14

An Internet Planner

AS YOU HAVE LIKELY NOTED FROM THE PRECEDING CHAPTERS, THE INTERNET can be a great tool for businesses to improve communications, save on costs, find information, increase customer reach, and even increase sales. But even after knowing what is available, it is difficult to know just where to start.

This chapter is designed to help you decide where to get started. You will find information on how to prioritize your needs, decide on the right Internet connection for your company, choose the right Internet Service Provider (ISP), or find a designer for your website.

Your Internet Plan

BY NOW YOU ARE THINKING, "HERE WE GO AGAIN WITH THIS PLANNING thing." Well, before you can get started it is time to sit down and determine what you want to do on the Internet.

Writing your Internet plan should not be difficult. You should have a good idea of what you want to accomplish from the last few chapters. But the first thing that you need for your Internet plan is the inventory list of the computers in your company. This information will provide a starting point, helping you to know what may need to be changed or added to make your equipment Internet ready. You will want to keep your inventory list handy when you call an ISP. If you have not already taken inventory, refer to Chapter 8 for help and use Forms A-1 or A-2 in Appendix A.

The second step for your Internet plan is to write down your Internet needs and justification. This can be done on a single page, so start up your word processor or pull out another piece of paper. Write "Internet Plan" at the top, then list what you want to do and your justification of why you want to do it. Table 14-1 shows an example of how you may want to format your plan (Form A-3 from Appendix A is a clean slate you can use to start your own plan).

This simple document, along with your inventory, will help your Internet Service Provider or network consultant to determine your needs and the best solution for you. If you are working on your own, you can use your plan as your own guide.

Table 14-1. *Sample Internet Plan.*

Need	Priority	Time Frame	Justification
Internet Connection	One	This month	We have 10 people who need a connection to surf the Internet. They include five people in marketing who need to do research on new products and competitors, the four members of the executive team, and the company controller. Will cut down on the number of trips from marketing to the library and help our controller find tax information on the Internet.
Internet E-mail	One	This month	We have a total of 23 persons who need Internet e-mail to communicate with customers and suppliers. Communicating on the Internet should cut down on some of our postage and long-distance telephone expenses.
Internet Fax	Two	Within six months	Since we signed on our distributor in England, our long-distance fax bills have increased 50 percent. We want to investigate vendors for Internet faxing to get the costs down. We are planning three more distributors in Europe this year and need to investigate a solution soon.
Internet Website	Three	Within six to nine months	Both marketing and sales claim that we need an Internet website. Marketing feels that it will help increase interest in our newest product. Sales says that with a website we can cut back on all the literature we are sending out by as much as 20 percent, by sending people to the website for information.

Choosing the Right Internet Connection

WHETHER YOU ARE LETTING AN ISP OR NETWORK CONSULTANT SET UP YOUR Internet connection or you plan on doing it yourself, you should have a pretty good idea of what type of Internet connection you need before you get started. Your connection requirements depend entirely on what you want to do on the Internet, the number of persons in the company using it, and what types of connections are available in your area. Review these factors before you decide (or let your ISP decide) what is right for you. Too often ISPs offer the same technology solution to everyone because it is what they are used to. If you feel that what you are being offered doesn't meet your needs, move on and talk to another ISP.

As discussed in Chapter 10, there are essentially two types of connections to the Internet. An individual dial-up connection lets users dial up to the Internet from their individual computers. The second type, a networked connection, gives everyone access to the Internet through a single, faster connection on the network. There are several technologies used to access the Internet, including analog modems; ISDN lines; dedicated connections such as frame relay; and some future technologies such as ADSL, cable modems, and wireless, which are emerging now and may be available in your area.

Table 14-2 gives a summary of each technology used for Internet connections, along with a description of the circumstances when they are most appropriately used. Review the different characteristics of each technology and compare it to your needs. In particular, you should consider the following when weighing your needs:

■ **Number of employees.** The number of people that need to get on the Internet will have a large effect on the speed of your connection. If you only have one or two people who need access, you are better off purchasing individual Internet access accounts. However, if more than two people in your company need to get on the Internet you should consider using a connection through the network. Network connections can be as slow as an analog modem, up to ISDN, frame relay, or a full T1 line.

Remember that not everyone needs access to the Internet, but deciding who gets access is a management quagmire if ever there was one. The Internet is a powerful tool that can help your business to communicate better and become more informed. However, it is also a potential productivity killer, luring in workers to play games, surf through mindless drivel,

Table 14-2. *Internet Connection Types*

Technology	Speed	Cost	Access	Recommendation
Analog Modem	33.6 Kbps or 56 Kbps (not bad)	The price of a phone line	Individual connections or networked	Very good for individuals and small groups
ISDN	128 Kbps (fast enough)	Low to moderate, depending on area	Individual connections or networked	Excellent for individuals or good-size networks
Dedicated or Leased Line	Up to 1.5 Mbps (greased lightning)	High, at least several hundred dollars	From the network only	For many users and fat wallets
ADSL	Up to 8 Mbps (upload speed slower)	Moderate	Individual connections or networked	New technology; use it if you can get it
Cable Modems	Up to 35 Mbps (but shared with others)	Moderate	Individual connections or networked	Initially for residential users; Use it if you can get it; many areas don't support network connections
Wireless	Up to 52 Mbps	Moderate	Individual and some networked connections	Still very new; use it if you can get it

or follow other unproductive pursuits. However you decide to dictate who does and doesn't have Internet access in your business, make sure that there is some rationale to it.

■ **Applications.** The second determinant your Internet connection needs is the type of applications that you will be running. If you are going to use the Internet just for e-mail, you may be able to get by with a 33.6 Kbps analog modem, even for a networked connection to the Internet and many users. However, if you plan to transmit video or download large files, you will need a faster connection such as frame relay. General web surfing and e-mail for a small number of users can usually be done over analog modems or an ISDN line.

If you plan on hosting a website at your company, you must have a dedicated connection such as frame relay or a T1 line from your website to the Internet that is up 24 hours a day, 7 days a week.

■ **Availability.** What you want and what you can get may be two different things. Because most telecommunications providers didn't anticipate and plan for the Internet many years ago, some technologies may not be available in your area. However, even if a particular technology doesn't exist in your area, you should be able to find an equivalent technology for your needs.

Choosing an Internet Service Provider

ONCE YOU HAVE A GOOD IDEA OF THE KIND OF INTERNET CONNECTION YOU need, you can now look for an Internet Service Provider to get you connected. There are almost too many places to turn for Internet service: the telephone company, small independent Internet providers, large national Internet providers, online services, cable companies, and even utility companies are all selling connections. It makes for a difficult decision to even know whom to go with, but it also means competitive pricing and service.

Although they all offer the same basic service—Internet connections—not all ISPs are created equal. Some are large, national companies that service tens of thousands of people with Internet connections; others are small, one- or two-person companies that offer service to a few hundred people in a local area. Some ISPs are reputable providers while others are fly-by-night organizations running modems and phone lines in the basement of their house and may be out of business the week after you sign on with them. They all range in the customers they target, as well as the services they offer, so make sure you shop around before choosing an ISP. The following is an overview of some of the basic types of Internet Service Providers available.

NATIONAL ISPS

National ISPs are large companies that offer access in many cities throughout the country. Examples of ISPs that fit into this category are AT&T, MCI, PSINet, UUNet, and Earthlink, among others. These national ISPs offer a broad range of services, including individual dial-up accounts, higher-speed connections, and website hosting. In general, national ISPs may be more trustworthy and may offer more ways to connect than a local ISP. In addition, most national ISPs have local numbers throughout the nation, so you will often be able to connect to the Internet with a portable computer while traveling for the cost of a local phone call.

Many national ISPs are also located closer to one of the Internet's access points, or points of presence (POP), which increases the speed of their Internet access. Also, they are often more stable businesses, so they will probably be around in the future.

However, one of the downsides to the larger ISPs is that they sometimes don't offer personalized help or service needed by Internet neophytes. If you are looking for someone to hold your hand in setting up your connection or help you when it goes down, then you might want to look to another source. Large, national ISPs can also be busier than the local service providers, so you may get a busy signal more often than you'd like.

LOCAL ISPS

Local ISPs provide Internet connections for a smaller geographic area than national ISPs. Their stability, knowledge, support services, and the quality and speed of their connection can vary greatly.

However, local ISPs may be able to focus better on specific needs. Some are small-business oriented and can offer specialization with targeted packages and fast access even at peak usage times. Also, many smaller, local ISPs aren't as busy as larger ISPs, so it is easier to connect when dialing in.

However, choose carefully when working with local ISPs. Many are run by people who know more about the Internet than running a good business. Often, one of the first areas to suffer is customer service. Most smaller ISPs actually lease their Internet connections from the larger providers, so their connection isn't quite as fast, but the truth is that you probably won't even notice.

ONLINE SERVICES

Online services, such as America Online (AOL) and CompuServe, are in a different class from other Internet Service Providers. Like ISPs, online services provide connections to the Internet. But they also differentiate themselves with services such as discussion or special interest forums on everything from running a small business to movie reviews. These services are available only to the online subscribers and not to other users on the Internet. Accounts with companies such as America Online cost about the same as a regular Internet connection, or about $20 per month per person, including an e-mail account and access to the extra services they provide.

One of the advantages of online services is their focus on ease of use. Their services are generally very easy to set up. Chances are you that have already received in the mail a diskette or CD that gives you everything you need to set it up. The software automatically sets up your PC and modem so that you can start surfing in minutes. Because of this, many people start out with an online service.

Online services are a great place to start if you are new to the Internet and you want all of their private discussion areas and special services. However, most of the information and special sections they offer are also available in one form or another on the Internet. Many users start out with an online service but quickly outgrow them and move to a regular Internet connection.

Choosing an Internet Service Provider should be as important a decision as choosing a telephone carrier or an overnight service, and it should be given as much thought. It is important to find an ISP with the right customer focus, the services you need, and the right connections. Unfortunately, most companies do not look very far before choosing an ISP. As a result, they may end up with a provider that does not adequately fulfill their needs or provide consistent quality service. When looking for a good ISP, you should look for the certain services or characteristics.

SERVICE CHARACTERISTICS OF A GOOD ISP

■ **ISDN or other high-speed services.** Most ISPs are able to offer basic dial-up services through an analog modem to access the Internet. But if your requirements go beyond just having a few employees dialing into the Internet with modems, you will have to look deeper to see what they offer.

Many ISPs now offer ISDN, ASDL, or dedicated lines as options. Check around for pricing—options and prices differ significantly for services such as ISDN or dedicated lines. Also, some ISPs may support a certain connection technology, such as ISDN or ADSL, whereas others, even in the same city, don't.

■ **Web hosting.** Just about any ISP can help you set up a website. Many consumer-oriented ISPs offer free space on their servers for a website. But if you want to set up a professional website with your own domain name, then you may be better off with some national providers or local providers that specialize in hosting business sites. Make sure that the ISP can offer you statistics on your website, such as how many people have accessed your site and what pages they have visited. Many will make that reporting information available to you on a regular basis as part of the cost of hosting the website.

If you are going to set up a website, make sure that the ISP has a fast connection to the Internet and that the ISP's servers are sufficiently fast enough and will not be weighed down by other traffic. Ask what the ISP's backbone speed to the Internet is. Also, find out about redundancy—that is, how many connections it has to the Internet. If the ISP only has one line, even if it is T3 (45 Mbps) or faster, it won't do your website any good when a construction worker accidentally cuts through it and brings their connection down. ISPs should have two or even three different connections to the Internet to balance traffic and ensure that when one connection goes down, the other will still be up. Finally, check to see if the ISP will register your domain name for your company and if it has web designers who can help you design your website.

■ **Support services.** If you have never even seen the Internet before, then you may want a little more hand-holding to get started, as well as good customer support when a problem arises. This may require you going to an online service such as AOL or CompuServe. They offer more than just plain web access and e-mail and usually have easy setup software that gets you going. If you don't want an online service, but still want help, you might consider some national services that have software setups that automatically configure your computer to access the Internet. Other local ISPs will offer special help for first-timers.

Once your computers are connected, some ISPs will also provide more assistance than others when it comes to setting up a website. They may help with domain name registration, hosting your site, training, consulting, and even providing statistics on who is accessing your website. You may want to also look into their customer support hours and response times.

■ **Traveling access.** If you or anyone in the company travels and needs to access the Internet on the road, you should plan to use individual dial-up accounts with a national ISP. National ISPs have connections in most major cities that allow you to use a local number to dial into the Internet. Some even have connections in other countries that can be used for international travel. Most local ISPs don't offer connections outside their area. Those that do generally charge extra to use an 800 number or use another, partner ISP in the area where you are connecting.

■ **ISP tiers.** Internet Service Providers are rated on a tier system, which indicates how close they are to an access point or point of presence of the Internet's true backbone. There are several ISP tiers:

Tier One ISPs:	These are the big daddies closest to the Internet backbone (the main pipeline of the Internet). There are very few Tier One ISPs; they include MCI, Sprint, BBN Planet, and UUNet.
Tier Two ISPs:	Generally lease connections and possibly other services from Tier One ISPs.
Tier Three ISPs:	Lease connections from Tier Twos.

Obviously, most ISPs are in tiers two and three. Tiers go as high as five and six, but few ISPs would admit to being that high. The higher the number, the farther the ISP is from the true Internet backbone. You shouldn't settle for anything less than a Tier Three ISP. Tier Ones have connections from 45 Mbps up to 622 Mbps. The small companies (e.g., Tier Threes or Fours) may be running access lines of 1.5 Mbps. However, even this needs to be taken in context; these speed differences may have absolutely no bearing on your access if you are running a slow little modem connection to the Internet.

■ **Utilization rate.** While the tier structure has to do with how fast and how close the ISP's connection is to the Internet backbone, utilization rate has to do with how much of that connection the ISP is using. The utilization rate measures how much traffic is going through the ISP's connection. You might be better off with a higher-tier ISP that has a 50 percent utilization rate than a lower-tier ISP with a 90 percent utilization rate.

■ **Connection rate.** If you plan to use ISDN or analog modems to dial into the Internet, one of the most critical things to check out with ISPs is their connection rate. Connection rates compare how many times someone tries to connect to the ISP and how often they actually connect. This may not sound critical, but it is frustrating trying to dial in and getting nothing but a busy signal time and time again. Make sure that your ISP can give you an accurate explanation of their connection rate.

■ **Small-business programs.** When deciding on an ISP, you should look for one that offers special services or packages for small businesses. Often these packages include a number of dial-up Internet accounts or access through a LAN connection, with a number of mailboxes for a reduced price. The ISP may also be willing to provide additional mailboxes for a nominal fee, say, $5 to $10 per month. As part of the package, the ISP should offer you a domain name (www.yourcompany.com) and may include website hosting on its servers.

Many ISPs also sell equipment such as routers for Internet access through a LAN. Some may even install equipment for you. Business-focused ISPs generally offer ISDN or frame relay access for a network connection. You will probably find many of these ISPs either offering or planning to offer electronic commerce solutions in the future.

Setting Up a Website

PLANNING AND PREPARING TO SET UP YOUR COMPANY WEBSITE IS NOT DIFFIcult. But it must be managed correctly for you to get the most from your site. If not, you will end up with a website that doesn't fulfill your needs.

There are five phases to setting up a website: planning, content creation, design, programming, and hosting. Each of these steps may be done in-house or outsourced, depending on your level of expertise.

1. *Planning.* Planning is the most important phase of setting up your website. At this stage you should decide on the goals of your website before you get started. If you don't, your site will never meet your needs. Your goals can include selling more products, providing information to your customers, decreasing your customer support costs, or improving your company image. Whatever it is, make sure that it is clearly outlined before you move ahead. Don't be afraid to open up the discussion of what should be on the website to different departments in the company. Each functional area may have its own needs and goals.

2. *Content creation.* This is the development of the information that

goes on the website. Your company's participation is critical at this stage, especially if you are using an outside web designer. No one knows your business as well as you do. For many companies, each department is responsible for the content of its own part of the web. Marketing may want to post product information and include background information about the company. Sales may want a section on where to buy the company's products or services. Customer support may want to create a section as well. Human resources may want a section for job postings. Let each area in the company contribute to the site's content.

Even though the company contributes to creating the content, you may want to use a professional copywriter to make your content crisp and easy to read. Glitzy graphics may get a visitor to stop and look at your site, but poorly written content will cause them to quickly move on to another site.

3. *Web design.* This step involves laying out how the site will actually look. This includes how the web pages fit together and how the graphics and content are used. Whether someone in-house or a professional is putting together the actual site, you should participate in how it is structured. A great structure should emphasize those areas that fit with your website goals and make the site easy to navigate. Make sure you or someone creates a map of how the pages link together.

The graphic design of the site should also be a big consideration. Make sure that the design fits your company image. If you have an in-house graphic designer or someone you use regularly, you may want to consider using that person to create the graphical elements for your site. The person designing the site should have experience in illustration, page layout, and photo manipulation software. Never use canned clip art graphics for your website. Visitors will recognize cheap graphics immediately and dismiss your site as shoddy. Your company image is too important.

4. *Programming.* The programming phase is the actual development of the website pages using HyperText Markup Language (HTML) code. In this stage, all of the graphics and content are laid out and the pages are linked together to form your website structure.

Programming can be done by a professional or someone in-house, depending on the person's talent level, patience, and an eye for design. Programming does not have to be done by the same person who designs the site. The best person to write HTML code doesn't necessarily have the best skills at creating the design, or vice versa. Because many HTML editors, such as Microsoft's FrontPage, NetObjects' Fusion, or SoftQuad's HoTMetaL, are available to make HTML programming easier, the real differentiation between web designers is their layout skills. Experience in tools such as Java, Java Script, and ActiveX can add a splash of action to your site.

Websites are highly graphical in nature and are designed to attract people to stop and look at your site. Most web designers today have a background in graphic design and know how to create something visually appealing. Some people are tempted to do it themselves because it has become so easy to use HTML editors to create web pages, but if the person doing the website wouldn't feel comfortable designing the company's brochures, then they shouldn't be creating the company website.

If you decide to go with a professional designer and programmer, make sure that you choose someone who is credible and will design a site that fits your company image. Because HTML tools are so easy to use, anyone can claim to be a web designer, but a truly good designer is hard to come by. Make sure that your designer has some experience: Ask for examples of what he or she has done in the past, and ask for some references by other companies. Check out some of the designer's work on the Internet for quality.

As you review your potential designer's work, make sure the designer's style matches what you want. For example, if you are a law firm, don't use the same designer that recently did a "Wired"-style website filled with fluorescent colors. It is best to use design elements that you normally use for your printed materials, including your logo. Web designers, like graphic artists, tend to fall into a design style. If the designer's portfolio reflects one type of design look and it doesn't fit your needs, find someone else.

5. *Hosting.* This final step involves the actual posting of the website on a server so that it can be accessed by users on the World Wide Web. There are two choices for web hosting: on a server at your company's location or off-site on an ISP's server. Factors to con-

sider before deciding where to host your site include cost, management, security, and speed. When all these issues are considered, most businesses choose to host their site with an ISP. It is generally cheaper, faster, and more secure, and relieves the business from the task of maintaining the server. It is also easier to monitor traffic and make updates with the help of an ISP, even though the web server is located off-site.

Some businesses opt for collocation, which is basically using your own web server and locating it at the ISP's facility. It will allow you to use your own equipment, without the need to maintain an expensive dedicated line to your company. Collocation is safer than having your network connected directly to the Internet, and it puts the burden of maintaining the server on the ISP.

So, if I have convinced you to host your site with an ISP, how do you tell them apart? It's easy. First, when evaluating pricing, get an ISP's entire Internet service package, not just information on web hosting services. Many ISPs will offer you a special deal on a website, a number of e-mail addresses, and web access. Second, find out how fast the ISP's connection to the Internet is. The biggest ISPs (i.e., Tier One and Tier Two) are closer to the Internet's backbone, so find out what their backbone speed is. Then, look for redundancy—make sure that they have multiple connections to the Internet so that your site is always up even if one of the connections to the Internet goes down.

Making Your Site a Hit

No matter how you decide to set up your website, make sure that your site is compelling enough to get visitors to stop and take the time to look around. Web surfers have a short attention span. If you want them to stick around, you need to make your site attractive. Here are some tips to help you develop a site that others want to visit.

HOW TO CREATE A COMPELLING WEBSITE
1. *Focus on the customer.* You may know what you want your website to do, but do you know what your customers want? Put yourself in your customers' shoes and think about what content and features they would want.

2. *Make your website visually interesting.* If you want people to come to your site and stick around, you have to make your website interesting to visit and return to. That means using a splash of graphics on your website, a professional layout, and content that your visitors want to read.

3. *Update your site often.* Imagine that your website is nothing but an electronic version of a yellow pages ad. No cool graphics, no real content, no new information. Potential customers come to your site during month one and look it over. They come back in month two: nothing new. They come in month three: nothing new. How much longer do you think they will keep coming back? Not changing your website is like asking visitors to read and reread the same company brochure over and over again. If you want to keep people coming back, you've got to make it interesting and change information often.

   As you budget for your website, plan on using a web designer or having someone in-house spend a few hours every month to make changes. Even the best sites need periodic updating to correct mistakes, reflect changes in the company, and keep the site interesting.

4. *Invite feedback.* If your website is only there to feed visitors your information, then you only have half of the equation. To have a successful website, be prepared to receive feedback from visitors. This means having links on your site that let visitors communicate with you through e-mail or even interactive feedback forms. Feedback may include complaints, ideas for new products or services, inquiries to the sales department, and even suggestions or corrections for your website.

   You will find that web surfers tend to be vocal and often provide good feedback. The best option is to have feedback delivered to various departments on specific topics, using a separate e-mail address called an alias. Aliases include sales@yourcompany.com, questions@yourcompany.com, marketing@yourcompany.com, and webmaster@yourcompany.com (for comments on your website design and operation). Each alias goes to an individual in the company that serves as a conduit for e-mail to that department or topic.

5. *Make it fast.* Make sure that your site downloads quickly, even for users with slow Internet connections. Graphics, interactive designs, and Las Vegas–style glitter may make your site look nice,

but they also take a while to download through a web browser. You want to make sure that your site has enough cool graphics to grab someone's attention, but if it takes too long to download your home page, surfers will move on before they read the first word. Use a dial-up connection with a 33.6 Kbps modem to check it yourself. If it is too slow for that modem, it is too slow. You'll want to consider options for speeding it up, including removing some graphics or fancy Java applications.

Promoting Your Website

NOW THAT YOU HAVE SPENT COUNTLESS TIME AND MONEY DEVELOPING YOUR website and publishing it on the Internet you are finished, right? Wrong. Getting your website on the Internet is only a fraction of the effort of building your web presence. You are now only one of a million other websites on the World Wide Web. If you want anyone to find you, you need to promote your website, and that means spending a little time and possibly a little money to get your name out there. Table 14-3 lists several useful resources to help you promote your site.

To promote your website effectively, you need to have an Internet marketing plan.

TIPS FOR GETTING YOUR WEBSITE NOTICED

1. *Pick a good domain name.* A domain name is the name used for your web site's address (sometimes called a URL, for Uniform Resource Locator). Pick a domain name that is easy to remember so that people can easily find your website. The best domain names are often your company name, because it keeps the link to your company and is easy to remember. However, other domain names sometimes work as well or better than your company. For example, Hank's Lawn Mower sales may find that www.mowers.com is much more memorable (and easier to use) than www.hankslawnmowersales.com. With so many Internet sites going up daily, many names are already taken. If the domain name you want is already being used by someone else, be creative in finding one that meets your needs. If you have access to the Internet, you may see if the domain you want is available at sites like www.internic.com or

Table 14-3. *Resources for Promoting Your Website*

Name	Site	Description
Be Here Now	www.beherenow.com /spider	Submit your site to search engines and other sites
Commonwealth Network	www.contentzone.com	Trade links
Link Exchange	www.linkexchange.com	Trade web banners with other sites
Net Announce	www.erspros.com /net-announce	Announce your web-site online
PR2 Newsletter	www.pr2.com/newsletter	Free e-mail newsletter on how to promote your website
Promote It!	www.net-promote.com	Submit your site to search engines
Register It!	www.register-it.com	Submit your site to search engines
Submit It!	www.submit-it.com	Submits your site to search engines
Web Ring	www.webring.org	Join your site to a web ring of similar sites
WebStep Top 100	www.mmgco.com /top100.html	Top 100 website list; submit yours
Yellow Pages Superhighway	www.action2000.com	Links to websites where you can link your site for free

www.register.com. If it is available, you can even reserve your domain name on the same site.

One note of warning when registering your domain name is appropriate here. Because so many good domain names have been taken, many registrars are encouraging companies to go with top level domains (TLDs) other than .com. Many are even offering TLDs from other countries such as Tonga (.to) and the Cocoa

Islands (.cc). Try to stay with .com for now, at least until other TLDs become more established. If your domain is www.my-company.cc, many people may mistakenly try www.my-company.com and never find your website.

2. *Put your web address on all your company literature.* You are your website's best promoter. Use your web address on everything your company produces, including business cards, yellow pages ads, advertisements, and anything else that you hand out. The more that you use it, the more users will find your website.

3. *List your site with different search engines.* The most popular way for people to find your site is through a search engine, which are websites that index other websites so that users can find them with keyword searches. Examples of search engines include Yahoo!, Excite, AltaVista, HotBot, and others. To list your website you can go to each site and follow the instructions for listing your website address. Most search engines then send out robots or spiders that search through the content of your website and register it in their vast database. When others then search for certain words, topics, or phrases, the search engine matches those terms to your site and returns your website address as a possible site to visit.

If you don't have time to register with each search engine, you can use a registration service such as Submit It!, Promote It!, Register It!, and others. Some sites will help you promote your website, but for a price. To find others, look up "website promotion" on any search engine.

There are other places to get your site listed as well. Several small-business-oriented sites let you list your website and company description for free. For example, the websites of American Express, *Inc. Magazine,* and CitySearch feature sections where small businesses can set up a small home page. You can include a description of your business and provide contact information. Other national, regional, or local search directories allow more detailed information to help people find a specific business in a local area or nationwide. These types of websites often charge a fee for posting information on their website. However, they act like Internet yellow pages and may offer your small business an inexpensive web presence. You may also be able to link your listing to sites that are dedicated to topics that relate to your business.

4. *Use META tags in your HTML documents.* META tags are HTML tags embedded in your website code. They include keywords or phrases placed in your website by the web designer and are used to describe your website. People who surf your site will never see your document's META tags, but many search engines may use them to rank how closely your site matches someone's search. For example, if you are a specialized mountain biking shop, your META file may include such words as "mountain bikes, bicycles, cycling, outdoors, adventure, sports, extreme sports, sporting goods, exercise." The META tag could also include names of bicycles, components, and clothing you sell. If your website designer has not asked you about what to include in your META file, speak up and make sure relevant descriptors are embedded in your code and cover what your business does.

5. *Encourage bookmarks.* Bookmarks are used by visitors in their web browsers for keeping shortcuts to their favorite websites. Encourage visitors to bookmark your site for future reference. By bookmarking your site, users will be able to find your site in their browser's little address book of Internet sites and keep coming back often.

6. *Trade links with other sites.* Trading links means adding a hypertext link to someone else's site on your site, and asking that they put a link from their site to yours. When looking to trade links, stick with sites that appeal to a similar target market as yours. But be cautious of what sites you trade links with; you don't want to promote sites that will lure people away from your website. There are several websites that serve as a clearinghouse for trading web links with companies in similar markets. Sites such as Link Exchange and Commonwealth Network will help you find trading partners. You can also get into a web ring, which links a group of common websites together to facilitate surfing from one site to the next.

7. *Advertise your website.* This is only viable for a select number of sites that can attract heavy traffic, but if you have the money, you can pay to advertise your website. There are plenty of places on the web to purchase advertising that will allow users to click on an ad for your business and show up at your website door. Most sites that do advertising will allow you to buy a banner ad—a strip of space on their website that advertises your website or a

product or service. But be forewarned: Online advertising isn't cheap, especially at high-traffic websites such as search engines. For most sites you pay a rate for the number of "views" your ad gets and a higher rate for the number of times someone clicks on your ad (yes, they can track clicks). If you decide to pay to advertise online, make sure your banner ad appears on sites that attract the target market you want.

8. *Promote with newsgroups and e-mail.* Some newsgroups will let you post information about your website, as long as it isn't just blatant advertising. The best way to post your site with a newsgroup is if you have valuable information that can help others solve a problem or learn more about a topic, then you can point them to your site for help. Be careful, because some newsgroups are hostile to businesses that promote websites. Check each newsgroup's rules before you post anything.

   Likewise, e-mail can be an effective way to promote a site, particularly if you can get people to register on your site with an e-mail address. You can then e-mail them with updates about your business. Make sure that you always get permission before you start sending out junk e-mail (called spam), and always give people a way to respond to let you know if they don't want to receive future e-mails.

9. *Use publicity and goodwill.* Publicity is another good way to attract visitors. Any articles written about your company in any publication should include your web address. Include your URL on any press releases. Also, some news-based Internet sites focus on a particular industry or area of interest. If your company regularly sends out press releases, make sure to include these companies on your PR mailing list. You can often send releases to them by e-mail.

   Goodwill may sometimes be an option for getting a mention or a link on someone else's website. Many times a company with a website may give your company a mention in exchange for some of your products or services. For example, you may find that there is a special nonprofit group that is sponsoring an exploration group to the Andes Mountains. The group is publishing a website to detail the expedition. Your company, a manufacturer of global positioning system (GPS) products, offers the group four GPS devices in exchange for a mention and a link from the expedition website to yours. When like-minded explorers visit the website, they will see the link and go to your site as well.

Dealing With Data Security

SECURITY IS ONE OF THE BIGGEST CONCERNS WITH THE INTERNET TODAY. Although most security fears are severely exaggerated, there is a risk when exposing your computers or your entire network up to a public network such as the World Wide Web. Hackers—whether computer nerds at the local university or criminals targeting your business for company secrets—are great material for movies and adventure novels. While they do exist and you need to guard against cyber break-ins, bigger threats to Internet security come from viruses in the form of files downloaded off the Internet. Chapter 15 contains more information on how to protect yourself from security threats including viruses.

ELECTRONIC MAIL SECURITY

Let's say that you want to send some information to someone on the Internet through electronic mail. You write a nice letter, hit send, and there it goes right to the other person as safe as can be, right? Or let's say that you receive an e-mail from your best customer telling you to cancel all current orders. Should you go ahead and take all orders off the books? Are you sure that message came from the customer? With regular electronic mail, you can never be 100 percent certain that people arc who they say they are, or that anything that is sent isn't being read or changed by someone else.

The vast majority of Internet e-mail is sent in plain text format. That means that if someone intercepts your e-mail, that person can read your message just as easily as the intended user. These interceptors can also change the message or even send e-mail under someone else's name. However, there are two technologies that provide for secure e-mail: encryption and digital certificates.

Encryption

Encryption is the ability to scramble information in a way that someone cannot intercept your transmission and read it, except for the intended person at the receiving end of the transmission, who can then decrypt the information and read it. This is particularly important on the

Internet, where data passes through public channels and can be easily intercepted.

The theory behind encryption is simple. Remember writing secret messages as a kid, where A=C, B=D, and C=E? Only your best friend understood the message because he had the key to unscramble the message. This same technique is used today for Internet transmissions through dual-key encryption. Keys are used to encrypt and decrypt messages. A private key sits securely on the computer of the originator of the message, while the public key is distributed to intended recipients. When you want to send a message, you encrypt it with your private key. The recipient, who already has the sender's public key, then receives the message and decrypts it using the sender's public key. Since no private keys are ever transmitted, it is difficult to crack the encryption. In fact, the current standard for "strong" encryption, which is 128-bit, is impossible to break using today's computing power—for now. Most current e-mail applications support "weak" encryption, which is 40-bit. It is not impossible to crack, but it is difficult enough to discourage most potential hackers.

Digital Certificates

Encryption solves the problem of e-mail information being read or changed. However, how can you determine that the message you received came from the correct person? That is where digital certificates come in. A digital certificate or digital ID is an electronic identification that proves to someone else that you are who you say you are.

When you send a message to someone using your private key (remember that the recipient has your public key for decryption), your private key is also used to send your digital certificate, verifying your identity. The person on the other end uses your public key to check your ID. Since that digital ID is created by the private key on your computer, no one can forge it. Certificates offer a sense of security because they are validated by a certificate authority, or a third party, verifying that you are legitimate. Two of the leading certificate authorities are VeriSign, Inc. (www.verisign.com), and the U.S. Postal Service. Certificates are inexpensive, so they are worthwhile if you need them.

A popular technology for encryption and digital certificates is Secure Multipurpose Internet Mail Extensions (S/MIME) from a company called RSA Data Security, Inc. S/MIME is already included in most popular e-mail applications such as Netscape Messenger and Microsoft's Outlook Express, so it is readily available. However, a competing encryption standard is Pretty Good Privacy (PGP) created by Phillip Zimmerman, which comes with Eudora, another extremely popular e-mail application. While its name makes it sound mediocre, PGP is the most popular encryption software around and can be used for e-mail and other transmissions. A version called OpenPGP is available on the Internet. Note that PGP and S/MIME are not compatible. If you want to use encryption software, the person on the other end needs to use software that supports the same encryption standard.

Now that we have gone through this cryptic encryption explanation, let's put the need for encryption into perspective. First, while it is possible that someone will intercept and read your e-mail over the Internet, it is unlikely. The chances of someone intercepting and reading your e-mail message is probably lower than someone at the post office opening your letter and reading it. Second, unless you are sending credit card information or other confidential information over the Internet, do you really care if someone reads the information? If not, don't worry about securing your email.

WEB SECURITY

When you surf the World Wide Web, you usually don't need to be too concerned about the information that is passed back and forth between a web server and your browser. However, once sensitive data starts being transmitted for the purpose of electronic commerce, you need to understand how secure web servers work.

Whether you are buying or selling over the Internet, it is critical that you use a secure connection before any sensitive information, such as credit card or financial account numbers, are ever transmitted. Like e-mail security, secure server technology basically ensures three things:

- What you are sending can't be read
- What you are sending can't be modified
- The parties you are talking to are who they say they are

One of the ways that you (or your customer) can tell that a website is secure is that the website URL starts out with "https://" instead of the usual "http://." (The "s" ending indicates it is a secure website.) In addition, the Netscape Navigator browser shows a closed lock on a yellow background in the lower left corner when securely connected. Microsoft's

Internet Explorer has its own security notification: a little closed lock in the lower right corner.

There are two primary standards for secure transmissions with web servers today: SSL and SET. SSL stands for Secure Socket Layer. It handles the details of encryption, sending digital certificates and making sure that the message sent hasn't been altered en route. SSL is typically used for sites that use electronic commerce to encrypt credit card information or other sensitive information. SET is short for Secure Electronic Transaction. It is a newer security protocol created by MasterCard and Visa for the transmission of credit card information across the Internet. The advantage of SET is that credit card numbers are never decrypted at the merchant's location, so there is no risk of someone breaking into your server and stealing your customer's credit card number. A third protocol, Private Communications Technology (PCT), is also sometimes used. Today almost all secure servers use SSL.

The Internet is the hottest tool around. It can help almost any small business to cut costs and increase communications. It can give your company the image of a large professional organization at a fraction of the cost of other marketing efforts. But good planning is essential to making sure that you are optimizing the benefits of the Internet for your specific needs. The next section will help you wrap up your plans; it includes ideas for fool-proofing your Internet plans and getting your business wired.

Planning and Justifying Your Network

CHAPTER 15

Steps to a Successful Network

BY NOW, I HOPE THAT YOU HAVE DISCOVERED SEVERAL OPPORTUNITIES TO use networking to help your business become more successful. For some companies, a computer network is one of the largest investments they will ever make. In all cases it is an investment that is large enough to warrant significant attention to ensure that it is set up properly and runs well. This chapter is designed to help you make important decisions about your network, whether it is a LAN, WAN, or a connection to the Internet. It contains information on managing your technology investment, securing your network, protecting your precious data, training, and other tips to making sure your network runs smoothly.

Managing Your Network

UP TO NOW YOU HAVE SEEN THAT A NETWORK REQUIRES A CONSIDERABLE investment in capital resources. A network is not a static device like a calculator; a network changes, grows, and even goes down from time to time. Your company will quickly become reliant on the network, and the network will require someone to manage and maintain your investment. Deciding up-front what needs to be done and by whom will help you in the long run. You don't want to wait until something needs to be done or something goes wrong before you find someone to manage it.

How much management is required depends on how you use your network. If you have a basic peer-to-peer network for sharing files and printers, or several dial-up Internet connections, it may not require much management at all. However, servers, advanced applications, e-mail, intranets, websites, and Wide Area Networks often require more time and maintenance. Some regular activities that are performed on a network include:

■ **Protecting data.** Backing up and protecting data on desktop computers and the server is critical. Backup can be automated, but someone needs to ensure that it is being done and that the backed-up data is stored in a safe, secure location.

■ **Maintaining the server.** Maintaining the server includes regularly checking utilization and hard disk capacity, ensuring reliability, loading applications, adding devices, and optimizing server performance.

■ **Maintaining printers.** Any printer needs regular maintenance, but networked printers tend to be used more, so they need more regular maintenance. This job is best left in the hands of a printer maintenance company.

■ **Adding users.** Anytime you add a new user, someone must set up their computer; add the networking hardware and software needed; and set up user passwords, e-mail accounts, and so forth.

■ **Managing users.** Someone should keep track of all network activities. Any new hardware or software being added to the network must go through that person. Some network managers liken their responsibility to that of a network watchdog, barking at anyone who tries to load any additional software. Often this approach is necessary. If not, the network can become chaotic as everyone in the company puts any and all programs or files they want on the server. Having someone to watch over the network not only prevents your server from filling up with mysterious applications, but also gives you someone knowledgeable about the network in case it ever goes down or problems develop.

■ **Upgrading.** What happens when the next version of Windows comes out? What if someone needs more memory or a new modem? Does your company need a faster Internet connection? It is the responsibility of the network manager to determine what upgrades and changes are necessary for the network and individual computers.

■ **Solving problems.** When there is a problem on the network you need someone who can take charge, diagnose the problem, and resolve it. This is the time when network managers would like to pretend that they don't exist, but their role in solving network problems is critical.

■ **Being the visionary.** As your company's needs change, your network should change also. Planning for the future means not only anticipating what you will need in the future, but also knowing what to use today that won't be obsolete tomorrow.

■ **Tracking inventory.** Tracking the network inventory means documenting each piece of equipment on the network.

MANAGEMENT ALTERNATIVES

At this point you may be wondering who is going to manage all these network-related tasks. After all, if your business is like most others, resources are usually pretty tight and you can't afford to hire another person. Network managers may be internal or external to the company, and their experience may range from the very technical to slightly technical, depending on your needs. Your management alternatives include:

■ **Part-time network manager.** A part-time person in-house may be the least expensive alternative. It is the best alternative when the network is not very complex or is used by a single department of the company, such as finance. For most companies, a part-time person is someone with other responsibilities in the company, but who has the time, interest, and willingness (some say stupidity) to take on the additional responsibility of managing the network. In many smaller companies, the part-time manager often is the office manager, controller, facilities manager, or an engineer.

This scenario works well when the employee has a good understanding of computers. Often it is good to have someone in-house part-time for the little projects and rely on an outside reseller or consultant for the big jobs. The in-house person can handle minor tasks, such as adding a new user, installing network adapters, loading software, or fixing a printer that is down. Bring the outside expert in for big problems and installing new equipment.

■ **Reseller/consultant.** As your network becomes more complex and grows beyond the time or knowledge of an in-house person, a reseller or consultant may be your best option for managing the network. Resellers and consultants, including moonlighters, are great for performing regular maintenance on your network as well as solving crises. They can handle complex installations and are invaluable for regular maintenance of servers. Also, because they work with networking vendors and keep up to date on future technology, they can help you make network purchasing decisions with an eye to the future.

213

Resellers and consultants usually work on a project by the hour, and their services are not cheap. Expect to spend between $50 to $100 or more per hour for their time. Many can offer you a service contract at a reduced hourly rate if you prepay for a set number of hours.

■ **Full-time MIS manager.** When your network becomes larger and more complicated and requires frequent maintenance and troubleshooting, it is time to consider hiring a full-time network manager. At this point you probably have many users and need someone who knows your network inside and out, can provide regular maintenance, and can do it more affordably than calling your reseller all the time.

Among the biggest qualifications to look for in a good network manager are a disdain for nontechnical employees and a healthy appetite for snack foods. Levity aside, however, good network managers also bring experience, previous training, and a certified understanding of networking and specific operating systems such as Microsoft Windows NT and Novell NetWare. Chapter 8 includes a list of popular certifications for networking professionals.

Network managers are expensive employees and may cost more than a small business can afford. They are also in short supply in many areas and are easily lured away once they are working for you. Some more experienced network managers may not even be interested in working for a smaller company when they can have bigger budgets and bigger toys in a larger company.

TIPS FOR THE IN-HOUSE NETWORK MANAGER

If you have an in-house person to manage the network part-time, in addition to other responsibilities, it is often difficult for that person to keep up with his multiple jobs. Unfortunately, that often means that the network suffers from lack of attention until something goes wrong.

If you are the poor soul who has the responsibility of managing the network, you may be asking yourself, "Why me?" The first thing you should do is decide if your boss has it in for you. If not, and you still feel overwhelmed by the task of managing your company's network, don't give up yet. With a little time and effort you will know everything you need to know about running a network. Follow the tips below and you will be praised around the company as a network guru:

■ **Study on your own.** If you haven't read this book all the way through, read it from cover to cover. Then, pick up some other networking books that go deeper into the "how to" details. Some of the best books are those that focus on your network operating system. Once you have collected so much material that you realize you are reading the same information over and over again (or your brain turns to Jell-O), you've studied enough. You'll know it's time to read another book when the number of acronyms you use per sentence starts to decrease.

■ **Get training.** Most general network training will be similar to what you can read out of a book. However, you may want to get training on specific network operating systems that you are using on your network, such as Novell NetWare or Microsoft Windows NT or Windows 98. Other options include local training organizations, traveling seminars, and Internet-based training.

■ **Learn from a professional.** One of the best ways to get trained is to let your reseller's technical people provide informal training. When your reseller sends someone out to install equipment or make a software change, make the technician stay for a few extra minutes and teach you how to do it. You should learn how to do some basic tasks from your reseller, such as adding a user, installing a network adapter, and diagnosing simple problems. Each time you learn something, it will be one less thing you will have to pay the reseller to do the next time.

■ **Stay up to speed.** Staying up to speed with what is happening in the world of networking may seem overwhelming. There is so much happening in computing and networking technology that it is hard to know what to look for, where to look for it, and what is relevant. Even if you are really into computers, networking may not be high on your list of things to learn about. But one of the best ways to stay up to speed is to subscribe to several periodicals that cover networking technology. Some magazines, such as *LAN Times, Internet World, Network Computing,* and *Communications Week,* focus primarily on corporate managers who have very large, complex computer networks. Other general computer magazines, such as *PC Magazine, PC Computing,* and *Small Business Computing,* have a great deal of information on computer technology with a smattering of articles on network products.

The Internet is a great source for networking information. Many of the magazines mentioned have online editions. Many other websites offer tips and white papers on how to use technologies such as ISDN. You will also find many user groups where you can ask advice and get help from others.

Another good source of information is computer trade shows. While the big ones—Comdex, NetWorld+Interop, and PC Expo—are held once or twice a year, they don't focus enough on what you need. Instead, look for smaller shows in your area. If the city you live in is large enough, it should be on the computer trade show circuit. Keep your eye on the business section of your newspaper or call your local chamber of commerce for information.

No matter where you turn for your network information, make sure that you keep up to date with what is happening. The computer world moves fast; you need to keep your eye out for what can help your business. It doesn't take long to stay up to speed, and it will help you and the company in making good decisions about your network.

Doing a Network Inventory

AS YOUR NETWORK GROWS, IT BECOMES MORE DIFFICULT TO KEEP TRACK OF what you have. For that reason you want to start now with an accurate inventory list of everything connected to the network. Yes, everything connected to the network: all computers, servers, printers, and other devices. While this sounds like a daunting task, it is easy to do if you start your inventory as soon as you install the network and maintain it consistently.

Before going into what you need to do, I'm betting that some of you still don't see the need for an inventory list of your network. After all, your time is precious. Well, consider the following situations when your inventory can prove to be invaluable:

1. *Initial planning.* When making initial plans for installing any type of network, a detailed network inventory of computers and other devices will help in determining whether you have the equipment you need. For example, someone's computer may not have enough memory or the right operating system to run on the network. It is preferable to find this out before someone actually sits down to install the network.
2. *Upgrading.* When making software or hardware upgrades, the inventory list can be used to determine if the computers on the network have the right requirements, such as an adequate processor, hard drive, memory, or a video card. This will save you from go-

ing from machine to machine to check this information or, worse yet, finding out after you have tried to install the software.

3. *Disaster planning.* Hurricanes, floods, earthquakes, a disgruntled employee, all are threats to your network. If anything happens to your company premises, your network, or any of the computers, you will want to be prepared to get things back to normal as quickly as possible. A list of the equipment on the network will be the fastest way for you to replace what you have and put everything back to normal. It is also helpful to keep invoices and receipts for all computer equipment together and even have photographic evidence of all equipment for insurance purposes.

   This also means that you should keep a second copy of your network inventory off-site so you will have a protected copy if anything happens to your building.

4. *Computer swapping.* Someone in marketing gets a screaming new computer. What do you do with their old junker? Most companies give the computer to another employee with a less powerful computer and then give their computer to someone else. You can save yourself some time and hassle and use your inventory list of each employee's computer to make swapping easier.

5. *Service/support calls.* Anytime you need to call your reseller or a networking vendor's technical support line, your inventory gives you all the information you'll likely be asked for. This information will help the service technician in troubleshooting equipment or resource problems, and avoid potential conflicts with other equipment.

Now that you have been overwhelmed with all the great reasons why you should keep an inventory of your network and have conceded that it is an inventory list is a good idea, you are ready to start. Your inventory list should include a detailed view of every computer on the network. A simple one-page form on each computer should include the computer type, model number, serial number, processor, memory, hard drive size, operating system version, number of slots and what's in them, and even the versions of applications running on the computer. Form A-2 in Appendix A gives you a detailed list to follow. You will want to use the same format for any servers on the network.

In addition to the computer inventory lists, you should also keep a generic form for other devices on the network, including hubs, printers, and routers. This information will allow you to have reference to any device on the network in one location. Form A-3 in Appendix A is an inventory sheet for other networking equipment.

Once you complete your network inventory, it should remain in your binder or notebook for future reference and update. Remember to keep an up-to-date copy off-site.

Training

TRAINING IS ONE OF THE MOST OVERLOOKED COMPONENTS OF ANY NEW technology. Companies are willing to spend hundreds, thousands, or even tens of thousands of dollars on new equipment but don't bother investing in training their employees on how to use it. Failure to train employees almost certainly leads to poorly used or completely unused technology. Leaving employees on their own to figure out the network will only lead to a backlash from frustrated employees and amount to a waste of time and money.

Training choices vary depending on the topic and how much money you are willing to spend. Your reseller or consultant should be able to formally or informally train users after the network is installed. Training is particularly helpful when it is a very specific, somewhat complex solution. If your reseller isn't available or is too expensive, you may also opt for training classes held by actual training companies. Some training companies are local organizations, but many are part of the traveling training circuit that goes from city to city offering one-day training on general topics, such as specific network operating systems or the Internet.

Training can be as formal or informal as needed. If you are installing a large application that everyone in the company is using, such as e-mail, then it is better to have everyone trained together in a more formal setting. If you are working with a smaller group of people or installing a simple solution to share a network printer or do basic file sharing, you may just want to give employees informal training at their desks so they have some hands-on experience at their own computer. One of the best techniques is to train someone in-house as the expert in a particular area and then let your resident expert help and teach others.

No matter how you train employees, follow a few basic guidelines:

1. *Keep group training to the lowest common denominator, covering information every employee needs to know.* There are always those who want to know more about an application. Let them learn on their own or set up a little extra time for them afterward.

2. *Give employees something to take away.* Whether it is a few steps on how to copy a file across the network or a document on how to use remote access with a notebook computer, employees should have something to reference after training is over. Any training materials should also go in the training section of your network notebook. It can be used later for refresher training, new employees, and those that lose their original copy.

3. *Assign several employees as informal trainers.* Teach specific tasks to one or two people in the company who can be the experts to train other employees. You probably already have this informal arrangement within your company with other technologies. When employees have a problem with a spreadsheet, who helps them? Who knows everything about programming the fax machine? With training, these same people can help the more technically challenged in the company with network problems.

4. *Give employees a chance for follow up.* The real work begins after any initial training is complete. Employees will experiment, try new things, and forget what they learned. Give them the opportunity to ask questions on what they have learned and also give suggestions on what they have found that is a different or better solution.

5. *Train the network manager.* If you have someone in the company who manages the network part-time or full-time, then you should plan on regular training to keep that person up to speed on new products and technologies, product upgrades, and network management skills.

As mentioned previously, there are many sources of training, including your reseller, training companies, the Internet, and networking books.

Introduction to Security

CHANCES ARE YOUR COMPANY ISN'T A VERY SECURE PLACE. YOUR IDEA OF security may consist of having the last person to leave the office at night check the door on the way out, or locking the metal file cabinet in your office. If this sounds like your company, now is the time to change the way you think about the security or your data.

Network security is almost a contradiction in terms. Networks are open systems designed to share information and resources. Security is on the other end of the spectrum—its goal is to limit access to information and resources. Network security tries to balance the two, allowing you to protect information and resources in a shared environment.

SECURITY RISKS

If you think that your company has no need for network security, think again. Anytime you share anything with anyone via your computer, you are open to computer security problems. Consider the following scenarios.

Two computer hackers break into your electronic commerce server, obtaining a list of recent customers and their credit card numbers. They use the numbers to charge thousands of dollars on your customers' credit cards. You lose hundreds of thousands of dollars in orders and your company's credibility.

An employee gets onto a shared hard drive from another employee and accidentally clicks on the wrong document, opening it up. The document is an offer letter to a potential new hire, including compensation information.

A coworker has access to the files on your hard drive. You and she are working on a presentation for a big pitch to a new prospective customer next week. After modifying the presentation, she copies the presentation to your hard drive and deletes her own copy. Only days later do you discover that she accidentally wrote over the latest copy with an older version of the presentation, losing valuable days' worth of work.

An employee downloads the latest game from the Internet. Before the day is over he has shared the game with five other employees. Then, he tries to play the new game only to find out it was really a computer virus that erased everything on his hard drive. Before he can warn the others, three of the five employees have also tried to play to game, with the same disastrous effect.

Three weeks ago the vice president of sales fired one of the sales representatives in the company. Today she discovers that the terminated employee gained access to the company server and, in retaliation, deleted the entire sales database of customers before leaving the company.

As you can see, security threats can come from many different sources and can range from an inadvertent inconvenience to a devastatingly malicious act that brings the entire company to a screeching halt. Threats come from many different sources as well, including:

■ **Employees.** The number-one threat to the security of your network will not be the hotshot computer hacker out of the movies, who cracks your network like a walnut and sells your secrets to a foreign government. Whether through curiosity, malice, or plain stupidity, the people within your company walls have the most potential to cause damage to your network. Before you put cameras throughout the company, realize that most problems stem not from malice but from inexperience. For the protection of the company's physical and intellectual assets, you need to guard against both advertent and inadvertent threats to your network by employees.

■ **Hackers.** Hackers are persons who attempt to break into your network for fun or profit. Hacking "pranks" include breaking in to send e-mail to others under your company name, bringing your server down, posting phony pages on your website, or simply leaving you a message to let you know that they got in. Others may do it for financial gain by stealing your latest product idea or customer database to sell to your competitor. This sounds like something out of a James Bond movie, but it happens more often than you think.

■ **Viruses.** A virus is a generic term for one of the biggest problems with computers today. These threats come in several forms, including Trojan horses, worms, and viruses.

A Trojan horse is a virus with devastating effects. Its purpose is to completely erase all the information on a hard drive. A Trojan horse is potentially one of the worst types of viruses because you probably won't recognize the problem until it is too late. This type of virus appears to be one thing, but is really something else. Trojan horses are often disguised as games or other applications.

Worms are similar to viruses but they are self-replicating. Rather than waiting for users to download the files from each area, worms are designed to find their way through the network, going from computer to computer, infecting everything in their path.

221

Viruses are pieces of code that attach themselves to other files. Once inside your computer they may affect the functionality of the computer itself or only a particular application. One such virus is the Microsoft virus, which is a macrovirus. Transmitted through shared files, it only allows users to save their Word documents as templates.

Most viruses are passed from machine to machine through some shared, common component. For example, a virus may attach itself to a computer diskette or a file that is passed from computer to computer. One example is a boot-sector virus that is transmitted through diskettes. The virus is activated when someone accidentally boots up a PC with a diskette in the drive. Shared diskettes and files are a commonplace method of infecting every computer.

LAN SECURITY

Using proper procedures on the Local Area Network is vital to ensure its security. While your local network may not look vulnerable, it is critical to make sure that users only have access to what they need and that unwanted users don't have access at all. To do this, there are three types of control: user accounts, authentication (or passwords), and access privileges or rights.

User Accounts

User accounts determine whether a user has the authorization to connect to the network's services. They give individuals the ability to use a server, printer, or other device. Unauthorized individuals may be able to physically connect a computer to the network, but without an account they can't actually access anything on the network. This is often known as user-level security.

User accounts are set up by the network administrator. Each user is given the ability to access specific resources on the network. User accounts can be set up with different privileges, which are explained a little later on. Most operating systems can also control the time accounts can be used. For example, you can set up accounts so that individuals cannot log on to the server at midnight, or possibly only certain users can remotely dial into the network between five and ten at night. Use caution with putting limits on the time people can work.

Authentication

The use of passwords for authentication is the second form of security. While user accounts allow you to connect to a resource, a password is still needed to prove that you are who you say you are. For example, when you first log onto the network, you are automatically given access to certain things, but you must first log on with your user account name and password.

In addition, passwords are used in share-level security. For example, in a Windows 95 or Windows 98 environment, you may need a password to access a specific network printer. In this situation there is no user account. Security is created for a specific device, with a password to protect it from unauthorized users. Anyone with the right password can access the printer. Obviously, if someone starts handing out a password, anyone can use it to get to that printer.

As with most security measures, password protection is only as good as employees make it. To make sure that passwords are effective, follow some simple password rules. First, don't use passwords that someone can easily guess. Examples of bad passwords are your first name, last name, spouse's name, dog's name, the word "password," and birth dates. Second, try to use both letters and numbers in the password to make it more difficult to guess. Third, change passwords every few months—some operating systems can even be set up to force users to change passwords periodically. And fourth, don't write down the password anywhere in the office. Users should choose a password that's easy to remember but hard enough for anyone else to guess.

Access Privileges

Finally, after accounts and passwords there are access privileges. Privileges, also known as user rights, are what you can do once you are connected. For example, three people may have access to a specific folder on a server. While only one person has rights to make changes to the files, the other two people have read-only privileges. This gives them access to important information, but prevents them from accidentally deleting that 30-page marketing plan. Also, some people may have access to a printer, but all they can do is check to see when their document will print, not delete the print jobs ahead of it. Access privileges are the last vestige of a class system left in our society.

INTERNET SECURITY

The Internet brings its own set of unique security challenges. The Internet has its share of virus-loaded files and hackers trying to break into any network they can. While your risk of security problems increases by connecting to the Internet, the value of working on the Internet far outweighs the risk. However, to minimize that risk, you must take proper security precautions.

Encryption and Digital Certificates

Encryption brings to mind those old World War II movies, where the British were always trying to crack the Germans' communications code. Encryption is basically the scrambling of information so that others will not be able to use it if they intercept it. "Keys" are used to decipher the information at the other end. Encryption is similar in theory to the secret codes you made up as a kid, where A=C, B=D, and C=E, and so on. It is used for everything from e-mail to electronic commerce.

Digital certificates are a way of proving you are who you say you are. Chapter 14 covers encryption and digital certificates in more depth.

Network Connections

Sharing a connection to the Internet through the network with a router is often a cost-effective way to spread the cost of an Internet connection over the entire company. It also connects your entire network to the Internet, possibly giving someone on the outside access to your network resources. You can minimize your risk with the use of either hardware or software that prevents outside users from gaining access to the network. Possibilities include using:

■ A proxy server that "hides" network users from the Internet
■ Firewalls that protect your network from unwanted attempts at getting to your network from the Internet by monitoring and filtering incoming traffic

Websites

Websites themselves do not pose any security threat if they are not using sensitive data. But where they are hosted may pose a security problem. Hosting your website with your ISP keeps your public website on the

Internet without jeopardizing private information on your own network server. If you are going to put your web server on your network, you need a strong firewall to prevent hackers from getting to the rest of your network.

Downloading Files

The Internet is a great place to obtain software for your business. You will find many great commercial applications that you may buy and download immediately, as well as shareware, which you may download and try out. In addition, there is much information that is available for your use by downloading to your computer. But when downloading applications and files, you also risk downloading viruses onto your computer. These viruses range from the benign joke to a file that can devastate your entire computer.

To protect yourself, you need to be careful of what you download from the Internet. As a general rule, download only from legitimate websites. Larger companies and some shareware sites such as www.Jumbo.com and www.shareware.com are examples of good websites, but even these popular commercial sites make no guarantee that their software is 100 percent virus free. For some of these shareware sites, the software you download isn't actually on their site; they are only a directory pointing you to the best sites where you can download freebies.

Antivirus Software

Anytime you share information with other computers or download from the Internet, you should have good, up-to-date virus protection software on your computer. The best antivirus software will regularly perform a check of your system for viruses. To be effective, your antivirus software needs to be used regularly and updated regularly also. There are many popular antivirus packages on the market, including McAfee VirusScan, Norton AntiVirus, Dr. Solomon's Anti-Virus, and others. Antivirus software will not save you from ever having a problem, but it will keep your system relatively free of problems.

Whatever antivirus software you use, make sure that it can be updated regularly so that the applications keep up with any new viruses that have emerged. An application that hasn't been updated since 1997 is only marginally effective since any virus younger than that may not be detected. Many antivirus applications now offer regular updates over the Internet.

SECURITY POLICIES

The reality of the situation is that passwords, antivirus software, and other security tools will not protect your company from problems if you don't have a clear security policy to get employees to use them. Your policies may be simple or complex, but they need to be written down, explained, and enforced. If not, employees will eventually deviate from them and a security threat will become a security reality. Simple policies should include information on the enforcement of passwords; types of passwords to use and not use, and when to change them; scanning for viruses; using outside disks and other media; downloading software from the Internet; and backing up data.

The objective of security policies is not to make your network impregnable; that is not possible. But by following some general ground rules you will make your network secure enough to deter most potential threats.

Disaster-Proofing Your Network

IRONICALLY, AFTER SPENDING HUNDREDS OR THOUSANDS OF DOLLARS ON computers and networking, you will soon realize that the most valuable part of your network is not the equipment but your data. If anything ever happens to the equipment, it can easily be replaced. Data cannot be replaced quite as easily. Think about what would happen today if every piece of data created in your company was wiped out. It would take months, perhaps years, to replicate it—if it could ever be replicated.

Possible threats to your network include natural disasters (e.g., floods, fires, earthquakes, asteroids), vandalism, electrical disturbances, disgruntled employees, or any number of other potential problems. While nothing can protect your network from ever having a problem, some anticipation and planning can minimize losses to your data.

Disaster planning encompasses two rules: minimize data loss and minimize downtime. Here are some of the things you can do both to prevent problems and smoothly get back on your feet after a problem.

BACKING UP DATA

Rule number one of disaster planning is to protect your data with your life. Many stories of companies that have literally gone out of business after suffering a significant data loss show the importance of this rule. All-important data, whether on your personal computer or a server, should be backed up on a regular basis.

There are three types of backup—full, incremental, and differential.

■ Full backup makes a complete copy of all the files on the disk being backed up. This is obviously the most complete form of backup, but it takes a long time to copy an entire disk.

■ Incremental backup only copies files that have changed since the last backup.

■ Differential backup is very similar to incremental, except that each file's archive bit, which indicates whether or not it has been modified, doesn't get reset when the file gets backed up as it does with incremental backups.

Many companies use a combination of two strategies. For example, a company may do a full backup every Monday. Then, Tuesday through Thursday the company does daily incremental backups of the data to save any changes made since Monday. On Friday, the company does another full backup.

STORAGE MEDIA

There are several media to choose from to back up your data. The most popular is tape backup. Tape backup allows you to write all of your data to one or more tapes that are removable from the drive and stored. Backup tape drives can hold a lot of data and come in different formats. Two of the most popular (and least expensive) formats are Quarter-Inch Cartridge (QIC) and Digital Audio Tape (DAT). Other formats include AIT, DTF, and Travan. QIC has a capacity of up to 13 gigabytes (GB) of data, whereas DAT holds up to 4.5 GB, depending on compression. Actual tape sizes are smaller. Tape has been around for a long time, and it is still the most cost-effective way of backing up. Most tape drives come with bundled software to facilitate the backup process.

A newer method of backing up is with compact disks. Compact disks (CDs) are more reliable and durable than tape, and they are fairly inexpensive, costing only a few dollars each. However, CDs still don't hold as much data as tape, so you may need several CDs to backup an entire server. New DVD-type drives will eventually be able to hold more than tapes or CDs.

A final popular backup method is Redundant Array of Independent Disks (RAID). RAID is really the stuff of large networks. Unlike regular backup, which essentially makes a copy of data on a separate media, RAID archives data by using a number of hard drives that act as one big hard drive. RAID is designed to protect against a disk drive error. If any disk goes down, the data on that disk can be reconstructed by assembling the data on the other disks.

FREQUENCY OF BACKUP

How often should you back up data? The question should be if you lost your data today, how much do you want to lose? Daily backup is the best path; that way, if anything goes wrong, the company never loses more than a day of productive work. Probably the most popular practice is to do a full backup twice a week and an incremental backup the other three days, as discussed previously.

You may be tempted to backup to the same tape day after day to save on costs. Don't do it. Sometimes things go wrong when you are backing up, so you don't want to go through the motions of backing up data on the same tape only to find that the disk or tape you used is bad. Instead, set up a rotation schedule for your backup tapes.

Remember to keep a copy of your backup off-premises. If your building burns down, your network and the backup tapes go with it. Take the one extra tape per week and rotate it out of the ones on-site. The tape that is rotated out should be kept in a safe off-site location, such as in a fireproof safe deposit box at a bank or at someone's home.

THE SHOCKING TRUTH: POWER PROTECTION

As a final protection, make sure that you use adequate power protection on your network. That means attaching an Uninterruptible Power Supply (UPS) on your server. UPSs are essentially backup batteries that kick in if the power goes out. Look for one that automatically shuts down the server when the battery runs down. It will prevent serious damage to your server. Also, use reliable surge protectors on each PC.

YOUR INVENTORY LIST

Remember the tip on keeping an inventory? Well, do it! If anything ever happens to the physical network, you should have a list of everything on the network. It is helpful to have it documented with invoices of hardware and software purchased, as well as photographic evidence. All of this should be stored in your network notebook, preferably in a copy that is off-site.

Choosing the Right Equipment

CHOOSING THE RIGHT EQUIPMENT IS AS IMPORTANT AS CHOOSING THE RIGHT partner to install it. Unlike a bad reseller or consultant, you are stuck with the equipment you buy once it is installed. When choosing equipment, one of the dangers that occurs is focusing too much on price and not enough on product quality and upgradability. When evaluating networking equipment, consider the fact that you will have to live with what you buy for several years, and that the equipment is only part of the total cost. Other costs to consider include installation, maintenance, upgrades, and other costs. A single product may look attractive because it has a lower up-front cost. However, in the long run it may cost you more money when the product is difficult to install, hard to maintain, or must be thrown out down the road because it can't be upgraded as your needs change.

There are three recommendations when it comes to finding the right equipment:

1. When purchasing any networking equipment, make sure the manufacturer has a reputation for quality products.
2. Compare warranties; they are not all created equal—minimum warranties should be for a year. Some products offer lifetime warranties, but don't let that fool you. With the pace at which products and technology change, a three- or five-year warranty is about the same as a lifetime warranty.
3. Check the company's customer support policy and hours of operation. If your network goes down, you don't want to be stuck with a nine-to-five customer support line when you are up all night trying to fix the problem.

Several companies are riding the wave of the small-business market, developing products specifically for smaller companies (i.e., those with less than 100 employees). They are courting small businesses with products that are specifically tailored to their needs, with special features and often at steep discounts over products aimed toward the higher-end corporate market. Big networking companies such as 3Com Corp., Intel Corp., Microsoft Corp., Novell Inc., and others have all come out with products that are aimed specifically toward you. The question is, should you be interested?

The answer is a qualified yes. Many of these small-business products may suit your needs well. They are often easier to use than high-end corporate counterparts and cost-effective. However, make sure that what you buy is not too limiting. If purchasing hardware products such as a hub, switch, or server, make sure that the product is adequate for your performance and size needs. For example, you may be able to purchase a server scaled down for the needs of small businesses, but make sure that it is powerful enough to serve the applications you need or has enough expansion slots for future growth. Likewise, make sure that as your needs change you can upgrade the software. Microsoft's BackOffice Small Business Server is a good example. The product is made for companies with up to 25 users, which is pretty limiting. However, Microsoft already has a program in place to offer discounted upgrades to the full-blown Windows NT when companies surpass the 25-user limitation.

Your Plan for Success

WHEN TALKING ABOUT IMPLEMENTING ANY TYPE OF TECHNOLOGY, A GOOD plan always includes putting your project in the best light possible. Sometimes this can be difficult. Often the network gets attention only when there is a problem. The Internet connection is down, the server is on the fritz, employees can't send e-mail—this is usually when people notice the network. To provide some balance, you need to emphasize the positive side, also. Building a positive impression of the network will not only help you feel good about the investment, it will also lay the groundwork for expanding the network in the future.

Many people are averse to technology. Some even fear it. New technology represents an unknown, even potentially threatening situation. Expect that your employees will react negatively to a network, and anticipate how to counter that response. At the same time, when your employees feel comfortable sharing the workplace with technology, they will be excited about their conquest of a new technology. You must build that excitement in the company and help ensure your network's success.

GETTING EMPLOYEE BUY-IN

1. *Get people involved early.* The more involved employees are, the more comfortable they will feel about a network. This could be as simple as a preliminary meeting or memo (on paper, until you get that e-mail system working) that explains what network is being implemented and what the benefits are. That involvement could go as far as forming a group to assess needs or asking for input as to what company needs are. If you are a real glutton for punishment, you could form a committee to assess company needs. Do whatever it takes to make employees feel as if they are involved in the decision.

2. *Ensure that everyone gets training.* Training cannot be overemphasized as a valuable tool in ensuring the success of your network. Whether you are installing a basic network for file sharing, simple Internet access, or the most complex groupware application available, don't assume that your employees will figure it out themselves.

3. *Share successes.* Keep in contact with employees throughout the process, especially those who are very enthusiastic about the network. Find out their success stories, and share them with others. Also, get those employees to informally train other employees. You will not only build confidence that the network is a worthwhile tool, but you will help everyone to be more productive by sharing knowledge.

Future-Proofing Your Network Today

BY NOW YOU ALREADY KNOW THAT TECHNOLOGY CAN BE A LARGE INVESTMENT. While a basic network or a single Internet account may not cost much, many networks can give you sticker shock. As expensive as your investment may be, resist the temptation to buy yourself into a corner, so to speak. Technology changes. As you make purchase decisions, you should always ask yourself whether what you buy will be usable in the future. Planning now may save you money in the long run.

Saving Money in the Future by Planning Today

1. *Buy big.* Remember when you were a kid and your mom took you to buy pants? She would always purchase the pants two sizes too big and say, "You'll grow into them." Learn from that experience when purchasing networking equipment. If you are putting in a LAN and only have seven computers, don't buy an eight-port hub. A 12-port hub will give you room to grow at only a slight increase in cost. Likewise, when purchasing a server, buy one that can expand—with extra bays for hard drives, extra space for additional processors, more room for memory, and extra slots for network adapters, modems, and other cards. By giving yourself a little room to grow, you will save yourself a lot of money in obsolete equipment in the long run.

2. *Buy the best cabling.* Network cabling is one of the worst areas to cut yourself short. When setting up a local area network, the wiring to use is Category 5 cable. Some people will opt for a lower grade of cabling to save a few dollars. However, most future technologies will only run on Category 5 cabling. It is far more expensive to tear out old cabling than it is to put the good stuff in the first time. When presented with a low- and high-grade cable option, always opt for the better cable.

3. *Focus on flexibility.* Use products that are flexible. For example, many network adapters today run both Ethernet and Fast Ethernet speeds. Adapters can switch from one to the other, depending on the network to which they are connected. The cost of these 10/100 adapters is only slightly higher than regular Ethernet cards. With these cards, your network adapters change with your changing needs. That additional investment today will save you time and money in the future.

4. *Check upgrade policies.* When looking at buying software or hardware, check upgrade policies. When is the next upgrade coming out? How is it available? Is it on the World Wide Web? Will they send it to you? Does the company make users pay for upgrades? How much will it cost? Don't be afraid to call the company and ask these questions before you buy.

5. *Check for flash memory.* Some products such as modems, routers,

and print servers store the software that runs the device in something called flash memory. Flash memory can be copied time and again. So, if the product has flash memory and a new feature or a fix for a "bug" (i.e., computer speak for a defect) comes out for the product, you can change the software very easily. Inexpensive products do not have flash memory, so they cannot be fixed or have new features added. You may pay a few dollars more for a product with flash memory, but you would rather pay more now than throw the product away.

Top Mistakes to Avoid

No matter what type of network you install and what you want to do with it, you want to avoid making the following mistakes. In the process, you'll avoid many problems.

■ **Thinking too small.** Don't think that just because you are not a major corporation you don't need technology. Most companies can benefit from technology, no matter the company size.

■ **Misjudging the size of the network management job.** Unless you have only a very small peer-to-peer network or a few dial-up Intranet connections, managing the network is going to take some time from someone.

■ **Thinking, "Disasters won't happen to our company."** More companies than you wish to know have gone out of business (really—I mean out of business) after suffering a large data loss. Don't be one of them.

■ **Ignoring security.** Small businesses are often lax on security because they think no one is interested in their information. If you are in business, someone, somewhere, wants the information you have.

■ **Failing to plan ahead.** Remember the old saying, "Pay me now or pay me later"? Failure to look ahead, or unwillingness to pay for the ability to expand with your future needs, will eventually be more costly in the long run.

■ **Failing to train.** Don't ever assume that anything you implement is so easy that employees don't need to be trained. Without proper training, you are just wasting money on solutions that will never be used.

KEEPING A "READINESS" TOOLBOX

Every network eventually has its problems. Servers go down, network adapters get zapped, cables break. Whether you are a full- or part-time network manager or the poor guy who got stuck with the job of getting the network running, you should have a few vital tools around just in case. They are:

- An extra network adapter
- Extra network cable
- Several copies of this book (Hey, I have to make a living.)
- One or two good books that explain your computer and network operating systems in depth
- A small toolkit with several screwdrivers, pliers, wire cutters, wire crimpers, tweezers, and a flashlight
- A document showing the network layout
- An inventory list of every piece of hardware and software connected to the network
- Copies of all hardware and software documentation
- Customer support telephone numbers for all suppliers of your network equipment
- Extra tapes or CDs for backing up your data
- Disaster recovery and disk utilities such as Norton Utilities
- The telephone number of your local computer reseller, along with pager and cell phone numbers
- The telephone number of the local pizzeria (for those long nights trying to get the network running again)

Follow these tips and you'll be able to plan for a better network operation in your company. We are now approaching the end. The next chapter will help you add final touches to your networking plan and build the justification for your plan with a financial analysis.

CHAPTER 16

Justifying Your Network

IF YOU HAVE BEEN AROUND ENOUGH PEOPLE WHO WORK WITH COMPUTERS OR play with them as a hobby, you have certainly run into enough (the author included) who like technology for technology's sake. There is no place in the business world, especially small business, for this wanton lust of technology. Time and money are in short supply. You would not make a significant investment in a new employee, a new storefront, manufacturing equipment, or anything else without a plan on how you will use it and a calculation of your return on investment (ROI). Investing in a network is no different. It is an investment in your company's productivity, communication, and future and must be planned for and watched carefully.

Planning has been stressed heavily in the book to get you to think through your technology needs and ensure your business will be more successful. If you have been following the planning recommendations as you should throughout this book, you already have notes on what you need and why. If not, slap yourself on the wrist and go back to the beginning. Put a pencil in your hand and put together a plan for what your company needs. When you have done it, come back here to learn how to put it all together so that it will make sense to you and everyone else.

Finishing Your Plan

YOU MAY HAVE BEEN ASKED BY YOUR BOSS TO INVESTIGATE THE POSSIBILITY of a network. Or you may just be looking into it on your own because you came from another company that had a network. You may even be the boss. Whatever your situation, you probably don't have carte blanche to spend whatever you want on a new network. Instead, you need to bring everything together into a cohesive set of recommendations with a justification to get approval to proceed. If you are the president of the company, you may not need a proposal, but you should still have something just in case someone asks why you are spending the money.

No matter what the situation, your chances for success will increase if you add professional polish to your plans. That means putting your proposal together in one package that clearly explains the objectives and implementation plans for your network. The ideal format should be the network notebook discussed in Chapter 8.

Review the plan that you have assembled in your network notebook. Remember that your plan should not just cover what you are going to do, but how it will help your business. Networking is a competitive tool to help you reduce costs, share information, increase communication and collaboration among employees. You need to demonstrate how it works specifically for you. Review each of the solutions you plan to implement and make sure that you have clearly outlined the justification for why it is important to the business. Finally, make sure that all of your needs are correctly prioritized. Your first need may be for a basic network, then a connection to the Internet for five employees, followed by a server for LAN e-mail. Start with basic needs and move up as your needs change or you can add secondary needs. Don't try to do everything at once; that will only cause you to spend a great deal of money at one time, increase the complexity of implementation, and make it more difficult to train your employees. Your plan should accurately reflect what you want to do and when you want to do it, within the guidelines of what you can do.

Financially Justifying Your Network

IF YOUR PLAN IS IN ORDER, THEN THE LAST THING YOU MUST DO IS FINANcially justify it. For some businesses, this may not be necessary. The financial benefit may be so obvious that you don't need to show this step. But for many companies, you can show that it is a sound decision and deflate the company skeptics. All you have to do is put pencil to paper and write a justification for your plan.

As with anything that you do with your business, any type of justification of your network should be built on a solid financial basis. In other words, if you cannot show financial reasoning for your investment in a network, then there is no reason for you to go forward. A network may seem difficult to justify. Throughout this book we have discussed many different solutions with somewhat intangible benefits, such as increased communication and coordination, that may be difficult to track.

However, without a plan that explains what you are going to spend and what type of return you expect on your investment, you could potentially spend more than your company can afford and make a bad investment for your company. The key to the financial analysis is not to overanalyze to the point of spending too much time, energy, and resources on the project. Rather, it is to show that there is an acceptable, measurable return on the financial resources being expended on the project. You shouldn't try to be fancy in your calculations or make complex comparisons and scenarios. Rather, keep it simple to compile, calculate, and communicate. Here are some tips for helping you through the justification process. The steps outlined are easy enough for anyone without a financial background to work through.

1. *Focus on cash flow.* For the purpose of this justification, focus on a cash basis rather than an accrual basis. In other words, analyze the costs from a perspective of when the costs are incurred, not by depreciating them over the number of years allowed. If something is purchased in a particular year, show the total cost incurred that year—don't try to use advanced methods to calculate the time value of money over a number of years. Leave the accounting work to the accountants and tax advisers, and focus instead on showing the benefits that the network is going to have on the company now.

   Of course, there may be tax benefits for technology products in taking the depreciation on the equipment. You should obviously take advantage of that, if it fits with your financial needs, but amortizing the cost of a product over numerous years is beyond the scope of this book. You may wish to consult an accountant or tax adviser before making any purchases.

2. *Follow a simple pattern.* To calculate the financial benefits of a network, it is important to calculate, within a reasonable amount of accuracy, the costs and benefits—in real dollar savings—and come up with a difference between the two. If you can show that the benefits outweigh the costs, the decision to move ahead should be obvious.

3. *Keep an acceptable time frame.* If your company needs to see a return on investment within a year, that is the time frame you should use when doing your analysis. Most small businesses need to see a quick return on their investment, within 6 to 18 months. The longer you extend the time period, the more unknowns you will run into, such as having to replace or upgrade equipment, adding more individuals, or maintenance costs. To keep things simple, show your work on an annual or semiannual basis.

A FINANCIAL JUSTIFICATION EXAMPLE

Now that we have some ground rules, let's construct a simple financial process that will help you calculate the return on your investment. Following this process will give you a reasonable amount of assurance of the validity of your investment. The three-step process is to 1) calculate costs, 2) calculate the benefits, and 3) show the return. This process assumes that you have already set your plan and determined an acceptable time period for your return.

To walk you through this process, we will go through an example investment for a network used for file and printer sharing by eight users. At the end of the chapter you will find other examples that show you how to calculate the benefits of an Internet connection and a website. Each example will help you understand better how the justification process works.

Step One: Calculating Costs

The first step in calculating the financial return on your network investment is to calculate the costs associated with obtaining, installing, and maintaining the network. Those costs include the charges for the actual equipment, as well as any other future costs incurred to keep the network running, including consulting and other fees. Costs are broken down into the following categories:

■ **Capital costs.** These are costs associated with the network hardware and software, including network adapters hubs, Internet routers or modems, cabling, operating systems, software licenses, and components needed to upgrade your computers to run on the network.

For our network for file and printer sharing, the costs of the network components include network adapters for all eight employees, a 12-port hub (to allow for future growth), cabling, and a print server to connect an existing printer to the network. The total cost for these items comes out to be $1,300.

■ **Installation/setup costs.** These costs include any consulting fees for designing your network and setting it up, and other up-front consulting fees or charges. Of course, if you opt to install the network yourself, you can save on these costs. You should also include other one-time fees, such as setting up Internet accounts, website design fees, or the fee to register a domain name for the Internet, as well as employee training costs.

In our network example, we will assume that the company decides to hire a reseller to install the network for file and printer sharing. The company buys the products from a reseller, who installs the network and sets up all eight PCs to use the network printer in three hours. The reseller charges $300 for the installation. As part of the fee, the reseller also trains all eight employees. The training time is one hour. Since the average hourly wage per employee (salary and benefits) is $20, that is an additional cost of $160 for one hour's worth of time for the eight employees. So, total installation costs are $460.

■ **Maintenance/support costs.** These costs are incurred after the network is installed. They include the service contract that you may have with a reseller to keep the network running or monthly fees for an Internet connection or a hosted website. Recurring costs may also include replacement components needed to maintain the network, including new network adapters, additional cabling, and another hard drive for a server. You should plan on at least a small amount of your budget being used to maintain and upgrade equipment as needed.

In our network for file and printer sharing, the reseller offers the company a service contract to do periodic maintenance on the network. The business declines the maintenance contract since the network is fairly easy to maintain. However, the company realizes that it will probably have several problems and will have to call the reseller in for help about two times that year. The company figures that the reseller will charge about $125 for each service call, for a total support cost of $250 for the first year.

Now that we have all of the costs for the year, we can calculate the total outlays for the network for the first year. In our example, the capital costs are $1,300, the training and setup costs are $460, and the support costs are $250, so the total cost of the network in year one is $2,010.

Step Two: Calculating Benefits

The second step in setting up your network justification is to calculate the benefits of what your investment will do for you. At times, these benefits may seem harder to add up and prove, but you will need to understand at least the most important ones to help determine if the investment is worth the cost. To calculate the benefits, you will need to look at how the technology investment helps you either to save money or improve your employees' ability to work. These benefits can generally be broken down into three areas: tangible savings, productivity savings, and other cost savings. Our shared file and printer network example shows how this works:

■ **Tangible savings.** These savings come from any assets that the company would have purchased, but can now forgo purchasing because it has installed a network. Examples of tangible savings include the costs of extra printers or larger hard drives that are no longer needed because the network allows users to share one printer or a hard drive on a server. You can also include software savings because your employees can now share software over the network with network user licenses.

For our example, the basic network allows the company to share its one existing laser printer and one color inkjet printer among all eight users. That saves the company from buying a second laser printer at a cost of $1,000, as well as another inkjet printer at a cost of $250. In addition, two employees have wanted removable storage drives to share larger files that won't fit on floppy diskettes. With a network, the employees no longer need the drives, which cost about $150 each. Therefore the total hardware savings for this project are $1,550.

■ **Productivity savings.** These savings are often some of the hardest to measure, but they can be the most dramatic and meaningful. They include the time it takes to perform tasks without the network—for example, the time it takes to share a printer on someone else's computer because you can't print across the network.

If you can, the best way to calculate this time is to take a burdened (including benefits) average hourly salary per employee and calculate it by the number of hours saved per year. You don't need to be exact with this estimate. This may be a sensitive area because of the disclosure of employees' wages and benefits, so it is best to work with an average hourly wage (multiplied by 1.2 to include employee benefits) for all involved and accept that it may be a little off.

More often than not, you will end up underestimating the time saved. Also, don't let anyone tell you that because the time is already paid for it is irrelevant. If all your employees sat around doing nothing with their time, you would not be happy. Why should you accept it when they lose productive time because of lack of technology?

For this example, it is estimated that the average employee prints or shares files twice a day, and it takes 10 minutes per print job or file transfer on disk (five minutes to copy from one computer to the disk and five minutes to copy from the disk to the other computer). This calculation means that the average employee copies files to share or use a printer for 7.3 hours per month, which equals almost an entire day per employee per month. That comes out to 58 hours per month for the entire company. If the average employee makes $20 an hour, including benefits, that comes to $1,160 per month, or $13,920 per year that can be saved by installing the network.

■ **Other savings.** This is a catch-all category for any other benefit that will come from the investment. For example, if you install an e-mail server, you could count reduced paper costs, long-distance phone charges, and postage charges as cost savings.

For our network for file and printer sharing, the only other costs that are saved are the maintenance contracts that the company normally buys on its printers. Because the company stays with only two printers rather than four, the company figures that it will save its $200-per-year service contract from doubling. However, the contract will go up by $100 to reflect some increased wear and tear on the two existing printers. Therefore, the company will save an extra $100 per year.

Finally, there are also intangibles— those savings and benefits that you really wish you could use, but are not quantifiable enough for you to measure and put into the equation. These are the things that you should hold in your back pocket as you do your analysis. Then you'll be able to pull them out later and say, "Oh yeah, we can save on this also." Intangibles include the benefits of collaboration and increased information flow in your company, or the increased credibility with other companies of having an Internet e-mail address for everyone in the office.

For our example, the company realizes that with easier file sharing, there will be increased collaboration as employees share documents and have greater access to information within the company. Although there will clearly be cost savings related to better communication, the company doesn't know how to put a real dollar figure to the benefit.

Thus, it is better left as an added benefit, but should probably be left out of the equation.

So, our total savings for the first year includes $1,550 in hardware savings, $13,920 in employee productivity, and $100 for a service contract that is not needed. Thus the company's first year savings due to a network for file and printer sharing are $15,570.

Of course, there is also the possibility that a network can actually increase your revenue, which brings an entirely different benefit to the equation. In this case you will need to justify that the revenue coming in is actually new revenue that you never would have without the new technology. An example may be an electronic commerce website that allows you to sell over the Internet and reach new customers around the world. In this case you would want to count the incremental profit that you normally wouldn't have gained as part of the benefits side of the equation.

Step Three: Showing the Return

The final step to the justification process is to take your final information on costs and benefits and come up with a total that shows whether or not the network is a sound investment. The example that we have used shows an obvious return, as follows:

Costs:

Capital costs	$1,300	(network equipment)
Installation costs	$460	(installation of network)
Support costs	$250	(service calls)
Total costs, year one	$2,010	

Benefits:

Tangible savings	$1,550	(two printers and two removable media drives)
Productivity savings	$13,920	(employees no longer carry floppies from place to place)
Other savings	$100	(no maintenance contract on two printers)
Total savings, year one	$15,570	

Total company return, year one: $13,560

This same scenario can be extended to a longer scenario, say, two or three years, by calculating the same costs and benefits for each additional year. To extend our example, we would assume that there would be some additional support costs of $250 per year and no additional costs beyond maintenance and some replaced equipment. The benefits, however, keep on rolling. The business would continue to receive the same productivity benefits and other cost savings. Thus, the total picture over a three-year period would look like this example below.

	Year One	Year Two	Year Three	Total
Costs:				
Capital costs	$1,300			$1,300
Installation costs	$460			$460
Support costs	$250	$250	$250	$750
Total costs	$2,010	$250	$250	$2,510
Benefits:				
Tangible savings	$1,550			$1,550
Productivity savings	$13,920	$13,920	$13,920	$41,760
Other savings	$100	$100	$100	$300
Total savings	$15,570	$14,020	$14,020	$43,610
Total return by year:	$13,860	$13,770	$13,770	$41,100

The total return of $41,400 is the number that the company would use to show how much it could save over a three-year period by using a network for file and printer sharing. As you can see, it is an excellent return on the investment of $2,500 over the same period, and the company should move ahead with the plan to put in the network.

The previous example showed how a very basic network can help a business become more productive and save not only hardware and maintenance costs, but also employee productivity. The examples that follow show how you can calculate the costs and benefits of other types of networks as well.

INTERNET COST JUSTIFICATION: EXAMPLE

Our next example shows how a company can do the same cost and benefit analysis to determine whether an Internet connection is a good investment for the company. For this example, let's take a consulting company with 15 employees that wants to set up an Internet connection to communicate with clients and do research on the Internet. The company already has all 15 employees on a network and is looking to install an ISDN router that will connect everyone to the Internet through the network.

Step One: Calculating Costs

The first step to putting together the company's financial analysis is to determine its costs for maintaining an Internet connection. The company has broken down its costs into three cost categories:

■ **Capital costs.** Because the company already has a network, the additional cost for the Internet connection is an ISDN router that connects the entire network to the Internet through one connection. The cost of the router is $500.

■ **Installation/setup costs.** Both the Internet Service Provider and the telephone company normally charge one-time fees for setting up an ISDN line. After shopping around, the consulting firm estimates that it will cost $50 to set up the Internet account with the ISP, which includes installation of the router, and $150 to set up the ISDN line with the phone company, for a total of $200. All employees already know how to use the Internet, so there are no training fees involved.

■ **Support costs.** Support costs include a $75 monthly fee from the phone company for the ISDN line. The Internet access fee, which includes e-mail accounts for all 15 employees, is $60 per month. In addition, the company plans to spend $50 per month for several subscription services on the Internet that will allow it to search for information on industries and even specific companies. So total fees for the ISDN line, e-mail accounts, and online subscriptions add up to $2,220 per year.

Combining all of the costs for hardware, setup/installation, and support costs comes to $2,920 for the first year for the networked Internet connection and Internet services.

Step Two: Calculating Benefits

Step two of the consulting company is to determine the benefits of the Internet connection. The savings include:

■ **Tangible savings.** In this case, there are no tangible savings associated with the Internet connection.

■ **Productivity savings.** Without the Internet connection, 11 of the consultants in the firm visit the local library for about 10 hours per week doing research. The consultants make an average wage of $35 per hour, including benefits. They feel that by using the Internet, they can cut that time to about five hours of searching on the Internet and some less frequent trips to the library and telephone research. That five-hour savings per week for 11 employees comes to a total savings of $7,700 per month. The annualized savings per year are $92,400.

■ **Other savings.** In addition to the above-mentioned savings, the company believes it can use the Internet to cut its long-distance telephone and postage charges. The company normally spends $1,000 per month on both costs. By communicating with clients and transferring files through e-mail, the company estimates it could cut those expenses by 20 percent, or $200 per month. That equals a savings of $2,400 per year on postage and long-distance charges.

Combining the total savings for consultant research time, long-distance phone charges, and postage charges shows a total savings of $94,800 per year.

Step Three: Showing the Return

After adding up the costs and the savings for the Internet connection for the company, the company is able to show a remarkable return on its investment, as shown below:

Costs:

Capital costs	$500	(ISDN router)
Installation costs	$200	(one-time ISP and ISDN setup fees)
Support costs	$2,220	(monthly ISDN, ISP, and online service fees)
Total costs, year one	$2,920	

Benefits:

Tangible savings	$0	
Productivity savings	$92,400	(reduced research time)
Other savings	$2,400	(long-distance telephone and postage savings)
Total savings, year one	$94,800	

Total company return, year one: $91,880

As you can see, the savings are substantial and easily justify the cost of the Internet connection. In addition to the cost savings, the company also receives other added benefits, including more up-to-date research information from the Internet and improved customer communication time with e-mail.

INTERNET WEBSITE COST JUSTIFICATION: EXAMPLE

The following example shows how this simple equation can also be used to justify a company plan for an Internet website. In this case, a manufacturing company plans to launch a website to give the company a presence on the World Wide Web. The goal of the website is to increase its marketing presence and reduce customer support costs. The analysis that follows illustrates how the company can show that the website is a good investment.

In this example, the manufacturing company has been overwhelmed with customer support calls on its newest product. In response to the calls, it has been forced to hire two new customer support people. Unfortunately, this has not solved the problem as more customers call in for technical information on how to use the product. The customer support manager estimates that unless something is done soon, he will have to hire two more customer support technicians to handle the additional calls. Likewise, the company's sales team has been inundated with calls for information on the new product, causing the company's 800-number, fax, postage, and literature charges to go up. The company also is considering hiring one additional salesperson just to take incoming calls.

Company executives feel that an alternative solution may be to establish an Internet website to help offload both customer service and sales calls. The website would contain information on the products, as well as customer support information on how to troubleshoot typical product problems. By providing product information on the web, customer service and sales employees can refer customers to the website as their first line of support. In addition, the website address can be printed on all sales literature, advertisements, and packaging to steer people toward the site when they need information. Company executives believe that this plan can significantly cut down on the number of phone calls coming in and the number of persons needed for sales and support. In addition, the company also feels that it will gain some additional market exposure by having an Internet website, allowing it to reach even more new customers and generate additional sales.

Step One: Calculating Costs

The first step is for the manufacturer to determine the cost of setting up its website. In this example, the company already has access to the Internet for e-mail and surfing the World Wide Web, and plans to set up the website at its Internet Service Provider. The total costs are:

■ **Capital costs.** Because the company plans to use its Internet Service Provider to host the website, there are no costs to the company for capital.

■ **Installation costs.** To establish an Internet website, the company must work with its ISP to have the website set up on the ISP's server. That setup fee includes registering for a domain name (www.companyname.com) and a fee for publishing the site. The fees for setup and registration are $400. In addition, the company hires a web designer to create a moderately complex website. The fee for the website design is $5,000. Total fees for setup are $5,400.

■ **Support costs.** Monthly fees to the Internet Service Provider for maintaining the website are $100 per month. In addition, the company plans to pay $100 per month to the web designer to periodically update the website with new information. The yearly fees add up to $2,400.

The total costs for setting up and maintaining the company website are $7,800 for the first year.

Step Two: Calculating Benefits

In step two, the company tries to determine the benefits that will be gained by implementing the Internet website. In this case, the main reason the manufacturer plans to implement the website is to cut costs on providing product information and product technical support to customers. A secondary benefit is to possibly gain more exposure and product sales. The savings are delineated as follows:

■ **Tangible savings.** There are no tangible cost savings with the Internet website.

■ **Productivity savings.** By using the website for general technical support information and some product sales information, the customer support manager and sales manager both estimate that they can forgo their hiring plans. The combined salary and benefits for these three employees would have been $90,000 per year.

■ **Other savings.** In addition, the company's executives believe that by using the website, they can move 15 percent of technical support calls and 10 percent of sales calls to the Web rather than calling into the company for information. They calculate that this will save 20 percent of their incoming 800-number calls, which currently costs about $800 per month. The savings come to $1,920 per year.

Adding up the productivity and other savings gives us a total savings of $91,920 per year.

Step Three: Showing the Return

Adding up the costs and the savings for the creation of a customer support website for the company shows a remarkable return on investment, as shown below:

Costs:

Capital costs	$0	
Installation costs	$5,400	(ISP setup fees and website design)
Support costs	$2,400	(monthly ISP fees and web design updates)
Total costs, year one	$7,800	

Benefits:

Tangible savings	$0	
Productivity savings	$90,000	(savings on salaries of three new employees)
Other savings	$1,920	(savings on 800 calls, postage, and literature)
Total savings, year one	$91,920	

Total company return, year one: $84,120

In this example, the Internet website saves the company more than 10 times the cost of the Internet website. By using a simple financial analysis, the company is able to show that it can cut its support and sales costs dramatically and more than compensate for the cost of the website.

As you can see, in many cases the benefits of a network can be calculated, and you can show a positive effect on your company's profitability. Now, with a plan and a solid financial analysis in hand, you are ready to show how a network can benefit your company.

Budgeting for the Future

A SHORT-TERM FINANCIAL ANALYSIS, AS ILLUSTRATED IN THE PREVIOUS examples, is important for getting your network started. Effective budgeting is also essential to keep your network running. If your company has an annual budgeting process, you will want to begin including a budget for computers and network equipment. If you already have a computer budget, add to it. Don't sell your technology future short by failing to fund what your company needs. The more you use your network, the more you will view it as an important business tool. However, like the company fax machine, copier, and telephones, the company network needs to be maintained.

How much you will need in the budget depends on what you're planning for the future. Review your network notebook for what you want to accomplish in the budgeting year. Call your local reseller and ask for some estimates over the telephone. If any employees will need a new computer in the next year, or you plan to add users to the network, factor in those costs. Management fees should be included, whether you have hired a reseller or consultant to manage your network for you or hired a salaried internal network administrator. Also, don't forget to include some budget for maintenance costs.

Conclusion: Getting Your Business Wired

NOW THAT YOU HAVE A COMPLETE PLAN FOR PRODUCTIVE NETWORKING solutions and an understanding of how a network will help your company, you are ready to join those businesses that are getting wired. As you finish this book, I hope that you have found the information contained within these pages to be helpful and insightful. If you can put this book down feeling more confident that a network will contribute to your company's success, then it has been successful. If you personally have a new level of comfort with the networking options available to your company, then it has been even more successful.

Whatever business you are in, whatever its goals, every employee has a responsibility to make the company successful. There are many paths that you can take and many challenges ahead. But the door to improving your business with networking and the Internet is in front of you. You now have enough knowledge to improve the quality of the business and make it more successful. You are still the one who must decide exactly how you want to use networking and the Internet to improve the way you do business. The technology is there; use it to your company's advantage.

Planning Forms

THIS APPENDIX WAS CREATED TO GIVE YOU THE TOOLS NECESSARY TO THINK and plan through your networks. Feel free to photocopy them and use them as they are or re-create them in your own word processor.

Form A-1. *Basic Computer Inventory Sheet*

Computer User	Computer Processor	Computer Operating System	Available Expansion Slots	Attached Peripherals

Form A-2. *Computer Inventory List*

Computer Name _____

User _____

Model _____

Serial Number _____

Processor Type _____

Hard Disk Size _____

Memory _____

Operating System Version _____

Monitor Type (EGA/VGA/SVGA/Monochrome) _____

Expansion Slots _____

Attached Printer _____

Other Attached Devices _____

Other Software (include version number) _____

_____

_____

_____

_____

_____

Form A-3. *Equipment Inventory List*

Device Type _____

Manufacturer _____

Model Number _____

Serial Number _____

Location _____

User (if applicable) _____

Purchase Date _____

Other Information _____

_____

_____

_____

_____

_____

_____

_____

_____

_____

_____

Form A-4. *Network Planning Form*

Necd	Priority	Time Frame	Justification

Form A-5. *Network Resources*

Resource	Priority	User Name:	User Name:	User Name:	User Name:

Instructions: List user names across the top row. Next, list available resources or network plans down the far-left column. Register a timeline priority for each resoure/plan in the next column. Finally, in the intersecting box of each resource/plan and user name, mark whether or not the user will have access to that resource.

Form A-6. *Networking Financial Justification*

Project _____

Justification _____

_____

_____

Costs	Amount	Description
Capital Costs		
Installation/Setup Costs		
Support/Recurring Costs		
Total Costs		

Benefits	Amount	Description
Tangible Savings		
Productivity Savings		
Other Savings		
Total Savings		

Return on Investment		Subtract Total Costs from Total Savings

Glossary of Networking Terms

THIS SECTION PROVIDES DEFINITIONS FOR SOME OF THE TERMS USED IN THE networking world, including some of those nasty acronyms. Use this reference for translation when speaking with someone who frequently uses TLAs (three-letter acronyms).

access method   The procedure used to communicate over the network set by a networking standard. The access method for Ethernet networks is CSMA/CD.

access rights   A security feature that defines what users can and can't do with networked resources, particularly files or directories. Also known as access privileges.

account   A network user's profile that allows the user to have access to the network and includes access rights or privileges.

acronym   An abbreviation comprising the first letters of the words in a technical term. Under networking rules, the person who can include the most acronyms in a sentence is considered superior to all others.

ActiveX   A technology from Microsoft Corp. used to embed animation in web pages.

adapter   A hardware device that is installed in a computer and used to connect to the network. Also known as a network adapter.

address   Used to identify a device on a network to allow it to communicate with other resources.

ADSL   Asymmetrical Digital Subscriber Line. A digital "always on" technology used for connecting to the Internet. Because it is asymmetrical, its download speed (i.e., speed from the Internet to you) is faster than its upload speed (i.e., speed from you to the Internet). One of many types of digital subscriber lines available.

antivirus software   Software that detects and removes viruses from computers and servers.

AppleTalk   Apple Computer's network operating system for the Macintosh.

ATM   Asynchronous Transfer Mode. A high-speed backbone technology for LANs and WANs that can carry data, voice, and video transmissions.

backbone   A section of cable that acts as the main connection for the network, with everything else branching off of it. Most backbones today are made from Fast Ethernet, FDDI, Gigabit Ethernet, or ATM.

backup   Method of creating a copy of files and storing them in a separate location in case something happens to the original. A critical component of networking.

bandwidth   The capacity of a network to carry data. Usually defined in bits (of data) per second.

banner ad   An advertisement created on an Internet website. Banner ads generally are linked to another website or web page so that viewers may get more information by clicking on it.

BNC connector   A twist-on connector used with coaxial (10Base2) cable.

bridge   A device that connects two network segments together. Bridges learn where devices are by memorizing their addresses. Thus, a bridge only forwards information on to a network segment if the destination device is actually on that segment.

bug   A deficiency or defect in a hardware or software product. A bug can have an effect ranging from minor inconvenience to debilitating your system. Bugs are common in computer and networking products. Most can usually be fixed with upgrades from the product's manufacturer.

bus   A type of network topology that uses coaxial (10Base2) cable. All the computers are connected on a single line of cable. A bus is also the series of expansion slots in a computer.

cable modem   A digital modem that uses coaxial cabling to connect to the Internet. Unlike most other technologies, cable modem users share the same bandwidth to the Internet.

cache   Memory used to place data and instructions in temporary storage so that it can be accessed quickly.

call back   Also known as dial back. A security method used for remote access.

When you dial into a device that supports call back, the device answers, recognizes you, hangs up, and calls you back at a predefined phone number. It is used mostly by telecommuters who work at home.

CD-ROM A high-capacity disk that is used to read and write information. It looks exactly like audio CDs.

certificate authority A third-party company that validates your identity and issues you a digital certificate for use on the Internet. Examples of certificate authorities include VeriSign and the U.S. Postal Service.

CHAP Challenge Handshake Authentication Protocol. A security protocol used for dial-up connections such as remote access or Internet access.

chat Real-time (dynamic) conversations that occur over a network, especially the Internet.

client A node or workstation on the network.

client/server A type of networking that includes both client computers and one or more central servers. The server acts as the central resource on the network used by the clients.

CNE Certified NetWare Engineer. Certification given by Novell Inc. that is evidence of someone's extensive knowledge of networking.

coaxial cable Cable used in a bus topology. Consists of an insulated wire core covered by braided metal and more black insulation. Although it looks similar to wire used for cable television, don't try to use your cable TV wire to connect a network; it is different cable with a different connector. And don't try to network your TV and your computer together--nothing will happen.

collision Occurs on Ethernet networks when two or more devices try to send data on the network at the same time. When a collision occurs, the devices stop sending data and wait for a period of time before retransmitting.

CompuServe An online service that provides different services and content as well as Internet access to users.

CPE Customer Premises Equipment. Any communications equipment that resides at the customer's (i.e., your business's) locations.

CPU Central Processing Unit. The main part of the computer that processes information.

CSMA/CD Carrier Sense Multiple Access with Collision Detection. The access method used by Ethernet networks to control how computers talk to each other. With CSMA/CD, computers listen to the network before transmitting data. If another device is already transmitting, the computer waits. If two devices communicate at the same time, a collision occurs, and both devices wait before trying to transmit again.

DAT   Digital Audio Tape. A common type of magnetic tape for backing up data.

decryption   Unscrambling of information that has been encrypted (scrambled).

dedicated line   Also known as a leased line. A full-time connection used for connecting resources over a long distance.

dial-up line   A communications link made over a telephone or ISDN line. Connects to resources only as needed.

differential backup   A type of backup in which only files that have been modified since the last backup are backed up. Also see incremental backup.

digital cash   A payment system in electronic commerce that uses electronic bank accounts for transactions.

digital certificate   A form of electronic identification on the Internet. Digital certificates gain their legitimacy by using a third party to validate identities.

digital subscriber line   A very fast "always on" digital technology used to connect computers or networks through common copper telephone lines to the Internet or other networks. Many different types of DSL are available at different speeds. The most common is ADSL (Asymmetrical DSL), which is often used to connect to the Internet.

DNS   Domain Name System. A TCP/IP networking standard that uses names to identify network addresses. Also Domain Name Server. A server that resolves a domain name into a specific address on the Internet.

domain name   A name used on TCP/IP networks such as the Internet that signifies a network address. Individuals and organizations often register their name as their domain name to easily identify themselves on the Internet.

DOS   Disk Operating System. Should stand for Difficult Operating System.

DSU/CSU   Digital service unit/channel service unit. Provides the connection between the telephone company's central office and a local area network, much like a modem for a dedicated or leased line.

DTF   Digital Tape Format. A type of tape used for backup that has very high capacity and is very fast.

dual key encryption   See public key encryption.

EDI   Electronic Data Interchange. Any number of systems used for business-to-business integration and transactions.

electronic business   The extension of the entire business process through electronic means. Electronic business includes conducting transactions over the Internet (electronic commerce), but it also ties into some "back office" functions such as accounting, billing, shipping, inventory management, production management, or purchasing management with suppliers.

electronic cash   A payment system for electronic commerce that uses electronic bank accounts to transfer numeric digital money.

electronic commerce   Selling products or services over a network, most often the Internet.

electronic wallet   A payment method for electronic commerce that uses encrypted credit card information and digital certificates stored on your computer. Customers can use multiple payment types and even save digital receipts of transactions.

e-mail   Electronic mail. A method of sending electronic messages over a network.

Ethernet   The world's most popular networking standard created by Digital Equipment Corp., Intel Corp., and Xerox. Runs at 10 Mbps.

EtherTalk   A version of Ethernet that runs over a network of Macintosh computers.

Fast Ethernet   A networking standard that is 10 times faster than Ethernet, or runs at 100 Mbps. Also known as 100BaseT.

FDDI   Fiber Distributed Data Interface. A network standard that runs over fiber-optic cable at 100 Mbps.

fiber-optic cable   High-speed cabling that uses light waves to transmit data through glass strands. Used as a backbone for very large and fast networks.

file server   A server that contains one or more hard drives and is used for storing and sharing files over the network.

file sharing   The ability to let others access and use your files across a network, and vice versa.

firewall   A device that protects a local area network from hackers on the Internet. A firewall can be software on a server, in a router, or a separate hardware/software device.

FRAD   Frame relay assembler/disassembler. Formats data to and from a frame relay network.

frame relay   A wide area network protocol that uses packet switching. Often referred to as a dedicated or leased line because it runs over a T-1 or fractional T-1 line.

FTP   File Transfer Protocol. A protocol used for transferring files over the Internet.

full backup   A type of backup where all files are backed up, regardless of whether they have been modified since the last full backup.

gateway   A device that connects dissimilar networks together.

Gbps   Gigabits per second. One billion bits per second.

Gigabit Ethernet   The fastest Ethernet standard. Runs at 1 Gbps, or 100 times faster than regular Ethernet.

Gopher   A hierarchical system used to locate information on the Internet.

groupware   Software that allows users to interact and coordinate and share information over a network. It's the next best thing to being there.

guru   What your colleagues in the office will call you after you spout off a few terms from this glossary.

HTML   HyperText Markup Language. The language used to create documents that are viewed through web browsers on the World Wide Web.

HTTP   HyperText Transfer Protocol. The standard for how web (HTTP) servers communicate with web browsers on TCP/IP networks such as the Internet.

hub   A network hardware device that connects devices together in a star topology. The most common device to connect a network.

hyperlink   Words or graphics that are "linked" to other web pages or websites. Users move from page to page by clicking on the links. Hyperlinks are designed to facilitate Internet surfing.

IEEE   Institute of Electrical and Electronics Engineers. The organizational body that publishes standards for networks. For example, the standard the IEEE (pronounced as "eye-triple-e") published for Ethernet networks is IEEE 802.3.

IMAP   Internet Messaging Access Protocol. An electronic mail protocol. A more flexible, sophisticated protocol than POP3.

incremental backup   A type of backup in which only the files that have changed since the last backup are backed up. Slightly different from a differential backup in that this procedure flags files to show that they have been backed up.

Internet   A vast collection of networks and computers that runs on the TCP/IP protocol. The Internet is used for just about any type of communication you can think of. Consists of different components including the World Wide Web, electronic mail, FTP, Usenet, and Gopher.

Internet Explorer   Microsoft's web browser used to access the Internet's World Wide Web.

Internet faxing   The ability to send faxes over the Internet using fax servers in order to save on long-distance charges.

InterNIC   The organization that maintains Internet addresses and assigns domain names to users.

interoperability   Network speak for "it works with other stuff."

intranet   An internal Internet used for creating websites accessed on a network. Used to share information within an organization.

IP   Internet Protocol. Ensures that information gets to a specific destination by using IP addresses.

IP address   A set of four numbers separated by commas, used to direct information to the right destination.

IPX   Internetwork Packet Exchange. The networking protocol used for Novell's NetWare.

ISA   Industry Standard Architecture. An older but popular expansion bus for adding cards such as network adapters and modems.

ISDN   Integrated Services Digital Network. A digital connection used for connecting a wide area network or the Internet. Basic rate ISDN runs at up to 128 Kbps, much faster than an analog modem.

ISP   Internet Service Provider. A company that provides Internet access and other services.

Java   A new language for web pages developed by Sun Microsystems, Inc., that is used for inserting animation and mini applications ("applets") into web pages.

Kbps   Kilobits per second. One thousand bits per second.

LAN   Local area network. A connection of computers and other devices within a close proximity used to share files and other resources.

LANtastic   A popular peer-to-peer network operating system from Artisoft, Inc.

leased line   A private, direct line used for connecting over long distances. Connected full-time, whether in use or not.

Linux   A very popular version of UNIX developed by Finnish programmer Linus Torvalds. A computer and server operating system that is popular because it's free and stable.

local resource   Any peripheral or device that is connected directly to a computer.

Mbps   Megabits per second. One million bits per second.

MCSE   Microsoft Certified Systems Engineer.

memory   An area where your computer stores data or programs that are being used.

Micro Channel   An expansion slot bus used for older IBM computers, often known as MCA.

micropayments A system of payment for electronic commerce that handles very small transactions between $.25 and $10. Used for purchasing inexpensive items from the Internet. Payment systems can draw money from credit cards or bank accounts.

MIME Multipurpose Internet Mail Extension. An e-mail transmission protocol.

MIS Manager of information systems. Another name for the network administrator.

modem A device (a modulator/demodulator) that converts digital data from a computer or other device into analog signals for use over the public telephone network. Another modem on the other end of the connection converts the data back to digital format.

NE2000 A compatibility standard for network adapters. If a card is NE2000 compatible, it works in most popular networks.

NetBEUI NetBIOS Extended User Interface. An enhanced version of NetBIOS used by Windows for Workgroups, Windows 95/98, and Windows NT for accessing the network and exchanging data. It is a commonly used protocol for simple peer-to-peer networks.

NetBIOS Network Basic Input/Output System. A protocol developed by IBM that allows dialog between computers.

Netscape Navigator A web browser developed by Netscape Communications. Another version, called Communicator, includes more features for communicating over the Web.

NetWare A client/server network operating system developed by Novell Inc.

NetWare Directory Services Also known as NDS, it is a feature of Novell's NetWare 4.0 and higher that pools the resources of all servers together so that when you log on to one server, it is as if you have logged on to them all. NDS isn't significant for small businesses with only one server.

NetWare for Small Business Novell's client/server network operating system for small businesses.

network A group of connected computers set up for communication and resource sharing. The word often is used to mean a local area network, but it can mean any network, including the Internet.

network adapter Also known as a network interface card. See adapter.

network appliance A server, often known as a thin server, because it uses an integrated "thin" operating system instead of Windows NT or Novell NetWare. Network appliances perform only a single function or several functions such as e-mail, Internet access, printer sharing, or network file storage. The advantage of network appliances is that they are less expensive and easier to install and maintain than a regular server.

network manager   The poor person who has to make sure the network operates efficiently and who has to remember all of this stuff.

network operating system   Software used to control and access resources on a network. Often called a NOS (rhymes with "boss").

network resource Any device or file or database that can be accessed and used through the network.

newsgroup   A resource on the Internet where people post and read messages on a specific topic.

node   A computer or other device such as a printer on the network.

Novell   A company that develops network software. Best known for its NetWare operating system.

offline   Disconnected from the network.

online   Connected to the network.

OSI   Open System Interconnection. A networking communications framework that includes seven different layers. Those layers are (from bottom to top) physical, data link, network, transport, session, presentation, and application. Each layer builds on the one before it. All networking standards are based on the OSI model.

packet   A unit of data used to communicate over a network. The size of the packet can vary depending on what networking protocol you use.

packet filtering   A technique used by firewalls to prevent some information from getting through. A helpful security feature for a network connection to the Internet that is often used with proxy servers and routers.

packet switching   The most common form of data transmission technology used in LANs and WANs. Information is bundled into "packets" of information that are sent and reassembled in their proper sequence.

PAP   Password Authentication Protocol. A security protocol used for dial-up connections such as remote access or Internet access.

password   A secret combination of letters, numbers, or other symbols that allows a user to connect to a resource.

PCI   Peripheral Component Interconnect. A newer, faster bus or expansion slot used in most new computers for adding cards such as network adapters and modems.

peer-to-peer network   A type of local area network in which all the computers run a portion of the network operating system and there is no server. All computers are "peers" to one another.

PGP   Pretty Good Privacy. An e-mail encryption software that secures messages. Created by Pretty Good Privacy Inc.

POP   Point of presence. A point of connection to a network.

POP3   Post Office Protocol 3. The message storage protocol for electronic mail.

port   A connector on a network adapter, hub, or print server that is used to connect to the network.

POTS   Plain Old Telephone Service. A normal phone line.

PPP   Point-to-Point Protocol. A communications protocol that enables a dial-up connection for IP traffic. Often used for connecting to the Internet or for remote access to a local network.

print server   A standalone device that is essentially a minicomputer used to connect a printer to a network.

private key   One part of a dual key encryption standard. The private key is held by the originator of the message and is used to encrypt (scramble) the message. The data is then decrypted by the recipient with the sender's public key.

protocol   A set of rules or a standard that allows computers and other devices to communicate in a common language.

proxy server   Software that runs on a server that is connected between a LAN and the Internet. The proxy server runs a modem or other connection to the Internet and hides all of the network users from the Internet so that an entire network appears as only one user or address. This prevents potential hackers from knowing what is on the network. A proxy server may sometimes also be used to prevent local users from going to certain sites on the Internet.

public key   One part of dual key encryption standard. The public key is sent by the user to the intended recipient so that the recipient can decrypt (unscramble) messages sent by the originator.

public key encryption   Also known as dual key encryption. A standard for encrypting or scrambling data for transmission over the Internet. Public key encryption uses both public and private keys (together known as a key pair) to scramble and unscramble data. The two most popular public key encryption standards are OpenPGP from Pretty Good Privacy and S/MIME from RSA Data Security.

QIC   Quarter-Inch Cartridge. A type of tape commonly used for backing up data.

RAID   Redundant Array of Independent Disks. A series of hard drives that are logically connected together to appear as one very large drive. Data is stored so that if one disk ever goes down, the information can be recompiled from the other disks.

RAM Random Access Memory. Memory in a computer, server, or other device that can be written to over and over.

repeater A network hardware device that connects devices together in a star topology. Similar to a hub, but a repeater strengthens the network signal as it sends it out.

ring topology A physical network protocol in which all computers form a closed loop that allows them to send and receive data.

RJ-45 A type of connector used for connecting twisted-pair network cabling to a port. It looks like a larger version of a phone connector (that's an RJ-11). Also used for connecting ISDN.

robot Software that automatically scans the Internet and indexes information on websites for search engines. Also known as a spider or crawler.

router A network device that routes network traffic based on network addresses. Used in larger, more advanced networks and for access to the Internet. Routers are often used to connect networks running different protocols.

SCSI Small Computer System Interface. A connection on computers used for hard drives, tape drives, and CD-ROMs. Pronounced "scuzzy." Often fun to use in any sentence about computers.

search engine A website on the Internet that allows you to search for information on many other websites by using keywords.

seat The number of licenses for software shared on a network—that is, the number of simultaneous users that can access the same application running on a server. Also the number of users a network operating system will allow. For example, Novell's NetWare for Small Business only allows a maximum of 25 seats.

segment A connection of computers that form a local network. Networks can have multiple segments by using a bridge, switch, or router to separate them.

server A large, powerful computer that acts as a central source in a client/server network. A server isn't used by anyone as a desktop computer.

SET Secure Electronic Transaction. A new Internet protocol for electronic credit card payments developed by Visa and MasterCard.

site A location on the Internet. Often known as a website.

Small Business Server Microsoft BackOffice Small Business Server. A version of Windows NT Server designed for small business networks with fewer than 25 users.

smart cards A payment method for electronic commerce. Cards are "charged" with money that is then spent each time you use the card.

S/MIME Secure Multipurpose Internet Mail Extension. A security method that encrypts e-mail messages, using public and private keys to encrypt and decrypt messages.

SMTP   Simple Mail Transfer Protocol. The standard e-mail protocol for transferring electronic mail on the Internet.

sneakernet   The cheapest form of networking. File transfers are done using floppy disks that the people in your office have to carry from computer to computer. Not a productive way to spend your time.

SNMP   Simple Network Management Protocol. A standard for managing your network. Don't worry about it until long after you hire a network administrator.

Spider   *See* robot.

SSL   Secure Socket Layer The most popular web server encryption protocol on the Internet. It supplies three services for security: encryption (so no one can read your message), certificate handling (to ensure that you are who you say you are), and message integrity (so no one can intercept and change your message).

star topology   A type of network that uses a central hub to connect all computers together.

STP   Shielded Twisted Pair. A type of network cabling used in a star networking topology.

switch   A network hardware device used to segment a network's traffic. It has many ports, similar to a hub, but each port is a different segment, as with a bridge.

T1   A dedicated or leased line that is capable of speeds of 1.5 Mbps. T1 lines are used for WANs and connecting to the Internet.

T3   A very fast 45 Mbps leased-line connection that is used for connecting LANs and for ISPs to connect to the Internet.

tape drive   A device that uses a tape storage medium, such as QIC, to back up data from the network server.

TCP/IP   Transmission Control Protocol/Internet Protocol. A protocol used on the Internet and by many local area networks.

teamware   Communication and collaboration software used over a network to get employees to work as if on a team. Less complicated and less flexible than groupware, it usually is a medium for electronic messaging, file sharing, calendaring/scheduling, online chats, and document management.

Thin Ethernet   An Ethernet network that runs in the bus topology. Thin Ethernet networks use coaxial (10Base2) cables.

TLA   A three-letter acronym.

TLD   Top-level domain. The letters at the end of a URL or web address that indicate the type of organization that owns the address. TLDs may also indicate the organization's country of origin. Common TLDs are .com, .gov, and .edu.

token   The repeating frame that gets passed around on a token ring network that allows computers to send and receive data.

token passing   The access method used by token ring networks. Devices on the network wait until a token is passed to them, allowing them to receive and send data.

token ring   A networking standard that uses a token passing scheme for letting computers and other devices communicate on the network.

topology   Describes the physical layout of a network.

Travan   A type of tape used for network backup.

Trojan horse   A type of computer virus that disguises itself as another software application. Most often a Trojan horse erases and reformats your hard drive.

Tunneling   The process of encapsulating one protocol (such as IPX) into another protocol (such as TCP/IP). Tunneling is used to facilitate the transfer of data and is often used with Virtual Private Networks.

UNIX   A powerful computer operating system used in high-end computer workstations and servers.

UPS   Uninterruptible Power Supply. A battery backup power source used on servers and other critical devices in the case of a power disturbance.

UPT   Unshielded Twisted Pair. A type of networking cable used in a star networking topology.

URL   Uniform Resource Locator. An Internet address that facilitates locating websites.

Usenet   An organization of newsgroups on the Internet.

VAR   A value-added reseller. Someone who sells computer, networking, or computer-related hardware and software. Often known as a reseller or dealer.

Virtual Private Network
Used for Wide Area Networks. VPNs use a public network, such as the Internet, to connect one or more private networks, like a Local Area Network.

Virus   Software that infects and affects the operation of a computer. Viruses include Trojan horses, worms, and macroviruses.

WAN   Wide area network. A connection between two or more local area networks that are in separate locations. WANs use the public telephone system to connect the two LANs.

web browser   A software application that reads graphical HTML pages and allows you to easily surf through the World Wide Web.

web server   A computer on the Internet that stores HTML pages and services HTTP requests from Internet surfers with the HTML-based text and graphics.

website   *See* site.

Windows for Workgroups   A pre–Windows 95 operating system from Microsoft Corp. for peer-to-peer networking.

Windows 95   The computer operating system from Microsoft that can be used as a peer-to-peer network operating system.

Windows 98   Microsoft's newest computer operating system with some improvements over Windows 95.

Windows NT Server   Microsoft's network operating system for servers.

Windows NT Workstation   A computer operating system from Microsoft developed for corporate desktop computers.

World Wide Web   The graphical portion of the Internet that uses computers and servers to let users graphically surf for information through a web browser.

worm   A computer virus that actively searches out victims over a network.

WWW   See World Wide Web.

zero-slot network   A type of network that doesn't use internal network adapters. It connects computers through a daisy chain of cabling that goes from serial port to serial port.

List of Vendor Companies

THIS SECTION LISTS THE COMPANIES THAT HAVE BEEN DISCUSSED IN THIS BOOK and a few others that may be of interest. Not all of the products or services offered by these companies have been thoroughly tested; therefore their presence on this list should not be construed as an endorsement of any kind.

NETWORKING HARDWARE VENDORS

3Com Corporation
800-590-3266
www.3com.com

Bay Networks
800-6BAYNET
www.baynetworks.com

Intel Corporation
916-377-7000
www.intel.com

COMPUTERS AND SERVERS

Compaq Computer Corporation
800-888-9909
www.compaq.com

Dell Computer Corporation
800-917-3355
www.dell.com

Gateway 2000
800-846-4208
www.gateway.com

Micron Computers
800-9-MICRON
www.micron.com

SOFTWARE VENDORS

Artisoft, Inc.
800-846-9726
www.artisoft.com

Microsoft Corporation
800-426-9400
www.microsoft.com

NetObjects
888-449-6400
www.netobjects.com

Netopia Incorporated
510-814-5000
www.netopia.com

Novell Inc.
800-453-1267
www.novell.com

SoftQuad
781-229-2924
www.sq.com

Symantec
800-441-7234
www.symantec.com

Visio Corporation
800-248-4746, ext. 89A
www.visio.com

INTERNET/INTRANET

HotOffice Technologies
888-4HOTOFFICE
www.hotoffice.com

Instinctive Technologies
617-497-6300
www.instinctive.com

The InterNIC
Internet domain registration
888-771-3000
www.internic.net

Intranetics
781-932-0960
www.intranetics.com

ELECTRONIC COMMERCE

IBM Corporation
800 IBM 4YOU
www.ibm.com

iCat Corporation
206-505-8800
www.icat.com

The Internet Mall
310-662-1900
www.internetmall.com

Lotus Development Corporation
800-343-5414
www.lotus.com

ViaWeb (Yahoo! store)
888-484-2932
www.viaweb.com

INTERNET SERVICE PROVIDERS

America Online
800-827-6364
www.aol.com

AT&T
www.att.com/business

BBN Planet
617-873-2000
www.bbnplanet.com

CompuServe
800-739-6699
www.compuserve.com

Netcom
888-316-1122
www.netcom.com

Earthlink
626-296-2400
www.earthlink.com

PSINet
800-395-1056
www.psinet.com

MCI
www.mci.com

UUNet
800-488-6383
www.uunet.com

If you would like a list of local Internet Service Providers in your area and you have access to the Internet, check out The List website (thelist.inter net.com). The List has thousands of ISPs listed by state, area code, or other search criteria, as well as information on services available and links to their home pages. If you don't have access to the Internet to check out The List, visit your local public library.

Index